AGRICULTURAL GEOGRAPHY

Agricultural Geography

A Social and Economic Analysis

BRIAN W. ILBERY

OXFORD UNIVERSITY PRESS

1985

Oxford University Press, Walton Street, Oxford OX2 6DP
Oxford New York Toronto
Delhi Bombay Calcutta Madras Karachi
Kuala Lumpur Singapore Hong Kong Tokyo
Nairobi Dar es Salaam Cape Town
Melbourne Auckland
and associated companies in
Beirut Berlin Ibadan Nicosia

Oxford is a trade mark of Oxford University Press.

Published in the United States
by Oxford University Press, New York

British Library Cataloguing in Publication Data
Ilbery, Brian W.
Agricultural geography: social and economic analysis.
I. Land use, Rural   II. Land use, Rural—Social aspect
I. Title
333.76   HD111
ISBN 0–19–874134–0
ISBN 0–19–874133–2 Pbk

Set by Grestun Graphics, Abingdon
Printed in Great Britain at the University Press, Oxford by
David Stanford, Printer to the University

To Mum and Dad at Manor Farm,
a thriving family business

PREFACE

The objective of this text is to provide some insights into the dynamic and complex nature of the agricultural landscape. Excluding traditional material on the physical environment, the spatial structure of agriculture is analysed in terms of various social and economic factors. The book takes a predominantly behavioural viewpoint, arguing that even in an industry which is economically orientated, it is the farmers' reactions to, and perceptions of, changing economic circumstances that have to be considered if a realistic understanding of agricultural land-use patterns is to be obtained.

Developed market economies provide the focus of attention and agriculture in the Third World is not discussed, except where it helps to demonstrate the importance of particular principles or methodological developments in agricultural geography, as in diffusion studies. The material selected for study was conditioned partly by the author's personal interests, but also by the need to provide insights into the 'modernisation' of agriculture. To this end, much of the illustrative material is taken from the USA and Great Britain, although case-studies from Australasia and mainland Europe are used where appropriate. Emphasis is placed upon farm-based research and information is drawn almost exclusively from the literature published in the English language.

In more detail, the first chapter sets the scene by outlining the nature of agricultural geography and demonstrating how approaches to the subject have changed over time. The major sources of data are described and problems with their use discussed. Chapters 2, 3 and 4 are behavioural in nature and cover a range of decision-making models and techniques, from the behavioural matrix, repertory grids and goals and values, to Game Theory and innovation diffusion. In each case the complexity of the decision-making process is highlighted, with wide variations between farmers being characteristic. The next three chapters deal with more economic aspects of agricultural geography, although in each chapter the varied reactions of different groups of farmers are discussed. Such trends as increasing farm-size and fragmentation, specialisation of production, government policy, and the growth of contract farming and agribusinesses are examined, with their spatial consequences emphasised. Chapter 8 attempts to combine both economic and behavioural approaches in a study of farming in the rural–urban fringe. The major processes affecting this dynamic zone are outlined before their varied effects in different areas are demonstrated in case-studies from many parts of the Western world.

Having an interdisciplinary flavour, it is hoped that the book will be useful for undergraduates of agricultural economics and rural sociology as well as geography. Farmers and all people with an interest in the forces creating change within the countryside should find many items of relevance. Although inspired by my family's farming traditions, I alone am responsible for the book. I gratefully acknowledge the help and guidance of an anonymous referee and Andrew Schuller of Oxford University Press, both of whom were responsible for making suggestions and improving my original draft proposal. I would also like to extend my gratitude to the Geography Department at Coventry (Lanchester) Polytechnic and pay particular tribute to Mrs Shirley Addleton for her skilful cartography and to Mrs Joy Summers and Joan James for typing the manuscript. Last but not least, I thank my wife, Lynne, for all her patience at a time of excessive demands from the two youngsters, Gareth and James.

December 1984   Brian W. Ilbery

CONTENTS

x *Contents*

ACKNOWLEDGEMENTS

We should like to thank the following for permission to reproduce copyright tables and figures. Source details are given at the foot of each figure and in the references. The numbers refer to the figs. and tables as they appear in our book.

Journal of Agricultural Economics: Tables 2.1, 5.2, 7.3: Figs. 5.8, 6.8

The Association of American Geographers: Table 8.2; Fig. 8.6 (from *The Professional Geographer*) and Table 3.3; Figs. 2.4, 7.7 (from the *Annals*)

I. R. Bowler: Tables 5.1, 5.2: Figs. 5.3, 5.10

D. K. Britton: Fig. 5.8

The Institute of British Geographers: Tables 2.2, 2.3, 5.3, 6.2 and Figs. 1.3, 3.2, 6.5 (from *Transactions*): Figs. 4.1, 7.1 a,b, 7.6 (from *Area*)

Cambria: Table 5.4

The Canadian Association of Geographers: Table 8.1; Figs. 8.4, 8.5

The University of Chicago Press: Fig. 4.8

J. Doherty: Fig. 2.1 b

The East Midland Geographer: Fig. 7.3 a,b

Economic Geography: Table 4.1; Figs, 4.9, 4.10, 5.9

V. R. Eidman: Tables 3.4, 3.5

Food from Britain: Table 7.1

W. C. Found: Fig. 2.1 a

R. M. Gasson: Tables 2.1, 7.3

Geoforum (Pergamon Press): Figs. 2.5, 8.8

Geografiska Annaler: Tables 3.6, 3.7; Figs. 3.3, 3.4

Geographia Polonica: Fig. 1.4

The Geographical Association: Figs. 1.6, 4.3, 5.3, 6.6

The Guardian: Table 6.1

Harper & Row, Publishers, Inc: Fig. 2.2

William Heinemann Ltd: Fig. 2.3

Longman Group Limited: Figs. 6.3, 6.4, 8.1, 8.2, 8.3

McGraw-Hill Book Company: Fig. 1.1

Methuen & Co, Ltd: Figs. 1.2, 4.7

Ministry of Agriculture, Fisheries and Food: Fig. 5.1 a

E. L. Naylor: Fig. 6.8

The Open University: Table 4.2; Figs, 4.5, 4.6

Organisation for Economic Co-operation and Development: Fig. 6.7 b

Outlook on Agriculture (Pergamon Press): Fig. 1.5

Pergamon Press Ltd: Fig. 6.7 a

Regional Studies (Cambridge Univ: Press): Tables 3.9, 3.10; Fig. 3.6

Royal Scottish Geographical Society: Fig. 5.6

M. J. Sargent: Table 7.2

Southern Journal of Agricultural Economics: Tables 3.4, 3.5

Tijdschrift voor Economische en Sociale Geografie: Figs. 3.8, 7.4, 7.5, 8.7, 6.1;
Table 5.5

FIGURES

TABLES

1

CONCEPTS, METHODOLOGY AND DATA

1.1 The nature of agricultural geography

Agriculture accounts for the largest share of the world's economically-active population and is the most important contributor to the national income in many developing countries. Although accounting for only a small proportion of the gross domestic product and employing less than 10 per cent of the employed population in the Western world, agriculture is a major user of land and between 20 and 30 per cent of disposable income goes on food (Grigg, 1984).

Therefore, agricultural geography, which seeks to describe and explain spatial variations in agricultural activity over the earth's surface, is an important topic comprising two major parts. The first has location and context as central themes and is concerned with recognising and analysing spatial variations in agricultural and farming practices throughout the world (Coppock, 1968). The second attempts to explain the great diversity of agriculture. This is a complex task and, in the absence of data on social and economic aspects of farming, explanation has often been sought in terms of physical and historical factors (Coppock, 1964). However, a proper insight into the distribution of agricultural types can only be obtained by examining the nature of the relationships between a large number of relevant variables. These relationships are of many different kinds, which cannot be incorporated into a single system of laws (Morgan and Munton, 1971), and consequently it is difficult to develop a truly realistic model of agricultural land-use.

Whilst by its very nature agriculture is economically based, it can be distinguished from other forms of economic activity on two major accounts. First, unlike secondary manufacturing and service industries, agriculture relies on the physical environment and biological processes. Therefore, a farmer is faced with an environment of uncertainty and has to take calculated risks. He will choose a system which he perceives to have a reasonable chance of success and where failures will not put him out of business. This is known as the 'region of risk' and is exemplified by the Mid-West region of the USA, where the high yields of maize increase the risk threshold against such physical hazards as hail, frost and drought. Secondly, agriculture is the only economic activity, except for forestry and fishing, in which extensive use of the land is made. Consequently, agricultural geographers often talk in terms of the *distribution* rather than the *location* of agricultural practices, although there are exceptions like the development of intensive pig and poultry production and agribusiness.

McCarthy, and Lindberg (1966), in differentiating agriculture from other forms of production, noted five further distinguishing features:

1. Many producing units

Agriculture employs the largest share of the world's economically-employed persons (between 35 and 45 per cent), although figures vary enormously between countries and output per worker is lower than for other occupations. The world's agricultural land is subdivided into a very large number of various-sized and often fragmented units which, despite the scientific nature of agriculture, are run by a group of people with a lower level of formal training than for most other occupations. It follows from this that farm-size is one of the fundamental factors affecting the spatial distribution of agricultural activities and it is not uncommon for sizes to vary from between 2 and 2,000 ha. within relatively short distances, as demonstrated by Ilbery (1979) in north-east Oxfordshire. Farm-size can determine whether a farmer will choose an intensive or extensive system of agriculture and the degree to which he is able to specialise in just one or two enterprises (Chapter 5). As the distribution of farm-sizes varies enormously, due to such factors as land quality, population pressure and inheritance laws, it is logical for agricultural practices to vary accordingly. Individual farmers are also in a weak marketing position and can have little effect on market prices (Chapter 6), although co-operative and contract farming has helped to ameliorate this adverse position (Chapter 7).

The task of collecting and analysing data for these individual agricultural units is beyond the scope of most researchers, who instead often resort to aggregated secondary data for larger units such as the parish, county and Agricultural Development and Advisory Service (ADAS) district. This necessarily affects the manner in which studies are undertaken and the results obtained. An alternative solution is to sample farms but this too has many inherent problems (Clark and Gordon, 1980; section 1.3).

2. Multiplicity of products

Despite major technological advances in agriculture, such as the increasing use of artificial fertilisers and machinery and the trend towards greater specialisation of production, a majority of farms engage in the production of several enterprises. (An enterprise is a product for which the farmer receives some cash income). This usually involves the processes of substitution, of one product for another, and rotation, which together help to keep the land fertile, maximise the use of machinery and labour, and reduce the level of risk if one enterprise fails. One of the consequences of developing a diversified farm system is the difficulty of allocating costs to individual enterprises. The increase in fertiliser application, contract farming and protective government measures has greatly diminished the need for a system of interdependent enterprises. However, many rotations survive because of tradition and today are 'rotations of convenience' (Morgan and Munton, 1971).

3.   *Biological nature of production*

Agricultural production processes are necessarily geared to the life cycle of plants and animals, or combinations of both, which are raised on individual farms (McCarty and Lindberg, 1966). Time, in the form of the completion of the life cycle, is thus a fundamental consideration in the planning of the farm system. This cycle can range from the length of a growing season to a three- to five-year rotation. The farmer has little control over the production process, increasing his environment of uncertainty, and the dependence on heat, moisture and soil nutrients means that agriculture requires extensive space.

4.   *Locational decisions in agriculture*

Decision-making constraints in agriculture are different from those in manufacturing. In the latter, the choice of location is often flexible and dependent on the entrepreneur's decision of where to site his factory, whereas in agriculture location is fixed and the farmer has to decide what system to adopt within this framework. Therefore, the spatial structure of agriculture is the culmination of farmers' decisions of how to derive the 'best' use of the land which they control.

5.   *Self-sufficing production*

Production of food for consumption on the farm rather than for the market is common practice in many parts of the world. A relatively large proportion of the world's food output never enters commercial channels, which can create problems when attempting to analyse the spatial characteristics of agriculture. Production for use on the farm is not recorded in official data sources and its magnitude can never be satisfactorily measured. A second important point is that the decision-making process for self-sufficient production may be different than for commercial production and reflect the tastes and desires of the farmer and not the commercial market.

The preceding paragraphs have demonstrated that the farm is the primary decision-making unit in agriculture. However, in common with most geographical studies, agricultural geography suffers from a scale problem (Harvey, 1968). With an increase in scale, from micro to macro, the role of influencing factors changes, and physical factors become reflected in agricultural land-use patterns more than management and personal factors. This basic point must be remembered when considering the different scales of investigation adopted in agricultural geography. Morgan and Munton (1971) identified four levels at which data are collected and generalisations made. The first is the national level, which contains much published data and allows some regional comparison on the basis of administrative divisions. The second is the agricultural region, common in early geographical studies but without a consistent definition. These rarely coincided with administrative regions and were poorly provided with data. With advances in methodology and statistical applications in agricultural geography, emphasis has changed away from 'regions' and towards 'regional types' of agriculture, where types of farming do not have to be contiguous in space to belong to the same 'regional type' (Byfuglien and Nordgard, 1974; Anderson, 1975; Ilbery, 1981a). However, this movement has witnessed a return to the use of administrative units for spatial differentiation rather than 'natural' agricultural regions. The third is the farm level, or decision-making unit. The distribution of farms, the spatial layout of fields and variations in land quality are all central to studies in agricultural geography. Official data are only available in aggregated form and farm data have to be collected directly by researchers. This represents a growing trend in agricultural studies and reflects, in part, a more behavioural approach to the explanation of land-use patterns. The fourth is the field level: size and shape of fields reflect many historical factors and determine the use to which they are put. It is not a popular scale of study in agricultural studies primarily because it lacks the characteristic functional element of the farm unit.

One consequence of the scale problem has been the development of the systems approach to agricultural geography, which can analyse patterns and processes at various geographic scales. There is much variation between the broader agricultural systems of the world and the smaller-scale farm systems.

Agricultural systems vary enormously throughout the world, ranging from subsistence and peasant systems to commercial and redistributive (communist) systems (Hurst, 1974; Morgan, 1978). Contrasts between these systems can and do occur within relatively short distances, often separated by natural or political barriers. For example, subsistence and commercial systems are in evidence either side of the River Vaal in Orange Free State. The different types of agricultural system are characterised by certain features (Hurst, 1974):

1.   Subsistence agriculture

In this system the producers consume their own output and there is minimal capital input and little division of labour or specialisation of production. Agriculture is primitive and small-scale, with little technology, machinery or innovation, but a large labour input. Up to 70 per cent of a country's working population can be employed in subsistence agriculture, which can be subdivided into such sub-types as shifting agriculture, pastoral nomadism and rudimentary sedentary tillage.

2. Commercial agriculture

A system of exchange occurs: farmers respond to world market demands and there is greater specialisation of production. High capital inputs replace many labour inputs, which are low at less than 15 per cent of the working population. Agriculture is large-scale, mechanised and technically advanced in commercial systems, which can be divided into three sub-types: extensive crop, extensive

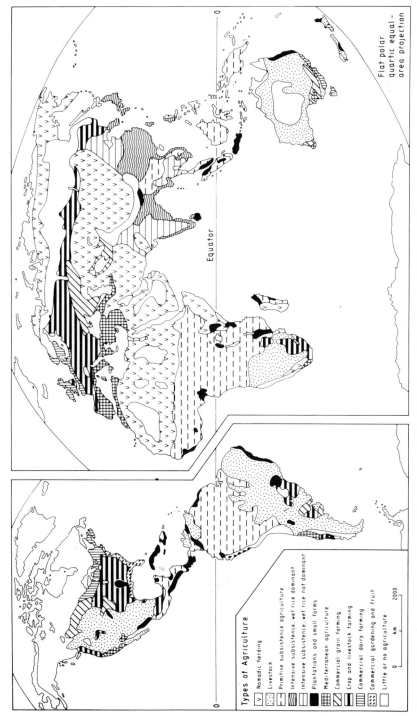

Types of Agriculture

V	Nomadic herding
	Livestock
	Primitive subsistence agriculture
	Intensive subsistence, wet rice dominant
	Intensive subsistence, wet rice not dominant
	Plantations and small farms
	Mediterranean agriculture
	Commercial grain farming
	Crop and livestock farming
	Commercial dairy farming
	Commercial gardening and fruit
	Little or no agriculture

0   km   2000

Equator

0

0

Flat polar quartic equal-area projection

Fig. 1.1   The agricultural regions of the world, after D. Whittlesey (Finch *et al.*, 1957 plate 8)

livestock and intensive livestock, to which can be added mixed farming and truck farming.

3. Redistributive agriculture

Tight controls are exercised through a socialist planned economy. Farms are often very large and of two types: state farms and collectives. The market-exchange system is controlled by the government, with the east European countries of COMECON providing a good example. Agriculture is relatively neglected, in preference for urban–industrial development, although Hungary provides a noted exception where the wealth of the country is based on its prosperous agricultural sector.

Agricultural systems are not mutually exclusive, but dynamic and in the process of change. This led Grigg (1974) to develop an evolutionary approach in order to understand the world distribution of present agricultural systems. Grigg considered nine agricultural systems (Fig 1.1), based on a modified version of Whittlesey's (1936) original typology of world agriculture. He felt that a proper understanding could only be achieved with knowledge of past developments and concluded that the distribution of world agricultural systems is related to the pattern of economic development. Four processes have been particularly important in this evolution:

(i) The increase in world population and more significantly, the regional differences in its growth.

(ii) Variations in the physical environment, which have aided population concentration and influenced types of agricultural development.

(iii) The diffusion of crops, livestock and farming techniques. Technical change in agriculture was very slow until the nineteenth century and has been adopted in relatively few areas in the twentieth century.

(iv) The combined effects of industrialisation, urbanisation, commercialisation, transport improvements and radical changes in agricultural technology over the past two hundred years.

Turning to small-scale farm systems, which form the main focus of this book, a simple descriptive model has been produced by Morgan and Munton (1971). This demonstrates some of the basic relationships between the four main elements of a farm system: inputs, outputs, enterprises and the environment (Fig 1.2). Inputs into the system are both fixed and variable. The former include items such as capital equipment, permanent labour, buildings and the land itself, the costs of which remain fairly constant except for the effects of changes in technology. Variable inputs affect individual enterprises directly, enabling costs to be more easily allocated; they include chemicals and sprays, temporary and casual labour, seeds, and livestock feedstuffs.

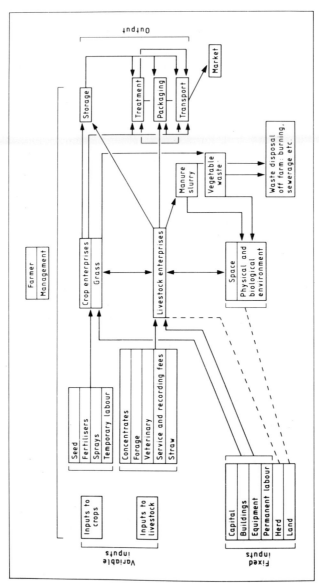

Fig. 1.2   A simple descriptive model of a farm system (Morgan and Munton, 1971 p. 22)

Outputs refer to those items passing through the farm gate and which are normally sold for some cash reward. Thus crops which are consumed on the farm by either livestock or people are not included, as for example with root crops grown for sheep. However, as Morgan and Munton (1971 p. 26) remark, reality is not so simple as there are 'hidden' forms of income. Farmers in Britain receive a subsidy payment for growing barley, which if fed to the beef herd is not a farm output. Farm systems can be very complex and it is difficult, if not impossible, to analyse all the influencing factors adequately or to allocate costs, especially those related to fixed inputs, to individual enterprises with little more than elementary precision.

Whilst farm systems may be similar, each is unique and a reflection of an individual farmer's perceptions, attitudes, ambitions, traditions and experience. This is accentuated by the varying levels of farmer knowledge and the stochastic nature of much decision-making behaviour. Therefore, the whole system is closely related to farm management (Chapter 5), the understanding of which is essential when unravelling the complexities of locational decision-making. In addition, it is the complex relationships between inputs, outputs, enterprises and the environment which determine the pattern of land-use on individual farms and in turn in different areas of the world.

1.2 Development of theoretical perspectives

A review of the mounting literature on agricultural geography reveals that most studies adopt one of two major approaches to their subject matter (Ilbery, 1979):

(i) *An empirical (inductive) approach*, which is concerned with describing what *actually exists* in the agricultural landscape. Explanation of the patterns is sought by inductive methods and generalisations are made on the basis of results from various studies.

(ii) *A normative (deductive) approach*, which is concerned more with what the agricultural landscape *should* be like, given a certain set of assumptions. This approach leads to the derivation and testing of hypotheses and ultimately to the development of an ideal theory of agricultural production.

The two approaches have never really merged and whilst this is difficult to explain, it relates in part to the complexities of the decision-making process in agriculture and the different times at which both have been popular within geography. It is primarily from the normative approach that models of agricultural location have been developed. Once again, model-makers have operated along one of two lines, with the latter emerging out of dissatisfaction with the former:

1. Optimiser models

These models are concerned with the notion of profit maximisation. Optimum land-use patterns rest on the assumptions that farmers are rational, have complete knowledge and an equal ability to use this knowledge. Such requirements are unobtainable in the real world and the approach has been criticised as unrealistic. Farmers, like other managers, cannot make perfect economic decisions and instead react to perceived conditions within an environment of uncertainty. Consequently, 'satisfaction' has been proposed as an alternative, leading to,

2. Satisficer models

These are a more realistic model, and take account of farmers' motivations, aspirations and attitudes. They include such items as a farmer's desire for leisure, a satisfactory income and social considerations, at the expense of profit maximisation. This approach stemmed from two classic geographical articles, by Wolpert (1964) in a study of Swedish farming and Harvey (1966) in a review of theoretical developments in agricultural geography, and forms the basis of the subsequent three chapters. There is much evidence of social factors playing an important role in the spatial structure of agriculture, as witnessed in the decline of dairy herds in Great Britain and the growth of hobby farming around major metropolitan areas.

As before, there is a noticeable gap between optimiser and satisficer models and it is becoming clear that the latter are also failing to explain the observed world adequately. The search for explanation of the distribution of agricultural activities would now seem to be based on empirical methods, but with a wide-spread usage of multivariate statistical tests (Fotheringham and Reeds, 1979).

Despite the different approaches adopted and the many methods of analysis available to the geographer, theoretical developments in agricultural geography have been slow. It could be argued that little real theoretical progress has been made since the work of Von Thünen (1826), yet theory can provide a framework for the explanation of spatial variations in agriculture. Existing explanations can be categorised into four main theoretical approaches, representing a continuum of thought in the post-war period and demonstrating how the focus of interest has shifted through time:

(i) *Geographical determinism model*, which assumes that the physical environment acts in a deterministic manner and controls agricultural decision-making.

(ii) *Economic determinism model*, which assumes that the economic factors of market, production and transport costs operate on a group of homogeneous producers, who in turn react in a rational manner to them.

(iii) *Socio-personal determinism model*, which assumes that there are further sets of influences which affect agricultural decision-making, including farmers' values, aims, motives, and attitudes towards risk aversion.

(iv) *Radical model*, which assumes that high technology and the rise of agribusiness are not signs of agricultural progress. Such an approach advocates that the future of agriculture in post-industrial societies is in the formation of economically-viable farm communities, which can exist in spite of agribusiness (see Chapter 7).

Before the 1950s, explanation was sought essentially in terms of the physical environment. Whilst this cannot be ignored in interpreting agricultural change (Grigg, 1982a), rarely does the physical environment act in a deterministic manner (Tarrant, 1974). It is the interaction of physical and human factors which determines patterns of agricultural land-use, especially as man interacts with, and increasingly controls much of, the physical environment. This interaction is in turn made more complex by two further sets of factors (Tarrant, 1974): first, the personal characteristics of the farmer, including his knowledge of new agricultural ideas and innovations and his attitudes toward risk avoidance; and secondly, the dynamic nature of agriculture, which may lead to an imbalance between physical and economic environments. Although the physical environment may remain relatively stable over long periods of time, the economic environment can be very unstable and fluctuate according to changes in such basic items as demand, price and government policy. The complexity of the situation is enhanced because farmers will perceive and react in different ways to changes in mechanisation, methods and crop varieties. As a consequence, geographers have added a behavioural element, to aid explanation of land-use patterns and complement previous physical and economic approaches (Ilbery, 1978).

A major characteristic of agriculture in many Western countries, especially those with diverse landscapes, is the tremendous variety in farming types practised. This is often true within relatively small areas where the physical environment may be fairly uniform. For this reason, economic factors have been emphasised in the spatial structure of agriculture and it is not surprising to find agricultural geography being classified as a branch of economic geography (Buchanan, 1959; Morgan and Munton, 1971). However, this is somewhat ironic for, as Coppock (1968) points out, agricultural geography is not only concerned with economic considerations. Indeed, a lack of suitable data has meant that connections with economics have not been strongly developed, whereas links with physical and historical geography have been more in evidence.

The nature of agriculture and the complexity of processes affecting its distribution has meant that agricultural geography has close links with many aspects of geography as well as with related subjects such as agricultural economics and rural sociology. For example, in an exhaustive review, Cloke (1980) considers agriculture within the broader field or rural geography. However, the perspective developed in this book is that agricultural geography has sufficient interest and methodological rigour to be considered as a separate branch of geography in its own right. Support for such a viewpoint can be found in the progress reports on agricultural geography which have appeared in recent years (Grigg, 1981; 1982b and 1983; Bowler, 1984).

Whilst economic and social considerations form the core of interest in this book, recognition of the importance of physical and radical approaches should be given. Traditional explanations of agricultural land-use patterns were related to the physical environment and have been fully discussed in standard texts (Symons, 1967; Coppock, 1971). However, one needs to emphasise that there are very few, if any, situations where physical factors are either all-important or of no account in the distribution of agricultural practices. Two contributory factors must be borne in mind: scale and enterprise type. On a large scale, it is possible to relate regional variations in agriculture to broad environmental contrasts, whereas at the micro scale, differences in farm management and decision behaviour are likely to be of prime importance. In addition, certain crops require specific physical and biological conditions, whilst others can be grown in a range of physical environments. For example, oats and potatoes can be grown in most parts of the USA, unlike maize which is restricted in its distribution by physical controls.

Maize is often used to demonstrate an important concept in relation to physical factors: the margin of cultivation. This is where environmental conditions restrict agricultural production to certain defined areas: the boundaries of maize production in the Mid-West relate to climatic controls and in particular to temperature and precipitation levels. However, changing economic circumstances could lead to an increase in cultivation in marginal areas, usually in former cultivated areas now abandoned. This was the justification advocated by Parry (1976) for more attention and detailed mapping of former abandoned farmland in upland areas of Britain.

Taking the Lammermuir Hills in south-east Scotland as his study area, Parry showed that over 11,440 ha. of existing moorland had been improved at one time; 4,890 ha. before 1860 and 6,500 ha. between 1860 and 1970. In an earlier study (Parry, 1975), the distribution of this abandoned farmland was related to secular climatic change. Using three indicators of climatic change—exposure (average windspeed), summer wetness (potential water surplus) and summer warmth (accumulated temperature)—Parry demonstrated how the climatic limit to cultivation may have fallen 140 metres over 300 years. By comparing the upper and lower climatic limits of marginal land with the distribution of abandoned land before 1800 (Fig. 1.3), a strong correlation was obtained, indicative of an indirect causal relationship. However, Parry was careful to point out that land abandonment in the marginal areas of south-east Scotland was due only in part to the deterioration in climate. A proper examination of the distribution of abandoned land would also have to consider soil exhaustion and such human influences as the decline in the monastic farming system and fluctuations in the demand for agricultural products.

The idea of physical margins to cultivation being partly controlled by economic factors was clearly demonstrated by Varjo (1979) in Finland, a country crossed by the limits of cultivation of numerous crops. Much of Finland is a marginal agricultural area which is hit by crop failures from time to time. Varjo plotted the changing cultivation limits of barley, oats, rye and spring wheat between 1930 and 1969, and the progressive southward movements were thought to be responses to deteriorating climatic conditions (Fig. 1.4). However, the climate had only worsened in the 1940s and the often-violent movements southwards, in the 1960s especially, were due to the influence of man. Varjo related these to the sharp decline in profitability of cereals and found that the limits of production were determined by a position where the output of cereals permitted profits to exceed costs. Laaksonen (1979) has extended Varjo's study period into the 1970s and provided a more detailed account of the role of physical factors in Finland's marginal agricultural structure.

Whilst a detailed account of the part played by physical factors is beyond the

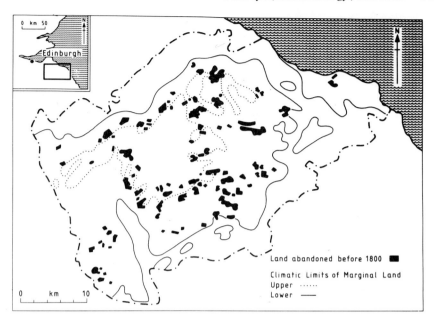

Fig. 1.3   Land abandonment in south-east Scotland before 1800 (Parry, 1975 pp. 4 and 6)

scope of this book, there has been a revival of interest in their effect on the spatial structure of agriculture. To a certain extent, this is a reflection of economic recession and the price–cost squeeze in agriculture (Bowler, 1982). As a consequence, the yield of agricultural products has become very important, encouraging farmers to seek the 'best' physically endowed areas for their enterprises.

Therefore, it is not surprising that part of this revival of interest centres on the effects of environmental conditions on the yields of certain cereal crops. Whilst Michaels (1982) has shown that long-term change in climatic and atmospheric pressure patterns is an important determinant of winter wheat yields in North America, Briggs (1981) found significant relationships between the yield of spring barley in England and Wales and edaphic and climatic conditions. Using multiple regression, Briggs demonstrated that yields of spring barley were related to four factors: sand contents, drainage conditions and available water capacity of the soil, potential summer soil moisture deficit, and annual accumulated temperature. These variables need to be incorporated into soil survey and land-use capability classifications, so that the discrepancy between actual and potential yields of cereal crops can be highlighted. Such information could be made available to farmers, with the possibility of the spatial pattern of spring barley being changed fundamentally.

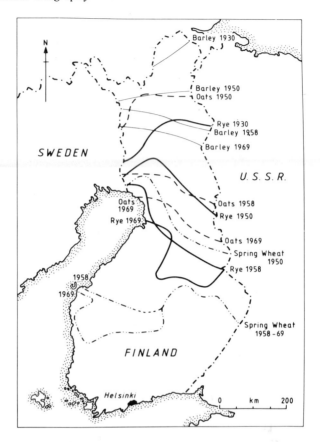

Fig 1.4   The northern cultivation limits of cereal crops in Finland, 1930–69 (Varjo, 1979 p. 227)

Similar inferences have been drawn by Gillooly (1978) and Gillooly and Dyer (1979) in their studies of spatial and temporal variations in maize production over South Africa, where yields have been successfully correlated with soil types and rainfall figures. Climatic conditions are also vital to the Californian raisin industry (Granger, 1980), especially during the drying period in September, and responsible for the instability of potato yields in the United Kingdom (Ingersent, 1979). The latter study advocates a spatial relocation of potato production to areas which are more physically suited. Although a reasonable suggestion, it is also an impractical one as the Potato Marketing Board controls production and is unable to differentiate between its members in different parts of the country.

A recent approach to the study of agriculture is to regard agricultural and farm systems as ecosystems (Simmons, 1979 and 1980; Bayliss-Smith, 1982), and modern ecological models, emphasising the flow of energy and nutrients, can be used as viewpoints from which to analyse agricultural systems. The idea of energy flowing through an agricultural ecosystem is not a new one, but the costing and quantification of energy used in agricultural production is. Such an approach gained impetus in the mid-1970s as a result of the energy crisis, when the sudden increase in oil prices highlighted the dependence of advanced farming methods upon energy from fossil fuels (Bayliss-Smith, 1982). The quantification of energy usage involves converting the various inputs of a farm system into energy values, so that the total non-solar energy necessary for the production of particular items can be calculated (Wood, 1981). A similar exercise is conducted for outputs and by comparing with inputs, ratios of energy efficiency for different kinds of agriculture can be obtained. From this one may be able to infer why the nature and magnitude of energy flows vary in different cultural environments.

Wood (1981) suggested two major themes concerning energy and agriculture that have particular geographical interest: first, a description, discussion and explanation of the spatial variations in levels of energy efficiency; and secondly, a focus of attention on the range of responses that have already occurred, or are expected, with worsening energy price/supply conditions. Responses to the energy crisis which include changes in the distribution, types and techniques of production will have far-reaching consequences for patterns of agricultural land-use. Whilst agriculture is not a major consumer of energy, it is inefficient in its use and the energy crisis has had adverse effects on modern farming systems, as demonstrated by Noble (1980) for British horticulture and glasshouse production in particular and by Buttel and Larson (1979) for corporate-owned farms in the USA.

Therefore, adoption of an ecosystem approach has emphasised the significant role energy consumption is likely to play in farmer decision-making. This is already evident in such trends as organic farming, reduced or minimum cultivation techniques and renewed interest in rotational systems. Actual changes in spatial behaviour and land-use patterns which have resulted, or may develop, from energy price rises still await detailed attention from geographers. However, as Bayliss-Smith (1982) warns, a strictly ecological perspective does not provide a very coherent framework for agricultural geography. An integrated approach, which related ecological pressures to farmers' responses, goals and values and the structure of social organisations, is required for a fuller explanation of variations in agricultural land-use patterns.

Before leaving this section, the emerging radical perspective to the study of the agricultural landscape needs to be considered. This approach condemns modern agriculture and its consequent effects upon the spatial distribution of crops and livestock. The essence of the radical viewpoint is that the increasing affluence of the Western world is not because of agriculture, but at the expense of it. This is justified in terms of a decline in food quality, a rise in centralised food monopolies, the destruction of the rural environment and rural depopulation and its consequences. The industrialisation of agriculture (see Chapters 7 and 8) has not produced a 'just, stable and fulfilling society' (Merrill, 1976), Agribusiness, or the diversification of big companies into agriculture, is thought to be dangerous because one is forced to think in terms of food supply systems and vertical integration, where the companies control production, processing and marketing stages of an agricultural product. Real farmers drift away from the land or remain as kinds of caretakers and far less attention is devoted to the conservation of natural agricultural resources.

In reviewing the subject, Merrill (1976) suggests that researchers have been working on three wrong assumptions: that the sole purpose of agriculture is the production of high yields; that fossil fuels will supply agriculture with all of its energy needs; and that agriculture will only operate efficiently within an industrial milieu. Merrill proposes that instead researchers should assume that fossil fuels are exhaustible and that an important role of agriculture is to sustain farmlands with ecologically-wise methods. Geographers have as yet been slow to develop these ideas within a spatial context, although there is a growing interest in landscape conservation and the detrimental effects of increased specialisation and intensification in agriculture.

Hopefully it has been demonstrated in this section how agricultural geographers' approaches to explanation have changed over time, from physical to economic, behavioural and finally radical/structural. It would be wrong to suggest that one approach disappeared completely when another approach became popular and researchers have continued to work in all fields, emphasising the complexity of processes affecting agricultural land-use patterns. Indeed, it is quite clear that these trends reflect changes in the methodology and philosophy of geography itself and in this respect agricultural geography is no different from many other branches of the subject.

1.3 Agricultural data sources and problems

The study of agricultural geography has been hampered by the nature and type of data available and early emphasis on the influence of physical factors on patterns of agricultural land use was due in part to the absence of usable data about the 'man-made framework of farming' (Coppock, 1964). A lack of suitable social and economic data for spatial analysis remains, although the problem has been mitigated by the growth of farm questionnaire surveys, where the researcher collects primary data in preference to relying on secondary sources which may be inadequate for his studies. At this early point, it is worth emphasising that data and statistics are only 'tools to aid the completion of study'. In this context they have three useful properties: they allow description of the areal patterns of agriculture; they allow some analysis and explanation of the patterns; and they allow the formulation and substantiation of hypotheses, leading to generalisations and theory.

There are four main agricultural data sources, the advantages and problems of which can only be outlined in this text:

1. Land and land-use classifications

An early exponent of land classification was Stamp (1940) who classified Britain's agricultural potential according to the physical characteristics of the soil. Three major land classes, based on inherent fertility and productivity, were produced: good, medium and poor. These were further subdivided in relation to the type of agriculture the land encouraged. As a data source, the classification has little value and is subject to much criticism. Agricultural land-use patterns are affected by a whole range of physical and non-physical factors and such a subjective classification could not hope to help unravel the complexities of agricultural and farm systems.

However, physical characteristics continued to form the basis of later land classifications, such as the land capability and land-use capability maps produced by the Ministry of Agriculture, Fisheries and Food (MAFF) and the Soil Survey respectively (Chapter 5). Both provide information which could be used as a basis for studies of agricultural differentiation and the latter lists management characteristics against each sub-class of land. Despite this they are subject to similar criticism as those levelled against Stamp. As Tarrant (1974) aptly remarks, 'good and bad quality farming is not restricted to good and bad quality land'.

In an attempt to link farming structure to land classification, Hilton (1968) classified land according to economic production data, which was modified first in terms of 'critical physical criteria' and secondly according to economic efficiency. Unfortunately, the only measure of efficiency available to Hilton was farm-size, an indication of the shortage of suitable management statistics on British agriculture. In addition, Morgan and Munton (1971) note that Hilton made little effort to ascertain whether land or management factors were responsible for varying crop yield levels. Therefore, land classifications offer limited potential as a data source to the agricultural geographer and a general critique has been provided by Boddington (1978).

A potentially more valuable source of data are land-use and type-of-farming classifications. In Great Britain, the former revolves around the first and second national land utilisation surveys. The first survey, begun in 1930 by Stamp, produced a series of one-inch maps based on a simple six-fold division of land-use. These were merely descriptive reports of land-use at one point in time, which emphasised the relationship between physical factors and agriculture. Their main value would appear to be as an information storage document, available for studies of agricultural change and as a basis for decision-making investigations. The second survey has been undertaken since 1960 by Alice Coleman. This permits comparison with Stamp's work, although the system of classification is more detailed and land-use is divided into twelve groups, including transport, industry and derelict land; resultant maps are published at 1 : 25,000. In addition, a new classification has been produced, placing land-use into five types of environment: wildscape, farmscape, townscape, marginal fringe and urban fringe. The maps are published at 1 : 400,000. Therefore, a wealth of information is provided, but the enormity of classifying every parcel of land in the United

Kingdom means that it becomes quickly dated and of restricted use. Its main value would again appear to be as a reference document and in certain cases as a sampling frame for more-detailed investigations. For example, maps of the urban fringe could provide a useful basis for studies of farming practices within the rural–urban fringe (Chapter 8).

Type-of-farming classifications, which attempt to combine both livestock and crop variables into one classification, offer more potential to the agricultural geographer. Whilst Whittlesey (1936) produced one of the earliest classifications, at the world scale, it is the MAFF who has been dominant in UK publications. After the development of the standard-man-days (SMD) classification (one SMD is equivalent to an eight-hour working day) by Ashton and Cracknell (1960/1) and Napolitan and Brown (1963), England and Wales was classified into six farming types. This was based on a one-sixth sample of individual holdings and results were mapped using equal-size squares (10 km) and published as type-of-farming maps in 1967. In 1968, Church *et al.* produced a colour version, also based on the 10 km grid-square. Each grid-square was classified into one of thirteen types-of-farming, on the basis of the estimated proportion of total SMDs devoted to each type of production, and a monochrome version of a section from south-east England has been reproduced in Fig. 1.5. The following year MAFF produced separate maps for each farm type and in the 1970s published a series of coloured type-of-farming maps, using individual farms rather than

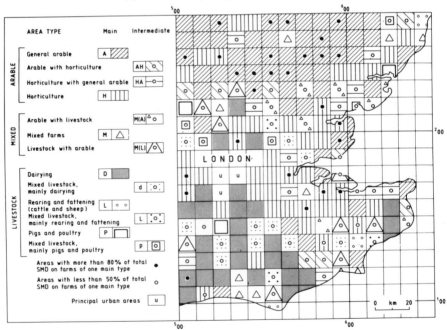

Fig. 1.5   Type-of-farming in south-east England, based on 1965 agricultural census (Church *et al.*, 1968)

grid squares as the basis for spatial differentiation. These were provided for each of the eight Ministry regions, at a scale of 1: 250,000. Two types of maps have been produced: first, type-of-farm by size of farm (acres); and secondly, type-of-farm by size of farm business (SMDs). The original 13 types-of-farming were reduced to 9 to facilitate mapping, and information for the exercise came from the 1968 Agricultural Census.

Geographers have also been producing type-of-farming maps, often making use of quantitative techniques in the process, such as principal components analysis and cluster analysis. Examples of this work include Anderson's (1975) classification of ADAS districts in England and Wales and Ilbery's (1981a) regional types of Dorset agriculture. However, it needs to be stressed that all classifications are means to an end and not an end in themselves. They are man-made and will vary according to the significance man attaches to them. The combined problems of scale, cut-off points between classes and the inter-dependent nature of farming activities have to be considered when interpreting the results of any classification (Chisholm, 1964). As long as these limitations are taken into account, type-of-farming classifications in particular can act as a valuable data source and can aid the agricultural geographer in his quest for a better description and explanation of land-use patterns.

2. Remote sensing of land-use

With increasingly sophisticated technology, remote-sensing techniques can provide the agricultural geographer with an important and unique source of data. This is because the aerial image gives a record of land cover over an area of any size, which is unobtainable by other means. Aerial and satellite imagery, such as that provided by the sensing systems of Landsat, show the type and extent of land cover in an area. The sensors actually record the reflectance from crops and vegetation, rather than the soil and other environmental features beneath (Allan, 1980), and as such are particularly useful for people studying land-use. This becomes acutely important in those parts of the world where the monitoring of crops and vegetation has in the past been totally inadequate for planning and resource management purposes (Cook 1979).

Remote sensors, which are not in direct contact with the objects about which they are collecting information, are very important data-gathering devices. Various techniques for collecting the data are available, ranging from reflective infra-red radiation to microwave sensing, and the interested reader is referred to the detailed exposition given by Tarrant (1974 pp. 92–101). These techniques are undergoing particularly rapid development, especially with the advent of Landsat (formerly the Earth Resources Technology Satellite) and the space shuttle. Landsat has been of overwhelming importance to land-use studies and was first launched in 1972 (then 1975 and 1978) to 'provide repetitive, high resolution, multi-spectral data on a global basis' (Rhind and Hudson, 1980, p. 80). The potential of gathering large volumes of data is enormous and by

1977 over half a million scenes of the terrestrial areas of the world were available either in digital or paper-print form. These data are collected at various ground stations and a number of distribution agencies have been set up, such as the EROS data centre in the USA and the Earthnet facility in Europe. Originally interpreted manually, the volume of data produced has initiated much research into methods of automated classification of data by the computer. These are relatively crude, when compared with aerial photograph interpretation, and are based extensively on tone rather than the size and shape of features; the latter are not easily used in a computer because the spatial unit is an abitrary one (Rhind and Hudson, 1980).

Whilst there are obvious advantages with remote sensing, such as the rapidity and repetitiveness of the imagery provided, no problems from other aircraft and the small number of skilled workers required, it would appear that the full potential of remote sensing is still to be realised and that its main value at present is as an aid to resource planning in Third World countries. This was demonstrated by Cook (1979) in a study of resource assessment in East Africa and confirmed in a detailed analysis of rural appraisal in Tanzania by King (1982). The very nature of remote sensing and its ability to record land-use over large areas suggest that it is not without certain problems and constraints. Apart from the problem of interpretation already mentioned, there are three groups of problems (Allan, 1980):

Environmental. Cloud cover is the main impediment to successful imaging in most areas and it can be extremely difficult to obtain a complete, cloud-free, Landsat coverage of a country within one season. Consequently, areas most suited to remote sensing—the low rainfall and semi-arid parts of Africa, the Middle East and Asia—are often those in less need of detailed resource assessments. Associated with, and exaggerated by, environmental conditions is the problem of resolution and artificial spatial units. Resolution remains coarse and unless one is dealing with very large fields, as in parts of North America, the spatial units will be of mixed land-use. However, the trend is towards higher spatial resolution and, with new sensors, it is hoped that a resolution of about ten metres will be achieved by the late 1980s. If obtained, this will naturally improve methods of automated classification.

Economic. The Landsat system of monitoring is appropriate in semi-arid areas for another reason: the relatively low productivity of many semi-arid regions. In such circumstances, an environmental monitoring system must be low cost because the productivity of the region could not sustain an expensive survey overhead. Similarly, many semi-arid areas are short of skilled census-gathering staff and so it makes sense to adopt a system that is undemanding on staff requirements. As Allan (1980 p. 42) remarks 'the inexpensiveness, the sequential and large area-covering capacity, and the capital, rather than labour-intensive character of the Landsat system all contribute to its appropriateness for the survey of renewable natural resources in semi-arid areas'. When discussing the costs of remote sensing, it is important to remember that aerial cover by aerial camera is by now an expensive survey method and is only possible where agricultural productivity will be high.

Political. For reasons of sovereignty, secrecy and ignorance, many countries, especially in the developing world, are aware and suspicious of the availability of Landsat imagery. This creates apparent security risks which, until the people living in these countries are educated, will be seen to outweigh any potential benefits in terms of planning and resource assessment. It is partly for this reason that the spatial resolution on early sensors was set at the coarse level of 80 metres; the consequences of the spatial resolution of just 10 metres are pure conjecture.

3. The agricultural census

Whilst many secondary data sources are available to the agricultural geographer, from historical documents to local government reports, the most commonly used is the agricultural census. This has been conducted in the USA since 1840/1 and in Great Britain since 1966; it has been held quinquennially in the former since 1920, but remains an annual event in the latter (Clark, 1982).

In Great Britain, farmers are obliged to complete a June 4th return, although for confidential reasons this information is not made available by MAFF at the farm scale. Instead, data are aggregated and published for larger administrative units such as the parish, county and region. The census provides information on crop acreages and livestock numbers, farm-types and sizes (the latter by acreage and SMD equivalents), the number, sex and type of agricultural workers, and land tenure. As a result it can be used to 'demonstrate the spatial variation in farming over wide areas and to study the evolution of these changes' (Clark *et al.* 1983 p. 155). The same authors point to four uses in particular:

 (i) The simple mapping of agricultural data, as demonstrated in Coppock's (1976) agricultural atlases of England and Wales, and Scotland.
 (ii) The derivation of agricultural regions, as shown by Adeemy (1968) for North Wales, Anderson (1975) for England and Wales, and Ilbery (1981a) for Dorset.
(iii) The study of change over time, as in Harvey's (1963) and Ilbery's (1982) analysis of the expanding Kentish and declining West Midlands hop industries respectively.
(iv) The diffusion of new developments over space and time, as exemplified by Tarrant's (1975) study of maize and Wrathall's (1978) investigation of oil-seed rape.

Despite this wide range of possibilities, much of the literature on the agricultural census has been devoted to the numerous problems associated with its use, especially at the parish level (Coppock, 1955, 1960 and 1965; Clark, 1982; Clark *et al.*, 1983). A review of this literature suggests that there are two main groups of problems: first, those associated with the use of the British parish or

US county as a statistical and geographical unit; and secondly, those associated with the reliability and comparability of census data. The first group included the following problems:

(i) The boundaries of civil and 'agricultural' parishes rarely, if ever, coincide, causing the area recorded for both to differ. This relates to the way in which farms are allocated to particular parishes and is clearly shown in Coppock's (1965) portrayal of farm boundaries crossing parish boundaries in part of the Chiltern Hills in 1941 (Fig. 1.6). Before 1949, MAFF used the farmer's place of residence to determine the parish under which farmland would be returned (Clark, 1982). Since this date, farms have been allocated to the parish in which the bulk of their land lies.

(ii) Parishes vary in shape, physical characteristics and size, as for example between 9 and 25,500 ha. in England (Clark, 1982). As parish data are

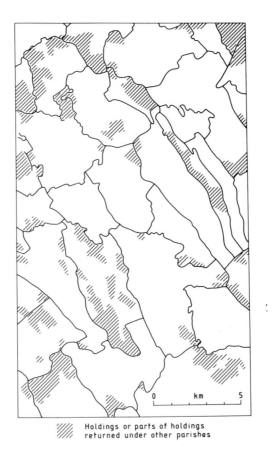

Holdings or parts of holdings
returned under other parishes

Fig. 1.6   Farm and parish boundaries in part of the Chiltern Hills, 1941 (Coppock, 1965 p. 104)

combinations of individual farm data, the level of aggregation and generalisation will differ. Therefore, the larger the parish, especially if it contains many small farms, the greater the degree of generalisation and the higher the chance that important enterprises might become 'hidden'. The problem can be partly overcome by grouping together smaller parishes, in an attempt to equalise parish size, or by aggregating groups of parishes to form similar-sized districts, as in Aitchison's (1979) study of Welsh agriculture. However, by definition this will increase the problems of generalisation and loss of information.

(iii) The number of parishes in Great Britain has been declining, making temporal comparisons difficult. Major changes occurred in the late nineteenth century and local government reorganisation in England and Wales in 1974 altered some parish boundaries. Clark (1982) has estimated that there are 26 per cent fewer parishes today than in 1870. This problem is compounded by the fact that parishes are not fundamental units of agricultural activity.

Problems concerning reliability, accuracy and comparability are more numerous, but in the main consist of the following:

(i) Whilst the holding of the agricultural census of June 4th each year permits the comparability of results, it means that spring crops may have already been harvested or certain crops not yet planted. Both go unrecorded, a problem which is intensified with double cropping and interplanting.

(ii) There is evidence of ignorance, uncooperation and bias on the part of farmers when compiling their census forms. Some farmers are genuinely ignorant of the size of their farm, especially in upland areas with common lands, whilst others appear to 'round up' to such convenient sizes as 1,000 500 or 250 acres. Even when the exact size is known, it is possible for the farmer to either under or over-record, in order to reduce liability to taxation or to claim extra subsidy respectively (Clark, 1982; Clark *et al.*, 1983). Co-operation by farmers has also varied spatially. Historically, south-east England had one of the highest refusal rates, whereas today the problem of poor response is likely to be greatest in districts with numerous small farms, common land or upland common grazing, or in areas with complex patterns of land ownership, as in the rural–urban fringe.

(iii) The definition of what actually constitutes a farm and farmland has changed over time. In Britain, five acres was the minimum size of holding in 1866. This was removed in 1867/8 and a new minimum of one-quarter of an acre was set in 1869. Although lasting for twenty-two years, a minimum of one acre was established in 1892 and survived until 1968. In that year the definition of a farm changed considerably, in order to eliminate holdings with little or no agricultural activity. Holdings were excluded if they had less than 10 acres (4 ha.) of crops and grass, no full-time workers or were smaller than 26 SMDs, (40 SMDs after 1973). Forty-seven thousand holdings were removed as a result of these changes, although 2,000 statistically-significant holdings of less than one acre (0.4 ha.) were included in the census after 1973 because they exceeded the 40-SMD threshold (Clark, 1982). Similar changes occurred in the definitions and census recordings of rough grazing and common lands, which hinders historical studies, especially as farmers in different areas have varying perceptions of what constitutes rough grazing. Since 1980, attempts to harmonise the British census with other members of the EEC has led to the progressive replacement of the SMD by the standard gross margin, another series of weightings applied to each enterprise. The total standard gross margin, expressed in European Units of Account (EUA), is converted into a new size classification of farms based on the European Size Unit (ESU). (1ESU = 1,000 EUA or approximately £500 of standard gross margin.) A consequence of this is that holdings of less than one ESU, under 6 ha. and employing no full-time labour were considered to be 'statistically insignificant' and excluded from the census. In Northern Ireland, this led to a 21 per cent decline in the number of enumerated holdings (Clark, 1982).

In an effort to reduce cost, the USA has also removed the number of small farms from its census. The definition of a farm was changed in 1976, to a business selling over $1,000 worth of produce regardless of the area of the farm; 300,000 farms were immediately excluded from the census.

(iv) Results of studies using census data will vary according to the scale of analysis and there is the associated problem of the ecological fallacy, whereby relationships between agricultural variables at the county and parish levels may not exist on individual farms. This situation is exaggerated by the failure of the census to collect information on decision-making processes, which would help the agricultural geographer provide better explanations of the spatial structure of agriculture. Indeed, the American census is now more concerned with farms as business enterprises rather than as distinct areas of land. As Clark (1982) has detailed, a long questionnaire is sent to the largest operators (over $2,500 worth of produce), which in 1974 accounted for 69 per cent of all farms and 99 per cent of the value of products sold, and a short questionnaire to the smaller operators. Questions are asked on the farmer's race, chemicals used, marketing arrangements, irrigation, farm income and expenditure, as well as on crop and livestock sales, subsidies and off-farm sources of income.

Despite the various problems associated with its use, the agricultural census continues to improve and remains an important data source. The greatest deficiencies relate to small farming areas and districts with complex land-tenure patterns, and there is an inverse relationship between scale and the degree of inaccuracy. With the trends toward larger farms, increased fragmentation and changing tenurial arrangements, the census authorities are faced with the awkward dilemma of either changing the bases of their classification system and so losing comparability or maintaining the old classification and losing the evolving character of farming. (Clark *et al.*, 1983). As these authors comment, 'the more the census reflects the current situation of farming the more difficult it is to map the results realistically' (p. 117).

4. Farm questionnaire surveys

With a more process-oriented approach to geography, the inadequacies of secondary data sources have become very apparent. The joint trends of improved explanation and behavioural studies have necessitated the use of personal questionnaires, which have become an important source of information in agricultural geography. Farm surveys provide primary data on enterprise structures and the workings of farm systems, as well as allowing detailed analyses of decision-making processes and farmers' attitudes and perceptions of the farming environment.

The wide literature on social survey techniques is now relevant to the agricultural geographer and whilst this book can only deal briefly with certain aspects, the reader is referred to such texts as Moser and Kalton (1971), Hoinville *et al.* (1978) and Marsh (1982) for greater clarification. At the outset, it is important to consider the choice of survey method and questionnaire design. With the former, the main distinction lies between postal and farm-based surveys. Postal questionnaires have a much lower response rate, rarely over 50 per cent, and farmers are often reluctant to complete 'more forms'. However, in certain cases they are unavoidable, especially in situations where national surveys are being undertaken, as in Bowler's (1982) study of pick you own (PYO) schemes in Britain and Ilbery's (1985a) renaissance of viticulture in England and Wales. A related problem with such studies is that they are dependent on lists of farmers and growers provided by various organisations.

The MAFF rarely releases lists of farmers for other people's research purposes. Farm-based questionnaires, where the researcher meets face-to-face with the farmer, can be more successful. Numerous approaches are possible, depending on the type of survey and farmer involved and the preference of individual researchers. These include prior appointment by telephone (if lists or Yellow Pages provide adequate coverage) or arrival on the farm premises, either to conduct the interview or to arrange a time suitable to both farmer and interviewer.

With survey method decided, questionnaire design is a second problem to be considered. Social survey texts stress the importance of the content, order, layout and wording of questions, all of which can be tested in a pilot survey. As well as being innovative, the questionnaire needs to be divided into distinct sections. This permits the collection of factual (objective) information at the farm scale, such as farm and farmer characteristics, enterprises and land-use, and changes over time, as well as attitudinal (subjective) information relating to motives, attitudes and decision-making processes. A combination of open (informal) and closed (formal) questions, carefully set out, can be useful as the former allows the farmer to express his own views, whilst the latter permits uniformity and easy coding of responses.

Certain problems are apparent with attitudinal information. Attitudes are complex and do not exist in a vacuum, and it is not clear with verbal responses whether the 'layer' of values being portrayed by the interviewee is the same as that used in productive decision-making (Gasson, 1973). However, learning theory suggests that values become internalised over time, with little difference between values expressed to the wider society and those internal to the individual. A further problem is deciding upon some adopted framework for recording attitudinal or 'soft' data, which will allow comparison both with the more objective information and between different farm operators. One typical method is to get the farmer to indicate either his degree of agreement/disagreement or level of importance to each item in a standardised list of statements. This is often achieved by adopting semantic differential scales or techniques like point score analysis and repertory grid procedures (Chapter 3).

A more general problem with farm surveys concerns sampling. The sheer number of farms means that it is virtually impossible to obtain an adequate coverage of them all and some method of selecting a representative sample is required. An early application of farm sampling in agricultural studies was made by Birch (1954), who considered the parish to have too much internal variation to be satisfactory for his examination of agriculture on the Isle of Man. However, sampling has certain inherent problems which have to be solved, unless a detailed survey of either a small area or a specialist crop is to be undertaken. Three problems in particular need to be considered:

(i) Lists of all farmers in an area are not available and those kept by MAFF are inadequate because they list agricultural holdings and not farm businesses, and a farm business may comprise more than one holding (Clark and Gordon, 1980). This leads to difficulties over the sampling frame, which cannot be satisfactorily overcome with reference to Yellow Pages or lists of farming organisations as they under-record both small and part-time farmers.

(ii) With most sampling techniques there is a bias towards the selection of large farms; the probability of being sampled is proportional to farm-size. In some circumstances this may not be a real problem for as Clark and Gordon (1980) remark, large farms are often the most innovative and 56 per cent of farm output in the United Kingdom is produced by the 15 per cent of farms comprising the largest holdings with over 1,200 SMDs. However, if one wishes to sample all farms with equal probability of selection, difficulties are encountered which have to be resolved.

(iii) The methods of sampling available have to be examined and the most appropriate for the specific task selected. A precise outline of different techniques has been presented by Clark and Gordon (1980), who suggest certain cluster methods of sampling to overcome the twin problems of bias and travelling distances in the field. However, each is hampered by difficulties and researchers may still resort to the simple, if unsatisfactory, method of using random numbers to generate random grid intersections within the study area and interviewing those farmers on whose land the selected intersections fall. Tarrant (1974) has similarly outlined a stratified systematic sampling method which incorporates a degree of randomness, but this results in a regular distribution of sample points and thus a large increase in distances travelled during fieldwork.

In the last resort and with all other methods failing, the geographer has no alternative to producing his own list of farms and selecting from this list at random. Whilst not ideal, the researcher will have collected information on farm systems and decision-making processes which is not available from secondary data sources.

AGRICULTURAL DECISION-MAKING

2.1. From economic to behavioural approaches

The preceding chapter established two fundamental points about agricultural geography: first, land-use patterns are complex in nature and causation; and secondly, the development of agricultural location theory has been slow and a poor descriptor of reality. The failure of traditional location theories, with their assumptions of rational economic behaviour, complete knowledge and profit maximisation, to adequately explain spatial variations in agricultural land-use patterns led to the development of behavioural models which stressed the satisficing characteristics of economic behaviour.

Traditional economic approaches to agricultural location centred on examining the effects of selected factors, whilst holding other possible influences constant. Although unrepresentative of the real world, these partial-equilibrium models formed the basis for explaining the spatial structure of agricultural activities. Foremost among traditional model-builders were Ricardo (1817) and von Thünen (1826) who both developed the concept of economic rent, defined as the 'return which can be realised from a plot of land over and above that which could be realised from a plot of the same size at the margin of cultivation'. According to Ricardo, variations in economic rent were caused by soils and rural population density. However, as Tarrant (1974) observes, Ricardo made two false assumptions in his work: first, that the margin of cultivation was determined solely by physical factors; and secondly, that agricultural production was homogeneous. Also, by concentrating on a single crop, Ricardo ignored the contrasting environmental requirements of different crops.

Whilst Ricardo's ideas rested on production advantages, von Thünen developed a model based on transfer advantages, where economic rent was controlled by distance from the market and transport costs. Von Thünen's work, which has been fully discussed in standard texts (Symons, 1967; Morgan and Munton, 1971; Tarrant, 1974), was based on empirical evidence of agriculture in his own locality and intended as a method of analysis rather than a theory of location (Chisholm, 1979). Economic rent was shown to decline with increasing distance from the market and this provided the necessary framework for both intensity and crop aspects of the model (Norton, 1979). The former stated that intensity of production would be inversely proportional to distance from the market, whilst the latter used different economic rent curves to show the tendency for agricultural land-uses to become concentrated in concentric rings around a central market.

Despite the many limiting assumptions of his work, von Thünen's ideas and the effects of distance on land-use patterns in particular continue to interest agricultural geographers. The zonation of agricultural activities, in relation to distance from a farm or central market, has been reported on numerous scales (Chisholm, 1979). These range from De Lisle's (1982) study of intra-farm variations in cropping patterns among the Mennonite cultural group in Manitoba and Blaikie's (1971) and Richardson's (1974) investigations of agricultural practices around north Indian villages and rice cultivation in Guyanan villages, to Horvath's (1969) and Griffin's (1973) work on land-use around the cities of Addis Ababa and Montevideo and Ewald's (1976) and van Valkenburg and Held's (1952) surveys in colonial Mexico and north-western Europe. Two further applications of von Thünen's ideas are worthy of brief mention: first, the development of Thünen's model in a dynamic context; and secondly, macro-scale zoning of agricultural land-use. The former was demonstrated in Peet's (1969) classic paper on imports into Great Britain in the nineteenth century, which came from an ever-expanding but logical von Thünen system, and in Day and Tinney's (1969) application using linear programming. The latter, assuming an extensive urban area and a continent-wide hinterland, was reported by Valkenburg and Held (1952) and Belding (1981) for western Europe and the EEC respectively, and by Muller (1973) and Jones (1976) for the USA, with megalopolis the central city. However, not all evidence of large-scale land-use zoning has been conclusive and Kellerman (1977) could find no such pattern in the USA, despite the observations of Muller and Jones.

Although a plethora of studies has been produced on von Thünen's model, the effects of distance and transport costs on agricultural location have declined in importance. Transport costs are offset by tapering effects and physical distance is less important than time, cost or perceived distance. Agriculture has also witnessed numerous technological developments, including the use of tractors, aircraft and fertilisers, which, along with major improvements in modes of transport, have relegated distance and transport costs to a more minor ranking in the list of locational and decision-making factors affecting farmers. These changes, together with the related problems of normative approaches to decision-making, macro-modelling techniques and aggregate studies of farmers, are responsible for the failure of traditional economic models to provide realistic explanations of agricultural land-use patterns. The need to look at sup-optimal solutions to decision-making, micro-modelling techniques and individual studies of farmers was apparent and agricultural geography began to experience a gradual replacement of economic models by a range of decision-making models and techniques. These recognised that the spatial structure of agriculture is affected by a multitude of factors, including social and psychological aspects of the decision-making process.

Behavioural geography is an elusive term to define, as demonstrated by Gold's (1980) 'the geographical expression of behaviouralism'. However, the objective of the behavioural approach is clear: to reject the notion of economic man and replace it with a model that is closer to reality. It is noticeable that the first behavioural studies in geography included the classic work of Wolpert (1964) on Swedish farming (section 2.3) and the review of theoretical developments in agricultural geography by Harvey (1966). The latter summarised the situation admirably:

If we recognise the all-important fact that geographical patterns are the result of human decisions, then it follows that any theoretical model developed to explain agricultural location patterns must take account of psychological and sociological realities, and this can only be achieved if the normative theories of agricultural location are made more flexible and blended with the insights provided by models of behaviour. (p. 373)

Variations in economic behaviour cannot be explained in terms of the availability of resources and a greater appreciation is required of the importance of social conditions and human motives in farming, as warned 57 years ago by Ashby (1926) and in the early 1960s by Williams (1963).

Gold (1980) outlined four distinguishing features of the behavioural approach:

(i) As an individual shapes and responds to both physical and social environments, the concept of environment, previously restricted to physical conditions, needs to be widened to include the social environment in which an individual lives.

(ii) Behavioural geography tends to focus attention on the individual rather than approach problems at the level of the social group. Generalisations are obtained by 'building up' from the individual to the group.

(iii) Behavioural geography is multi-disciplinary in nature and borrows concepts developed in other disciplines.

(iv) Environmental cognitions upon which people act may well be different from the true nature of the real world. Space has a dual character, comprising objective and behavioural elements.

An early exponent of the behaviouralistic school of thought was Kates (1962), in relation to hazard studies. Kates developed a schema for the study of decision-making, based on four assumptions and of particular relevance to farmers:

Men are rational when making decisions. This is in relation to the perceived environment which may be quite different from objective reality. Therefore, rational decision-making is not necessarily the same as 'maximum' rationality assumed in neo-classical models.

Men make choices. Many decisions are habitual and given little thought, especially organisational or day-to-day decisions in farming. Even major policy-making decisions, such as the choice of enterprise, may become habitual as a result of learning theory. This helps to explain 'tradition' and 'follow the leader' characteristics in agriculture.

Choices are made on the basis of knowledge. Complete knowledge is not possible and farmers differ in the amount of knowledge assimilated. Any model developed must take account of the differing levels of knowledge, the varying perceptions of farmers and the choices they make under conditions of risk and uncertainty.

Information is evaluated according to predetermined criteria. Farmers may seek satisfactory rather than optimal decisions and these will be related to attitudes, perceptions and values as well as to past experiences.

It would appear from Kates's framework that most decisions in agriculture are rational, but made to satisfy some goal which will vary from farmer to farmer This helps to demonstrate the complexity of decision-making processes and the difficulty of incorporating life-like conditions into land-use models. Found (1971) pointed to three factors in particular which act as an obstacle to the development of behavioural theory:

(i) Although many studies have revealed genuine insights into the decision-making process, the universal application of their results have not been demonstrated. Results need to be presented in a conceptual framework which others can build upon.

(ii) It is difficult to observe human behaviour objectively. Farmers may be unaware of the bases of their decisions and can be influenced unknowingly by factors. Whilst this is complicated enough, decisions are likely to vary between farmers when conditions are identical. Consequently, a common feature of decision-making is stochasticism, or a tendency towards randomness.

(iii) Human decision-making is a very complex process.

More recently, Bunting and Guelke (1979) have voiced further criticism of the behavioural approach, in particular its failure to solve the explanation problem. They comment upon the slowness to develop realistic theories and the failure to relate attitudes to observed patterns of behaviour. Lack of coherence is apparent and there is over-concentration on studies of images and preferences and the way these relate to the socio-economic characteristics of individuals. Although partly valid, these criticisms need to be placed in perspective and some are unjust given the short time-span so far devoted to behavioural studies in geography (Cox and Gollege, 1981). Economic models of spatial location have proved to be unsatisfactory and the same time constraint does not apply. In addition, empirical studies have highlighted the importance of behavioural influences in farmers' decision-making (Wolpert, 1964; Saarinen, 1966; Bowler, 1975; Ilbery, 1978 and 1979; Hart, 1980) and it is only from such observations that a coherent framework and common method of approach can be developed. The objective of the following two sections is to synthesise some of the various ideas presented in this quest for a standardised base and a more realistic agricultural land-use model.

2.2 Development of decision-making models

In agriculture, there are two basic kinds of management decision: first, long-term, policy-making decisions, including the allocation of capital resources and the choice of enterprise; and secondly, daily, organisational decisions which ensure the smooth running of the farm system (Morgan and Munton, 1971). Land-use patterns are, in the main, affected by long-term decisions as the selection of enterprise types has to be made by particular dates, according to the seasons or adopted system of rotation. The relationships involved in this process are intricate, although Found's (1971) simplified model of the decision-making process provides a useful framework for analysis (Fig. 2.1(*a*)).

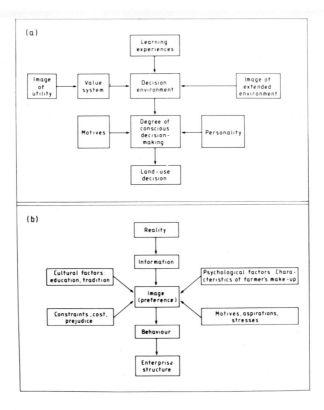

Fig. 2.1 Agricultural decision-making: (*a*) simplified view of an individual's general decision-making framework (Found, 1971 p. 166); (*b*) development of the image (Doherty, 1969)

The decision-making behaviour of farmers can be viewed as a reflection of a wide range of goals (Gasson, 1973), from family security and a satisfactory income to being creative and belonging to the farming community. However, many factors affecting decision-making are unpredictable, increasing the degree of risk and uncertainty involved and demonstrating the large chance element in the determination of land-use patterns (Hart, 1980). The causes of uncertainty are extensive, although Wolpert (1964) classified them into five sources: personal factors, such as a farmer's health, age and ability to work; institutional arrangements like government policy; technological changes in agriculture; market structures; and physical factors, such as the climate and other environmental controls. To these can be added the availability of labour and capital, machinery breakdown and disease. All farmers make choices within this environment of uncertainty, preventing the attainment of an optimising goal. However, actual decisions made will vary because farmers have different goals, levels of knowledge and perceptions of, and attitudes toward, risk (Wolpert, 1964; Tarrant, 1974). This is reflected in the spatial organisation of agriculture.

As a consequence, Found (1971) suggested that farmers proceed by a process of elimination when forming expectations. He felt it was important to distinguish between two types of environment (Fig. 2.1(*a*)): *the decision environment*, comprising information which is actually available to the decision-maker; and *the extended environment*, which consists of the complete set of information assumed in traditional economic models. The two are not the same, as farmers rarely feel the need to learn about the extended environment, and the amount of knowledge accumulated will depend on the farmer's education and his ability to search for information. A highly educated farmer, with more readily available information, will have a better image of the extended environment and his decision environment will begin to approximate it. However, in a majority of cases the difference between the two types of environment will remain large as farmers often lack formal education and training.

The decision environment, which affects the degree of conscious decision-making, is itself affected by a farmer's perceptions and value system. It is the way in which a farmer perceives the world which is important, rather than what is actually there. As Tarrant (1974 p. 47) remarks, 'the study of perception in geography ... is of considerable relevance to decision-making in agriculture'. Perception is important to the extent that it influences the learning processes whereby 'images' of the decision environment are determined (Saarinen, 1969). Therefore, one needs to consider the image an individual has of his own environment (Lynch, 1960). This image is developed by many factors, diagramatically portrayed in Fig. 2.1(*b*). Doherty's (1969) diagram shows how an individual's image of reality is determined by a whole series of influences ranging from cultural and psychological factors to motivations, stress, constraints and prejudices. The resultant image will condition behaviour and ultimately determine the enterprise structure of individual farms. As individuals will differ in their images of the environment, the collective result for farmers is the spatial contrasts observed in the agricultural landscape.

A further aspect for consideration is that a farmer's image of his farm environment will be modified by experience and past perceptions. Consequently, a dynamic element is involved in the degree of conscious decision-making and thus land-use patterns, again influenced by a farmer's motives and personality (Fig.

2.1(*a*). Learning theory plays an important role in the whole cycle and refers to the 'process whereby an individual or group develops a behaviour pattern in response to situations through time' (Found, 1971 p. 139). Learning may be conscious or totally unknown, but it is important because almost all human behaviour is learned. As Found continues to discuss, the differences between actual and theoretical land-use patterns can be explained by the degree of learning achieved by the farmers. Therefore, as geographers, it is important to obtain information on two things in particular: the learning stage of the farmers in an area, whether at an early stage or one of routine behaviour; and the conditional responses to information of the farmers, which reflect their learning experiences. From these conceptual ideas four important points can be established:

(i) Land-use patterns depend largely upon the decision environment within which a farmer operates.

(ii) The extent of the differences between decision and extended environments depends on the farmer's ability and motivation to search for information.

(iii) Decision environments vary spatially, causing spatial contrasts in agricultural land-use. The degree of variation relates to the extent farmers seek, learn and use information and to their perceptions, personalities and capabilities.

(iv) Social and psychological factors are important in the decision-making process and distribution of farming types.

These viewpoints add further weight to the argument that farmers cannot make optimal decisions and, whilst economic man can be retained as a yard-stick, it is not surprising that satisfaction has been proposed as an alternative to profit maximisation. In stressing the satisficing characteristics of economic behaviour, the *satisficer concept* gives more consideration to social factors and motives in farming and suggests that a farmer will seek decisions which yield satisfactory rather than optimal outcomes. The attraction of the satisficer concept is quite clear: the farmer lists the various alternatives in his 'subjective' environment according to whether their expected incomes are satisfactory or unsatisfactory.

If the elements of the set of satisfactory outcomes can be ranked, then the least satisfactory outcome of that set may be referred to as the level-of-aspiration adopted by the decision-maker for that problem. The theory suggests that as-piration levels tend to adjust to the attainable, to past achievement levels and levels achieved by other individuals with whom he compares himself. (Wolpert, 1964 p. 545)

As Blunden (1977) explains, the satisficer concept recognises the limitations placed on the farmer as a decision-maker, whose attitudes to his task will be constrained by age, education, experience of the world outside farming, socio-economic background, personal traits, personal ambitions, beliefs and interests, as well as the realities of the world in which he lives.

Simon (1957) was the first person to suggest that decision-makers are satis-ficers and should be considered as 'boundedly' rational rather than assuming that they have complete or 'omniscient' rationality. He based his ideas on two premises: information is not a free good and has to be searched for within the constraints of time and financial resources; and decision-makers have limited capacity to process the information as they acquire it.

It was Simon's ideas which formed the basis of later decision-making models. For example, Thornton (1962) produced a three-fold typology of the major aspects of the decision-making process:

1. Objectives in decision-making

As an individual rarely has all the information relevant to a decision at his disposal, social scientists have developed concepts such as goals and values, ends and means, motives, utility and satisfaction to help explain and compare objectives in decision-making. A decision-maker has a complex set of goals which are related to many aspects of his life, whether he is aware of them or not. To obtain an understanding of the formulation of objectives, a knowledge of these goals is vital (section 2.3). Objectives may be diverse and compete with one another, as demonstrated by the conflict between gain and security, but they have received insufficient attention from researchers.

2. Context of decision-making

Decision-makers develop a perceived view of reality which is often related to their past experiences. Therefore, in making their decisions, farmers will prefer to follow a pattern already established by themselves or somebody else; they like to avoid the risk of making bad decisions. This is so because farmers tend to adopt enterprise types which their neighbours have found successful, rather than experiment with new practices.

3. Methods of arriving at a course of action

Faced with the task of actually making a decision, a farmer must search for a plan or plans of action. How thorough and objective this search will be depends on various factors, such as outside influences (i.e. agricultural advisers), the amount of time available, cost and prejudice against a certain method of action. Thornton (1962) suggested that plans have two components: first, a target; and secondly, the date by which the target will be reached. In reality, many courses of action may be possible and comparison of alternative plans can be a very complicated procedure, especially in the uncertainty of the farm environment.

Implicit in the work of Simon and Thornton is the idea of decision-making being a search process. It was on this basis that Lloyd and Dicken (1977) developed a search-based model of decision-making, which has considerable relevance to agriculture. Like Thornton, they divided decision-making into three stages:

(i) The perceived stimulus to make a decision and definition of the nature of the problem.

(ii) The search for a satisfactory solution.

(iii) Evaluation of the consequences of alternative courses of action and choice of solution.

The interaction between farm and environment involves both inputs and outputs of energy (Fig. 2.2). The former comprises production resources and

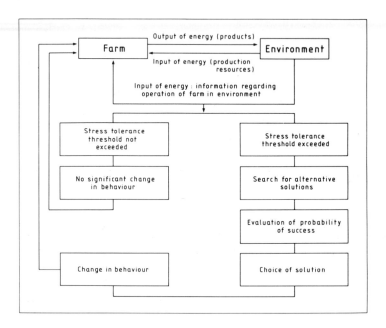

Fig. 2.2   A simplified search-based model of the decision-making process (Lloyd and Dicken, 1977 p. 322)

information whilst the latter consists of products flowing from the farm to the environment. As Fig 2.2 demonstrates, it is the input of energy from information which provides the platform for monitoring the farm's performance in relation to its predefined goals and values. Lloyd and Dicken refer to this as the aspiration level or *threshold of satisfactory performance*. However, the farm is dynamic and continuously adjusting its behaviour to minor changes in internal structure and the environment. A degree of imbalance will always exist between farm and environment, known as *stress*, and there will be a *stress tolerance threshold* which, if exceeded, will lead to a change in behaviour. Small stresses involved in the organisational or day-to-day decisions of the farm will have little effect on behaviour or the farm system. But if the tolerance threshold is exceeded (where the imbalance between expectations and experience is greater than the farm is prepared to tolerate) then stage two of the decision-making process—the search process—is initiated.

The search process tends to follow established lines. It invariably begins locally and is constrained by time and cost. Farmers, being conservative in nature, will try to find a solution which has proved satisfactory in the past. If this is not possible, Lloyd and Dicken suggest the adoption of one of two commonly followed procedures: first, a trial-and-error strategy; or secondly, the imitation of the behaviour of other farmers with similar problems. With the time constraint in mind, the order in which the search process is carried out is important. The satisficer concept becomes relevant as the first satisfactory solution encountered is likely to be chosen, on the principle of least effort, irrespective of whether it is the 'best' solution.

Lloyd and Dicken's model is really a simple learning model which is affected by experience. If a farmer is constantly faced with the same problem, a standard (satisfactory) response will be adopted which becomes learned. This is a habitual/ programmed decision and can be distinguished from genuine/non-programmed decisions, which initiate the kind of search procedure outlined above. In reality, many decisions occupy a 'grey' area between programmed and non-programmed decisions, adding to the complexity of the decision-making process and making agricultural land-use patterns so difficult to understand.

From a geographical viewpoint, it is the spatial dimension of farmers' behaviour which is of prime importance. A fundamental spatial decision is the choice of enterprise types and more specifically the allocation of crops and/or livestock to particular fields. Other spatial decisions relate to the changing nature of the farm system as new information and innovations become available, and the choice of possible marketing channels for disposal of farm produce, whether direct to the consumer or through local or distant markets. Most of these decisions will relate to learned patterns of behaviour, modified in the light of new information and technology. For example, the continued regional concentration of hop farming in the West Midlands and Kent can be linked to the spatial network of information supplied by the Hops Marketing Board Limited and to learned patterns of behaviour which have been found to be satisfactory in the prevailing environmental conditions (Ilbery, 1983b). It is the spatial aspect of decision-making that will be developed further in the next section.

2.3 Specific models and applications

In developing a methodological framework for analysing enterprise specialisation in agriculture, Bowler (1975) outlined some of the attempts to develop models of agricultural decision-making. These fall into four categories, ranging from purely theoretical approaches to empirical studies based on farm questionnaires, and will be used as the basis for the remainder of this chapter.

1. Pred's behavioural matrix

In the first of two volumes on behaviour and location, Pred (1967) proposed the 'behavioural matrix' as a means of understanding decision-making at the margin of transference (point of change from one land-use to another). The two axes of the matrix are the quality and quantity of information available (vertical) and the ability to use that information (horizontal); economic man is located in the bottom right-hand corner (Fig. 2.3). A farmer's position on the vertical axis will depend in part on his spatial location, reflecting the nature and importance of information flows, whereas on the horizontal axis his place will be determined by such factors as farm-size, education, experience and aspiration levels.

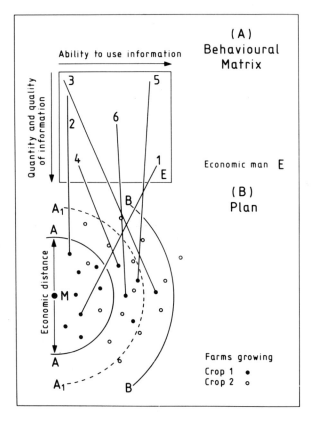

Fig. 2.3   The behavioural matrix and agricultural location (Knowles and Wareing, 1976 p. 43)

Pred emphasised the idea of 'boundedly rational satisficing behaviour', rather than profit maximisation, and whilst different farmers in different positions in the matrix will vary in their decisions, it is possible for two farmers at the same position to act on different bases and in contrasting ways (Johnston, 1979). As a consequence, land-use patterns overlap in an almost disorderly way (Hurst, 1974), reflecting variations in farmers' incomes and aspirations, farm-size, land-tenure and physical conditions; the result is a distribution of agriculture far removed from von Thünen's ideas.

In Fig. 2.3 a line joins each farmer's spatial location to the particular cell in the matrix which best describes his information and general receptivity. Six examples of farmers growing crop 1 are shown, with the following explanations (Knowles and Wareing, 1976):

 (i) Farmer 1 has made the right decision by using good information well. He approximates economic man.
 (ii) Farmer 2 has made the right decision purely by chance. This is because he has poor information and little ability to use it.
(iii) Farmer 3 is similar but not so lucky as he is growing the wrong crop for his spatial location. He is unlikely to survive for long.
(iv) Farmer 4 is making a profit but is not doing as well as he might because he has not made good use of the information available to him.
 (v) Farmer 5 is in a similar position, although unlike farmer 4 he is very able but lacks the right information.
(vi) Farmer 6 is an average farmer making a profit to the best of his ability and information.

An important element to emerge from these examples is that optimal decisions can be made by chance, demonstrating the emphasis placed on probability (Gold, 1980). To add to the complexity, Pred (1969) included a dynamic element in his behavioural matrix. Certain farmers will change their decisions, as they learn and acquire more information, and shift through the matrix towards the position of economic man; poorer farmers will become eliminated. However, changes in the external environment produce what Johnston (1979) calls parametric shocks. As a result farmers become less informed and less certain and so shift back towards the top left-hand corner of the matrix, before starting another learning cycle. Whilst parametric shocks outnumber learning experiences, optimal land-use patterns are highly unlikely and will occur only by chance. The behavioural matrix, which was never intended as anything more than a hypothetical conceptual device, has received little empirical application. It is virtually untestable and whilst possible to develop some index of the 'quality and quantity of information', measurement of an individual's 'ability to use information' is fraught with difficulties. Harvey (1969) criticised the matrix for being an over-simplification of the complex nature of behaviour and Morgan and Munton (1971) referred to the interdependent nature of the two dimensions of the matrix: information sought by a decision-maker and thus available depends on his perception of the environment, which in turn is related to his ability. Therefore, it is impossible to accurately locate the cell in the matrix to which a farmer belongs.

2. Deviations from an empirical model

Over twenty years ago, Butler (1960) produced a monograph on the attitudes and motives of farmers and their consequent effect on farming systems in the North Riding of Yorkshire. With data on a range of farm and farmer characteristics, Butler developed an empirical model in which he used the concept of a 'modal' farm to distinguish farm units that deviated from the 'norm' for the area. The features of the modal farm were determined by the mean values of different variables for all farms in the sample. Once these were established, Butler attempted to explain deviations from the norm in terms of three sets of factors: *physical*, especially local soil conditions; *economic*, especially capital availability, farm-size and tenure; and *social*, especially managerial ability and the desire to increase profits.

Whilst demonstrating the interrelated nature of factors affecting agricultural decision-making in North-Yorkshire, the model has received little testing and is severely restricted by its prerequisite of a homogeneous area in terms of farm type. Farming is often far from uniform, even within relatively small areas, and the model would be better applied to particular farm types rather than to a certain geographical area. Methodological developments in geography, and the use of statistical procedures in particular, have allowed more sophisticated calculations of the 'modal' farm. For example, trend surface analysis, with the production of regression surfaces, is most appropriate, especially as the resultant residual values can be used to measure deviations from the norm for an area or particular type or farming. This technique was adopted by Bowler (1975) and applied to hop farming in the West Midlands by Ilbery (1984d) (see section 5.3).

3. Deviations from a normative model

In his classic study of farming patterns in middle Sweden, Wolpert (1964) used both behavioural and normative analyses to test whether real-world decision-making accorded to satisficing or optimising principles. Wolpert's model was based on Simon's notion of bounded rationality and comprised three parts (Fig. 2.4):

Normative model of potential labour productivity. Using a linear programming analysis for 17 representative farm situations, optimum labour productivity values were determined which would result from the 'single most profitable combination of enterprises that is within the resource limitations, i.e. the potential productivity which the individual farmer could attain if his goal were optimisation and his knowledge perfect' (Wolpert, 1964 pp. 541-2). The major determinant of the potential values is the ratio of the supply of capital to land and labour resources and, assuming all farmers are economic men and use their resources optimally, the resultant pattern is as shown in Fig. 2.4(*a*). Potential levels are highest in the northerly zone of middle Sweden and in the extreme

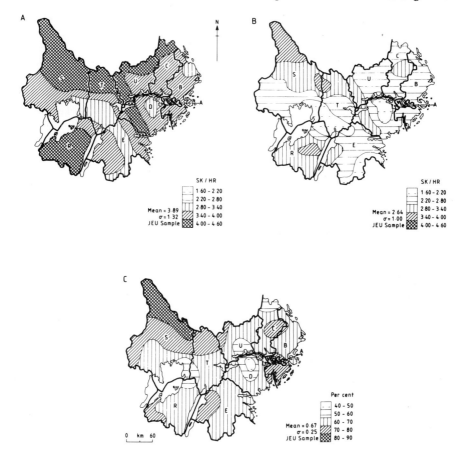

Fig. 2.4   Actual and potential labour productivity in middle Sweden's agriculture (Wolpert, 1964 pp. 540–2)

south-west (**R**); the overall distribution is closely related to structural variations in middle Sweden's farms.

Actual labour productivity. This reflects the net return to the farmers' labour during a four-year period between 1956 and 1959. It incorporates such factors as technology, finite supply of resources, individual goals and levels of knowledge, and the final surface demonstrates notable spatial variation, with the highest productivity in the north-west and south-west (Fig. 2.4(*b*)). High levels of actual labour productivity were found on relatively few farms.

Mean productivity index. In order to illustrate the extent of the difference between actual and normative patterns, ratios of actual to potential labour productivity were calculated. The resultant productivity index (**PI**) surface (Fig.

2.4(*c*) represents the 'human element' in farming as the average farmer achieved only two-thirds of the potential productivity that his resources permitted. With distinct variations in the PI surface, reaching a peak in the north-west, Wolpert surmised that there were significant spatial contrasts in the goals and knowledge levels of farmers and that the decision-making process had a spatial dimension.

In searching for an adequate explanation, Wolpert attributed the differences between actual and potential labour productivity to the provision of working capital, which gave greater flexibility in the choice of enterprise (Bowler, 1975b). Two additional factors were also isolated as being important: first, the amount of arable land; and secondly, spatial variations in the annual variability of crop yields. In turn these two could be held as indicators of variations in farmers' levels of knowledge and goals, constraints set by the resources of the farm and instability resulting from the uncertainty of the farm environment.

Wolpert concluded that actual productivity levels were guided by three factors: first, a farmer's desire for a satisfactory solution, which is sub-optimal; secondly, regional lags in the diffusion of information from the main urban centres; and thirdly, the degree of aversion to risk and uncertainty by the farmers. The work of Wolpert (1964) represented an important landmark in the development of a more descriptive behavioural theory of agricultural location. However, in line with the models developed by Butler (1960) and Pred (1967), it is unlikely to be reproduced for other areas or used as a framework for future studies because of its 'dependence upon sophisticated data at the farm level for the measurement of potential labour productivity by linear programming' (Bowler, 1975b p. 104).

4. Social survey analysis of farmers' goals and values

The four approaches outlined in this section have one thing in common: they all stress the satisficing characteristics of economic behaviour. Central to the satisficer concept are the goals and values of farmers, which help to provide a better understanding of their motivation. A review of post-war literature suggests that studies of farmers' goals and values have been popular (Taylor, 1949; Wilkening, 1954; Clarke and Simpson, 1959; Kivlin and Fliegel, 1968; Mitchell, 1969). Emerging from this work was the emphasis placed on the importance of non-economic values in farming, which is in strict contrast to the income-orientated values assumed by Butler and Wolpert.

Unfortunately, little attempt was made in the 1960s to synthesise the findings of these studies to form an overall methodological framework for analysing farmers' goals and values. This had to wait until 1973 when Gasson developed a useful method for studying values. Gasson's work was concerned with farmers' motivations, in an attempt to discover what farmers actually wanted from their occupation. Emphasis was placed more on *why* rather than the way decisions are made, on the basis that a better theory of farmers' behaviour would in-

incorporate behaviour as conditioned by customs, habits, perceptions, beliefs and goals and values.

A framework for comparative analysis was provided when Gasson listed twenty dominant values which might apply in a broad range of farming situations. These were classified into four groups (Table 2.1.):

Table 2.1
Dominant values in farming

Intrinsic Essenhan

Independence
Doing the work you like
Leading a healthy, outdoor life
Purposeful activity, value in hard work
Control in a variety of situations

Expressive

Meeting a challenge
Being creative
Pride of ownership
Self-respect for doing a worthwhile job
Exercising special abilities and aptitudes

Instrumental Helping

Making maximum income
Making a satisfactory income
Safeguarding income for the future
Expanding the business
Being able to arrange hours of work

Social

Belonging to the farming community
Gaining recognition, prestige as a farmer
Continuing the family tradition
Earning respect of workers
Working close to family and home

Source: Gasson (1973 p. 527).

(i) *Intrinsic*, where farming is valued as an activity in its own right.
(ii) *Expressive*, where farming is valued as a means of self-expression or personal fulfilment.
(iii) *Instrumental*, where farming is viewed as a means of obtaining income and security, in pleasant working conditions.
(iv) *Social*, where farming is carried out for the sake of interpersonal relationships in work.

It is the ordering of these groups of values relative to one another which influences farmers' decisions in situations of choice and in turn helps govern the spatial patterning of agriculture. After pilot surveys in East Anglia, Gasson concluded that farmers had a predominantly intrinsic orientation towards work, valuing the way of life, independence and performance of work tasks above expressive, instrumental or social aspects of farming; this confirmed the importance of non-economic values in agriculture. In addition, Gasson showed how the importance of values varied according to the size of farm business, with the 'smaller' farmers valuing intrinsic aspects of farming more highly than 'medium' and 'larger' farmers who placed more emphasis on instrumental and social aspects.

However, it is not clear from Gasson's work whether values varied according to the socio-personal characteristics and detailed production decisions of the farmers or the type of farming practised, the latter being particularly relevant to the geographer. If differences in values reflected differences in farming types, this could help to account for variations in the economic behaviour of farmers. There are two possible solutions to this problem: first, to examine farmers practising different types of farming and ascertain whether values vary accordingly; and secondly, to hold farm type constant and survey a relatively homogeneous group of farmers, to see whether or not significant differences in values still occur. The latter approach was adopted in a study of the goals and values of hop farmers in Hereford and Worcestershire (Ilbery, 1983c).

Before presenting the results of this work, it is appropriate to raise the problems relating to verbal indicators of values. Both Gasson (1973) and Bowler (1975) drew attention to the 'layering' of values, from the outer skin, which represents values upheld by society, through to the core, which comprises values an individual admits only to himself. It is not clear in social surveys which layer is being expressed and whether it differs from the layer used for productive decision-making. However, this is not an insurmountable problem as all values are socially learned and those expressed tend to become internalised over time and influence an individual's motivation. As Gasson (1973 p. 526) remarks, 'superficial answers are still meaningful and individual variations in what is thought to be socially acceptable can be highly revealing'. In response to the question 'How important are the following farming attributes to you?', the overall ranking of values by the West Midland hop farmers is presented in Table 2.2. Intrinsic values have again been emphasised above expressive and instrumental values, with social values having the lowest priority of all. As with Gasson's Cambridgeshire farmers, the hop farmers have placed more importance upon doing the work they like and being independent than on the income aspects of farming. A significant correlation (0.69 at $p < 0.01$) existed between the ranking of values by the two groups of farmers, although there were three notable exceptions:

(i) Earning the respect of the workers (social value), which was much more important to the hop farmers than to the Cambridgeshire farmers.

(ii) Self-respect for doing a worthwhile job (expressive), again of more significance to the hop farmer.

Table 2.2
Ranking of values by hop farmers

Value	Total score	Rank
Intrinsic		
Doing the work you like	342	1
Independence	340	2
Leading healthy, outdoor life	313	7
Control in variety of situations	302	8
Purposeful activity, value in hard work	250	14
Expressive		
Self-respect for doing worthwhile job	323	5
Meeting a challenge	317	6
Exercising special abilities	271	11
Being creative	268	12
Pride of ownership	247	15
Instrumental		
Making a satisfactory income	335	3
Safeguarding income for the future	295	9
Making maximum income	281	10
Expanding the business	220	17
Being able to arrange hours of work	218	18
Social		
Earning respect of the workers	329	4
Working close to family and home	266	13
Belonging to the farming community	238	16
Continuing the family tradition	196	19
Gaining recognition, prestige as a farmer	160	20

Responses were scored as follows:

Essential	4	Not really important	1
Very important	3	Irrelevant	0
Important	2		

Source: Ilbery (1983c p. 333).

(iii) Expanding the business (instrumental), which ranked lowly amongst the hop farmers but quite highly in Cambridgeshire.

These discrepancies can in part be explained by the nature of hop farming, a capital- and labour-intensive enterprise requiring particular labour skills. Hop farming in Britain is in decline and faces an uncertain future (Ilbery, 1982 and 1984a), and with the high level of capital investment required, expanding the business is in most cases a non-viable proposition.

With farm type held constant and Gasson's known differences in values between the operators of small and large farms, it is possible that different farm and farmer characteristics are associated with value orientations. Consequently, twelve variables, ranging from farm-size, hop acreage and the number of enterprises on the farm, to the age, education and status of the farmer and his experience of hop growing, were examined for possible relationships with values. No significant correlations were found, suggesting that farmers' values may vary more according to farm type than to farm-size. Whilst no significant differences existed in the ranking of values according to farm and farmer charactersitics, certain important contrasts were found between individual values. For example, the younger hop farmers placed greater emphasis on meeting a challenge, expanding the business and making maximum income than the older hop farmers (aged over 45) who stressed the importance of independence and belonging to the farming community. Similarly, owner-occupiers ranked independence and family tradition more highly than hop farmers who did not own their farm. Farmers with more than four enterprises felt that being creative and exercising special abilities were much more important values than farmers with three or less enterprises. Finally, the intrinsic values of doing the work you like and independence were stressed by those farmers who ranked hops as their number one enterprise.

Therefore, the more one delves into the nature of value orientation the more complex the pattern becomes. Indeed, a multivariate analysis of the twenty values and twelve farm and farmer characteristics, using cluster analysis (Ward, 1963), classified the 127 hop farmers into nine groups or 'types'. Results of this grouping process are summarised in Table 2.3. and their spatial expression portrayed in Fig. 2.5. Each group highlighted interesting correlations and stressed the importance of different values, demonstrating that farmers with an enterprise type in common have different values that motivate them. This complexity is aggravated by the apparently random pattern displayed in Fig. 2.5. and the lack of natural spatial groupings. It is clear that further and more detailed investigations are required before one can begin to generalise about farmers' goals and values. Alternatively, it could be that their significance is overridden by other factors. With studies in different areas and amongst farmers practising different enterprise combinations, a more realistic theory of agricultural land-use, emphasising the satisfactory nature of economic behaviour, may emerge.

Elements of the four approaches discussed in this section were combined into an alternative methodology by Bowler (1975b), who related deviations from the normal level of enterprise specialisation in Montgomeryshire to various physical, economic and social constraints on decision-making. This approach is discussed in more detail in section 5.3. and presents a possible way forward in studies of agricultural decision-making. With problems concerning the application of the first three approaches outlined here and the difficulty of generalising about farmers' goals and values, it is not surprising that other techniques have

Table 2.3

A typology of hop farmers in Hereford and Worcestershire

Group number	Number of farmers	Distinguishing characteristics
1	9	College/day-release trained farm managers/directors with little experience or tradition of hop growing. Family tradition/belonging to farming community not important.
2	7	Mixed farm and farmer characteristics, with much hop-growing experience. Independence, outdoor life and family tradition stressed. Being creative and making maximum income not important.
3	43	Mixed farm and farmer characteristics. Experienced hop growers where family tradition is not important. Independence, being creative and making maximum income all important.
4	13	Older, owner-occupier hop growers with much experience. Hops the major crop. Family tradition and making maximum income important, along with gaining respect of workers.
5	6	Large farm and hop acreages. Manager/director status, well-educated. Main training from hop-growing fathers. Expanding the business/meeting a challenge important, but not family tradition, being creative and arranging hours of work.
6	14	Mixed background/diversified farm systems. Most values important, except expanding the business and gaining prestige as a farmer.
7	13	Young, educated growers with small farms. Independence, challenge, pride of ownership, the farming community all important, unlike family tradition and working close to family and home.
8	17	Owner-occupiers, large farms with many hops. Being creative and working near family important, but not prestige, family tradition and belonging to farming community.
9	5	Part-time hop growers with little experience. Independence and arranging hours of work stressed. Expanding the business and gaining recognition of little importance.

Source: Ilbery (1983c p. 337).

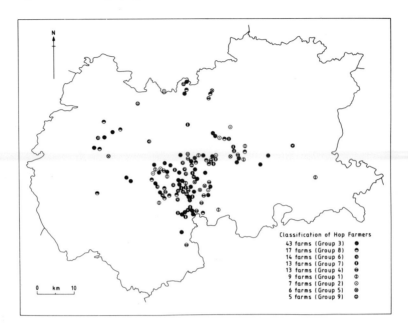

Fig. 2.5.   Distribution and classification of hop farmers in Hereford and
Worcestershire (Ilbery, 1983b p. 456)

been employed to analyse the decision-making process in agriculture. These
form.the focus of attention in the next chapter.

3

DECISION-MAKING TECHNIQUES

An understanding of decision-making processes is fundamental to obtaining a proper explanation of land-use patterns, and more sophisticated techniques of analysis have been developed to take account of the complexities surrounding farmers' decision behaviour. These range from the use of mathematical models for examining decision-making processes in a farm environment of risk and uncertainty, to studies of farmers' perceptions of certain factors affecting their decisions. A dichotomy between normative and behavioural approaches is once more apparent, as will be demonstrated in the subsequent discussion.

3.1 Game-theoretic models

Operating in an uncertain world, farmers have to make an important spatial decision: what kind of production is most suitable for their circumstances and where on the farm should each enterprise or combination of crops be practised? Game Theory, originally discussed by Von Neumann and Morgenstern (1944), can be used to predict the best choice of strategies (crops) available to the farmer and the proportions of each to be used; as such it is a potentially valuable tool in studies of decision behaviour. However, the mathematical procedures involved can become complex and this, along with other operational problems, has restricted the use of Game Theory in agricultural geography (Gould, 1963; Agrawal and Heady, 1968; Cromley, 1982).

Game Theory attempts to provide a normative solution to decision-making, in the light of farmers' incomplete knowledge and uncertainty. It introduces probabilistic formulations into decision-making and represents an extension to the behavioural bases on spatial theory. The probabilities are associated not with risk but conditions of uncertainty, which may relate to a host of variables ranging from weather patterns to market prices. Despite his lack of knowledge, a farmer will still seek optimal decisions and Game Theory is concerned with the rational choice of strategies in face of competition from an opponent, usually the environment. Therefore, the game is the farmer playing his environment in some form or another, with contrasting physical conditions resulting in different crop yields. This implies that a farmer will grow different crops, some which will do well in, say, wet years and some in dry years. Consequently, he will 'hedge his bets' as he only has a subjective image of the probability of future rainfall conditions. Given this situation, there are a number of possibilities open to the farmer, but the important thing is that his final decision will be reflected in the resultant patterns of agricultural land-use. The basic principles of Game Theory are best demonstrated by means of a simple example, where two assumptions are made: the farmer is confronted with three different strategies (crops) and can only choose one; and the income, or potential return, from these crops depends on weather conditions, of which there are again three possibilities. The actual strategies and returns (pay-offs) are normally displayed in a *pay-off matrix* (Table 3.1), which shows the outcomes of each possible move by the farmer against each possible move by the environment (Found, 1971). A high return is good for the farmer whereas a low return is good for the opponent (environment). The 'game' is to determine the best solution, which in the example in Table 3.1 would appear to lie between crops 2 and 3; crop 1 can be eliminated because it constantly gives lower yields. Crop 2 is the most successful when environmental conditions are right (wet), but runs the risk of complete failure with low rainfall. Alternatively, crop 3 is the most succesful in dry years; it also has the highest minimum yield (18), which means that it will give the best return under the worst environmental conditions.

Table 3.1
General pay-off matrix of crop yields

	Environmental conditions (rainfall)		
	High	Medium	Low
Crop 1	35	17	12
Crop 2	90	45	0
Crop 3	18	24	55

Source: Author's hypothetical example.

In reality there are various 'best' solutions, depending on the approach adopted. These have been summarised by Agrawal and Heady (1968) and can be illustrated with the use of the simple pay-off matrix in Table 3.1.

1. Wald's criterion, or the maximum–minimum solution

According to this criterion the farmer chooses the strategy which yields the minimum possible disadvantage. He is a pessimist and assumes that the worst will happen. In such circumstances he will consider the worst possible outcomes (12 for crop 1, 0 for crop 2 and 18 for crop 3) and select the least risky, i.e. crop 3. The farmer is choosing a course of action which gives the best result under the worst conditions. Consequently, he is a maximiser, assuring himself of a minimum return under the worst state of affairs.

This type of solution would be suitable for either a novice or a cautious and risk-averting farmer who is very conservative. It would appear to have greatest application in Third World countries, for subsistence farmers who often do not have the security offered by government grants and compensation for crop losses.

Although crop 3 is selected under this method, it may be better for the farmer to grow a combination of crops 2 and 3. This can be demonstrated in relation to Wald's criterion. To first confirm that crops 2 and 3 are the ones to be considered, the graphical device presented in Fig. 3.1 can be used. Vertical axes are drawn to represent yields or returns under the three rainfall conditions. Values for each of the farmer's strategies are plotted on the appropriate axes and then connected by straight lines. The lowest point on the uppermost boundary of the diagram indicates which two crops should be grown (Knowles and Wareing, 1976); in this case crops 2 and 3.

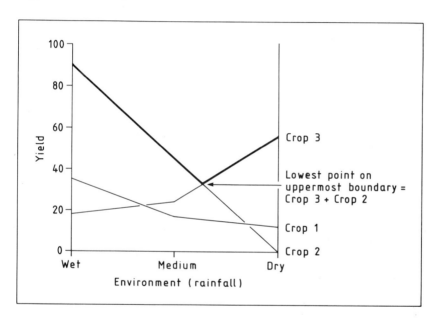

Fig. 3.1   Graphical solution to determine critical pair of strategies in Game Theory

With this established, the optimum combination of crops 2 and 3 is determined by use of the variance formula (Table 3.2). This is achieved in three simple stages:

(i) Determine the average yield of crop 2 and crop 3 and calculate the variance of each by the formula $\Sigma(x - \bar{x})^2$.

(ii) Calculate each variance figure as a percentage of the total variance. 83.7 per cent of the total variation in crop yield comes from crop 2, which basically is an unreliable crop carrying great risk of failure. However, it does produce very high yields in 'good' years, unlike the less exciting but more reliable crop 3 (16.3 per cent of total variance).

Table 3.2

Best possible solutions for pay-off matrix

1. Wald's criterion (maximum–minimum solution)

	Yields (x)						
	High	Medium	Low	Average Yield ($\bar{x}$)	$\Sigma(x-\bar{x})^2$	% Variation	% crop growth
Crop 2	90	45	0	45	4050	83.7	16.3
Crop 3	18	24	55	32.3	788.7	16.3	83.7
				Total variation	4838.7		

2. Laplace principle of insufficient reason

	High	Medium	Low	Yield
Crop 1	$35 \times 0.3 = 11.55$	$17 \times 0.3 = 5.61$	$12 \times 0.3 = 3.96$	21.12
Crop 2	$90 \times 0.3 = 29.7$	$45 \times 0.3 = 14.85$	$0 \times 0.3 = 0$	44.55
Crop 3	$18 \times 0.3 = 5.94$	$24 \times 0.3 = 7.92$	$55 \times 0.3 = 18.15$	2.01

3. Hurwicz's pessimism–optimism criterion

	Highest (α)	Lowest ($1-\alpha$)	Yield
Crop 1	$35 \times 0.7 = 24.5$	$12 \times 0.3 = 3.6$	28.1
Crop 2	$90 \times 0.7 = 63.0$	$0 \times 0.3 = 0$	63.0
Crop 3	$55 \times 0.7 = 38.5$	$18 \times 0.3 = 5.4$	43.9

4. Savage's minimum regret criterion

	High	Medium	Low	Total regret
Crop 1	$90-35 = 55$	$45-17 = 28$	$55-12 = 43$	126
Crop 2	$90-90 = 0$	$45-45 = 0$	$55- 0 = 55$	55
Crop 3	$90-18 = 72$	$45-24 = 21$	$55-55 = 0$	93

5. The benefit criterion

	High	Medium	Low	Total benefit
Crop 1	$35-18 = 17$	$17-17 = 0$	$12-0 = 12$	29
Crop 2	$90-18 = 72$	$45-17 = 28$	$0-0 = 0$	100
Crop 3	$18-18 = 0$	$24-17 = 7$	$55-0 = 55$	62

Source: Author's hypothetical example.

(iii) Invert the percentage figures to give the final optimum combination of crops. Consequently, the farmer will produce 83.7 per cent of crop 3 and 16.3 per cent of crop 2: a solution which assumes that the choice between the two strategies is on the basis of the best possible worst position—the maximum–minimum solution.

2. Laplace principle of insufficient reason

This principle assumes that the farmer has no knowledge of environmental conditions and that there is an equal likelihood of each 'state' of nature occurring. Therefore, equal probability weighting is given to each pay-off value; in the matrix in Table 3.1 the probability of occurrence of each of the three rainfall possibilities is 0.33. By multiplying pay-off values by 0.33, the expected yield of each crop can be determined (Table 3.2). Crop 2 is selected, with a best yield of 44.55.

Such an application of Game Theory is unlikely to be used, except in extreme situations, as it assumes complete ignorance of rainfall regimes on the part of the farmer. It could possibly have relevance to a farmer moving to an area about which he knows very little, but in these circumstances it is more likely that the farmer will, in the short-term, continue the system adopted by his predecessor or seek advice from neighbours.

3. Hurwicz's pessimism–optimism criterion

Hurwicz (1950) suggested that most people are neither optimists nor pessimists, but that their degree of optimism can be described by a coefficient called alpha (α) (Found, 1971). Alpha ranges from 0 to 1, depending on the degree of optimism, and can be used to calculate expected yields by multiplying the best return of each crop by α and the worst by $1-\alpha$. In Table 3.2., α is assumed to be 0.7., with $1-\alpha$ (pessimism index) being 0.3. Crop 2 is again selected, with an expected yield of 63. However, the solution has two obvious problems which restricts its use:

 (i) It only considers the extreme values and ignores other relevant data on yields.
(ii) The results will vary according to the degree of optimism–pessimism of the farmers.

4. Savage's minimum regret criterion

This approach assumes that a farmer will try to adopt a strategy which will minimise his regret. In such a situation, he attempts to minimise the difference between the yield that he obtains and the yield that he would have obtained had he known the environmental conditions. (Tarrant, 1974). This is made clear in the regret matrix (Table 3.2) which shows the difference between each actual outcome and the best possible outcome in a particular state of nature. The strategy with the lowest regret (crop 2 with 55) is selected. Being less pessimistic than Wald's criterion, the regret criterion can sometimes lead to a choice which will give higher yields.

5. The benefit criterion

Outlined by Tarrant (1974), this is a compromise situation between the regret criterion and Wald's criterion. Instead of selecting the best possible play by the farmer for each state of nature, as in the regret method, the worst play is taken such that all other plays would increase the benefit. A benefit matrix is created (Table 3.2), with crop 2 again being the selected strategy.

Of the five approaches outlined, the maximum–minimum solution is the most commonly employed. Gould (1963), in an application of Game Theory in the barren Middle Zone of Ghana, used it to determine the choice of strategies which would help win the basic struggle for survival. The study area had a very low population density and a severe agricultural climate where 'heavy precipitation ... is ... followed by the extreme aridity of the Harmatten, which sweeps south from the Sahara' (p. 291). For the farmers of Jantilla in West Ghana, Gould developed a pay-off matrix for five crops (Table 3.3). After selecting maize and hill rice as the critical pair of crops by the graphical method, he calculated that the former should be grown 77.4 per cent of the time and the latter 22.6 per cent of the time.

Table 3.3
Pay-off matrix for farmers of Jantilla, West Ghana

Crop choice	Environment moisture choices	
	Wet years	Dry years
Yams	82	11
Maize	61	49
Cassava	12	38
Millet	43	32
Hill rice	30	71

Source: Gould (1963 p. 291).

Gould proceeded to demonstrate that the questions raised by the 'game' are of equal importance to the geographer as the solution itself. For example,

Does the land-use pattern approach the ideal? And if not, why not? If the land-use pattern does not approach the ideal, does this imply a conscious departure on the part of the people, or does this less-than-ideal use of the land reflect only the best estimate they can make with the knowledge available to them, rather than any degree of irrationality? (p. 293)

A more recent and novel application of Game Theory by Cromley (1982) attempted to develop the principles in relation to von Thünen's land-use model. Patterns of land-use were deemed to vary according to the goals and values of farmers and Cromley tried to examine deviations from the idealised system which resulted from uncertain weather conditions. With the aid of linear programming, elements of Game Theory were used to show how a crop pattern (in relation to distance from market) that maximises the long-run economic return frequently differs from the pattern that maximises a guaranteed return every year. Cromley also showed that the long-run pattern generates a higher average annual return, thus creating a situation whereby farmers who can afford the higher risks dominate those unable to survive short-run fluctuations.

Cromley's work helps to demonstrate the mathematical complexity of Game Theory when pay-off matrices become large. With linearity a feature of the formal solution to such problems, linear programming is normally adapted to solve them (Found, 1971). The link between Game Theory and linear programming will be further pursued in section 3.2.

Therefore, Game Theory helps one to understand something of the 'complexity underlying decision-making, particularly because of its explicit focus upon uncertainty and upon attitudes towards uncertainty as key variables in the decision-making process' (Lloyd and Dicken, 1977 p. 314). However, a farmer could only assess Game Theory after much experience and even then it is unlikely that he will incorporate elements of it knowingly in his decision behaviour. A number of criticisms have been levelled against game-theoretic models (Found, 1971; Hurst, 1974; Tarrant, 1974), including the following:

 (i) They are psychologically and behaviourally unreal and fail to incorporate the whole range of factors affecting farmers' decision behaviour.

(ii) They simply simulate patterns without explaining why. Even if the predicted land-use pattern approximates reality closely this could be due to chance occurrences.

(iii) Although incorporating uncertainty and attitudes, they remain essentially normative and assume that the decision-maker, in creating a pay-off matrix, has a high level of knowledge and powerful computational ability.

(iv) The construction of pay-off matrices also depends on certain unrealistic assumptions (Found, 1971, p. 118), including linear production functions (i.e. doubling the land area doubles production), constant intensity of land-use and the ability to classify strategies as finite occurrences. With regards to the last point, it is quite possible for one year (i.e. 1983) to possess all the different 'states' of nature, ranging from very wet to very dry. Quite simply there is a lack of adequate data to construct pay-off matrices and it is virtually impossible to obtain information on the subjective assessment of probabilities by farmers.

 (v) There are too many sources of uncertainty in farming to be incorporated into a game-theoretic framework, some of which (e.g. machinery breakdown) farmers are unable to plan against.

(vi) In the applications of Game Theory discussed in this book it is assumed that the environment is a 'player'. This is a wrong assumption as the environment is not a true competitor because only the farmer can win or lose the game.

3.2 Simulation models and linear programming

Both linear programming and simulation techniques have been frequently used in agricultural studies, primarily as a predictive tool for agricultural planning and to show how future resources should be allocated to maximise some defined function. This approach is clearly demonstrated in the work of Heady and Egbert (1964) and Howes (1967), who used linear programming to allocate resource production between the different regions of the USA and the different sections of the Susquehanna river basin respectively. However, an increasingly important field of application of these techniques is concerned with farmers' reactions to changes in agricultural systems and their decision behaviour. This takes one into the realm of behavioural studies and necessitates changes or relaxations in the many limiting assumptions of purely deterministic models (Tarrant, 1974).

Linear programming has been used in case studies of agricultural decision-making in both developed and developing worlds. For example, Vasquez-Platero (1976) and Bourliaud *et al.* (1977) used linear programming to simulate the behaviour of peasant farmers under conditions of risk and uncertainty in Uruguay and Senegal respectively. Low (1974) was similarly interested in peasant farmers' behaviour in south-east Ghana. In order to incorporate elements of uncertainty into the production decisions of these near-subsistence farmers, Low integrated a game-theoretic framework into his linear programming model. This was not the first study to employ such an approach, as the bases of game theory had been previously integrated with linear programming models by numerous authors (McInerney, 1969; Tadros and Casler, 1969; Hazel, 1970; Heyer, 1972).

Low's main assumption was that farmers would maximise 'expected' income, provided the possibility of ruin was so small it could be neglected. He incorporated Wald's criterion to help minimise the cost of providing against ruin. Therefore, under conditions of uncertainty, farmers would provide against ruin by adopting 'a production strategy which at least satisfies their subsistence requirements under the most adverse conditions they consider likely to arise' (p. 312). The game-theoretic approach would enable farmers to minimise the cost of ensuring a subsistence level of production in all states of nature. Low felt that the incorporation of uncertainty formulations into his linear programming model helped to provide a realistic representation of farmer objectives and a good description of production patterns observed in the villages. This was confirmed by comparing predicted and observed behaviour patterns of particular households at one moment in time, and households in general at different moments in time. However, it needs to be recalled that Low's model was based on the assumption that the farmers would maximise their expected income in relation to yearly subsistence requirements.

Quadratic programming has also been used to represent peasant farmers' decision behaviour (Freund, 1956; Camm, 1962). Results tended to show a better correspondence between actual and predicted production plans than with linear programming. However, numerous theoretical and data problems increase the difficulty of applying this technique to peasant farming situations (Low, 1974).

In the Western world, simulation models have also been adopted to evaluate possible alternative strategies of the farm firm under conditions of risk and uncertainty (Johnsson, 1974; Hatch *et al.*, 1974). The former, in a study of European agriculture, developed a behaviouristic approach on the assumption that farm managers are more likely to look for solutions which satisfy a hierarchy of goals than to seek optimal solutions to their problems. This necessitated an understanding of farmers' goals and the proposed simulation model, designed to evaluate the consequences of random variations in the farm environment, appeared to work well in the cited examples.

A similar simulation exercise by Hatch *et al.* (1974) attempted to incorporate multiple goals into the study of decision-making processes of Texan farmers. The proposed model attempted to identify a hierarchy of goals and thus assumed that such a hierarchy existed and that each goal in the hierarchy had a quantifiable satisficing level. More specifically, the model was designed to determine the effects of selected factors on the survival capability and the growth of dryland and irrigated farms in the south central Great Plains. Seven factors were considered to be of major importance: goals of the farmers; initial tenure status; yield variability; consumption by the farm family; land requisition alternatives; initial farm-size and availability and cost of irrigation water. The 21 selected counties were all located in relation to underground aquifers (the Central Ogallala Formation) which could be used for irrigation purposes.

The actual model developed by Hatch *et al.* (1974) had three objectives: estimate a hierarchy of goals; evaluate a specified set of plans; and choose between alternative plans, taking into account the estimated goal hierarchy.

A list of 8 goals (Table 3.4) was placed in ranked order by the farmers, from which scalar values were estimated for each farmer. These were regressed on various farm and farmer characteristics (Table 3.4), including age, tenure and education. The simulation model was then used to compare the rate of growth for representative dryland farm situations in the study area. Three farm-sizes were selected (390, 648 and 1,036 ha.), the operation of which was simulated for full owners, part owners and full tenants. Each of the nine tenure-size combinations was analysed, assuming an operator age of 25 and 45 years. The final 18 situations were simulated for 20 years and replicated 15 times.

In relation to the hierarchy of goals (Table 3.5), results showed that 'to make the most annual profit' was a dominant goal about 80 per cent of the time in year 2. However, its relative importance declined over the other four decision years listed. In contrast, the goal of 'increasing net worth' became relatively more important and was dominant about 50 per cent of the year in year 18. The

Table 3.4
Goals and farm-and-farmer characteristics of Texan farmers

A. Goals	B. Farm and farmer characteristics
1. Control more acreage by renting or buying	1. Age
2. Avoid being forced out of business	2. Education
3. Maintain or improve the family's standard of living	3. Tenure
4. Avoid years of low profits or losses	4. Years of farming experience
5. Increase time off from farming (leisure time)	5. Number of dependents
6. Increase net worth from farm or off-farm investments	6. Off-farm income
7. Reduce borrowing needs	7. Farm income
8. Make the most profit each year (net above farm costs)	8. Assets
	9. Debts
	10. Net worth
	11. Debt-asset ratio
	12. Land operated
	13. Acres of owned land
	14. Proportion of land owned

Source: Hatch *et al*. (1974 pp. 104–5).

Table 3.5
Simulation of dominant goals observed in decision years for dryland farm situations, south central Great Plains (percentage)

Goals*	Decision year					
	Year 2	Year 6	Year 10	Year 14	Year 18	Total
1.	0.00	0.00	0.74	0.00	0.00	0.15
2.	2.97	0.00	0.00	0.00	0.00	0.59
3.	0.00	0.00	0.38	0.00	0.00	0.07
4.	16.67	35.19	32.96	30.37	27.41	28.52
5.	0.00	0.00	0.00	0.00	0.00	0.00
6.	0.00	30.00	32.96	47.41	50.74	32.22
7.	0.00	1.48	0.00	0.00	0.00	0.30
8.	80.36	33.33	32.96	22.22	21.85	38.15
* Order of goals as listed in Table 3.4						
Total	100.00	100.00	100.00	100.00	100.00	100.00

Source: Hatch *et al*. (1974 p. 109).

importance of 'avoiding years of low profits and losses' increased from years 2 to 6 but declined thereafter and was restricted primarily to full-owner and part-owner situations.

The two advantages of such a simulation procedure were that it allowed first, the goal hierarchy to change over time, in response to changing family and operator characteristics and changing economic conditions; and secondly, the data on the ranking of goals to be related to such farmer characteristics as age, tenure, experience and education. Farmers make decisions which are subject to uncertainty and for this reason simulation procedures are useful. Johnsson (1974) forwarded three major benefits of simulation models:

(i) There is no requirement of optimisation. The farmer is interested in a solution which satisfies a hierarchy of goals.
(ii) More aspects of risk and uncertainty can be handled than with many other analytical methods.
(iii) Simulation procedures facilitate a consideration of a firm's starting position with respect to resources and decision rules of the manager.

3.3 Regulation theory

Regulation theory, which is part of information theory (Ashby, 1964; Theil, 1967), offers considerable potential as a method of studying farmers' perceptions and decision-making behaviour. However, its rather complicated procedure has resulted in scant attention from agricultural economists and geographers. Chapman's (1974) study of the perceived farming behaviour of a group of farmers in Bihar, India remains the only geographical work to adopt such an approach.

Chapman demonstrated that a farmer is faced with an environment that comprises two parts: first, a physical environment which affects crops; and secondly, a human environment which provides the farmer with an opportunity of obtaining inputs and disposing of surpluses. Neither is known completely, creating uncertainty which the farmer must respond to. In his case study, Chapman made two assumptions: the individual entrepreneur was the prime decision-maker in the agricultural sector; and the decision of which crop to grow had already been taken—in this case rice.

Despite these restrictive assumptions, further management decisions have to be made during the crop's growth and these are based on personal assessments; for example, whether to spray or irrigate. In such circumstances three elements are involved: the physical environment, the crop and the farmer. The farmer can intervene and stop the environment affecting the crop, possibly by irrigating against drought, and is thus a 'regulator'. Consequently, the objective of regulation theory is to make a quantitative assessment of the farmers' capacity to regulate, but as Chapman remarks 'this measurement is dependent on the farmers' own definitions of environmental variability and their own expectations of crop yields' (p. 72).

Regarding the theory itself, the three principal information sources (physical environment, crop and farmer) can be in a number of alternative states and represented in vector form (Fig. 3.2). Two systems are shown in the diagram. In the first (A), an environmental disturbance (D) can transmit information as its state changes. For example, if there is a drought it can be seen in the withering of the crop (E); therefore, it is possible to assess the actions of the environment by observing the crop. The farmer (F) also receives equipment (T) to obstruct the flow of information from D to E; this equipment would include items like sprays, fertilisers and irrigation ditches. By observing the damage caused by pests and diseases, the farmer also obtains information from E. This acts as a feedback control, i.e. when F has not observed the disturbance in D and acted quickly enough. A similar situation is portrayed in the second system (B), except that inputs from the human environment (S) have been placed between F and T. If the farmer receives information about pest attack, for example, either from D or E, he may wish to spray. However, S states that no sprays are available in the market. Therefore, F cannot actuate T to spray because S has blocked the farmer's intended move.

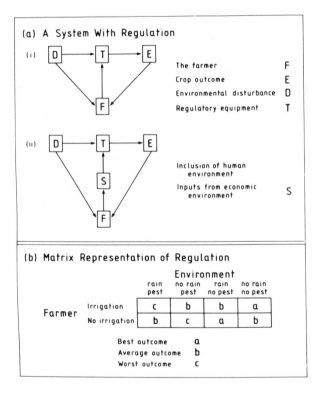

Fig. 3.2   Regulation theory and agriculture (Chapman, 1974 pp. 74–5)

To become operational, this information is translated into matrix form, as shown in Fig. 3.2. Very similar to a pay-off matrix in Game Theory, four possible disturbances by the environment (on the 'x' axis) and two possible regulatory moves by the farmer (on the 'y' axis) are portrayed. The cells of the matrix simply record the result of each combination of moves by the environment and the farmer. In his actual study, Chapman (1974) produced three such matrices, one each for the different growth stages of rice: germination, middle growth and flowering period. Each matrix consisted of aggregated individual farmer matrices, of which there were 92 (50 non-tribal and 42 tribal). Results of the pilot study suggested that 'there are differences between large and small farmers, between tribal and non-tribal farmers, in terms of their expectations of the benefits of regulation, and in the crop yields they are likely to obtain on the basis of their expectations' (p. 92).

Regulation theory provides an alternative and possibly more flexible approach than methods such as Game Theory and multiple regression. The idea of 'regulation' is that the farmer's response follows a known disturbance and is not the best estimate of the likelihood of one. However, in Game Theory both 'players' are committed to action at the same time, which necessarily means that each player is unable to see what the other does before responding. Regulation theory does not assume the environment to be static, but dynamic, because disturbance response continues through time. Apart from the data-expensive nature of the technique, there is also the problem of a lack of application. More studies adopting a regulation framework are required before one can hope to begin to draw valuable general conclusions.

Whilst acting as a valuable exercise in economic modelling and providing some insights into the complexities of agricultural decision-making, both simulation and regulation models have a large normative component and are fraught with operational problems. For example:

(i) They are restricted in use by data sources. Quadratic programming has produced a better correspondence between actual and predicted decision behaviour, but numerous data problems have restricted its use.

(ii) They quite often make unrealistic and simplifying assumptions, as in Low's (1974) study in Ghana.

(iii) They often tend to produce results which could have been reached using more straightforward techniques.

(iv) They are often far removed from reality and certainly too complicated for the farmers to even consider.

It would seem from this that more attention needs to be focused on Found's (1971) 'decision environment', as opposed to the 'real or extended environment' which is assumed to exist in most mathematical and traditional agricultural models. An important part of the decision environment is the collection of images of reality which relate to land-use. Therefore, a more behavioural approach to the understanding of the spatial structure of agriculture is required (Ilbery, 1978) and a number of techniques for assessing the importance placed by farmers on certain factors in the decision-making process are available. Two techniques in particular will be analysed in sections 3.4 and 3.5.

3.4 Repertory grid procedures

The 1970s witnessed a growing interest amongst geographers in images, hoping this would lead to a better understanding of man–environment relations and spatial behaviour. Unfortunately, the techniques derived to measure environmental images were divorced from relevant psychological theory and failed to specify the relationship between images and behaviour. However, the discovery of Kelly's (1955) 'Personal Construct Theory' by geographers offered a way forward and presented a method of measuring images via a repertory grid. The result was a range of studies on environmental images in many spheres of human geography (Hudson, 1980); agriculture was one of those spheres.

In examining environment–behaviour relationships, Personal Construct Theory believes that absolute truth or objective reality do not exist (Bannister and Mair, 1968; Harrison and Saare, 1971 and 1975). Instead, repertory grids are used to elicit information about people's attitudes and behaviour. The technique has been used to examine the perceived world of the farmer, especially in a Third World context (Floyd, 1976; Townsend, 1976 and 1977). Little work has been conducted in the Western world, except for an exploratory survey in mid-Warwickshire by Ilbery and Hornby (1983).

Farmers are not always able to identify all the factors affecting their decisions and so one needs a generalised cognitive view of the importance of possible influencing factors. The individually-completed repertory grid attempts to elicit information relating to attitudes, behaviour, motivation and perception of socio-economic issues in agriculture (Floyd, 1976). A repertory grid consists of a set of *elements* (different farms) and *constructs* (different factors perceived to have an effect on farming operations) (Fig. 3.3). The choice of elements and constructs can be determined by individual farmers, but in order to allow comparisons between individually-completed grids, a standard set of elements and constructs is advisable, possibly determined after a pilot survey. This standardisation is necessary for three main reasons (Hudson, 1980):

  (i) It reduces the time taken to elicit the grid, which allows the researcher to employ larger samples from widely scattered populations.

 (ii) It enables the researcher to test particular hypotheses and compile a super-grid, the underlying dimensions of which can be extracted using principal components analysis.

(iii) It permits temporal comparisons of images, although there is little work on this.

It is recognised that whilst standardised grids are preferred, freely elicited grids would ensure a more valid measure of 'the image'.

A standardised repertory grid was established by Floyd (1976) in a study of small-scale farming in the Caribbean. His objective was to test whether or not a meaningful measure of ideas and insights into agrarian problems could be obtained from the farmers themselves, as an aid to rational planning in the future. Floyd used three sets of constructs in his grid: physical, including soils,

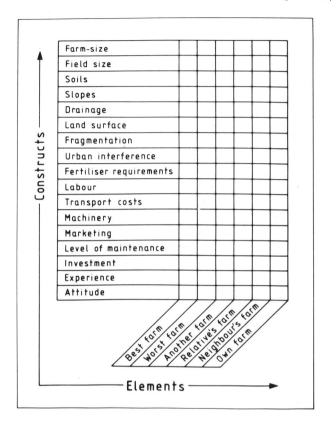

Fig. 3.3   A specimen repertory grid (Ilbery and Hornby, 1983 p. 78)

drainage and slope; agro-economic, including labour, machinery and fertiliser use; and personal-operational, including attitude and experience. Two hundred and fifty farmers in Trinidad and Tobago were asked to complete the grid, by allocating a score out of ten for each factor within the three sets of constructs, first for their own farm and then for the other 'types' of farm in the grid (elements). Additional information was collected on farm-size and type and on the age and ethnic group of the farmer.

Various statistical tests, from correlation to principal components analyses, were used to analyse the relationships between elements and constructs for four different groups of farmers. Results indicated a certain amount of variability among the farmer groups and the technique helped to demonstrate that farmers' decision-making behaviour was not irrational and traditional, but governed by economic constraints. Floyd concluded that the farmers were skilled managers and their experience of, and attitude towards, farming were very important in the functioning of small-scale farming systems. Similar conclusions were reached by Townsend (1977) in her study of the colonists of tropical rainforest in Colombia, where the skilled management of farmers was placed above physical considerations in the decision-making process.

A more recent application of repertory grids in the Western world (Ilbery and Hornby, 1983) also highlighted a number of significant relationships between elements and constructs. The objective of this study was to outline and apply the methodology of repertory grid procedures in an exploratory micro-scale survey of 35 farmers in 6 urban-fringe parishes of mid-Warwickshire (Fig 3.4). The selected parishes were of a fairly uniform agricultural potential, being classified as grades two and three land on the agricultural land classification maps of England and Wales, and permitted a mixed pattern of farming.

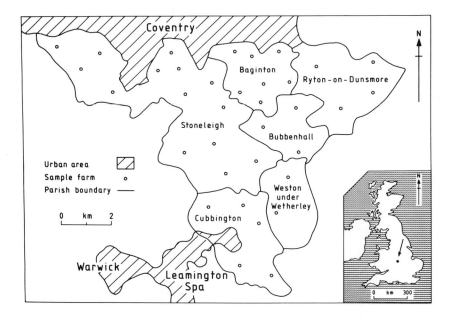

Fig. 3.4   Urban-fringe parishes in mid-Warwickshire (Ilbery and Hornby, 1983 p. 78)

After completion of a pilot survey, 17 factors were selected as constructs; these were very similar to those employed by Floyd, with the addition of variables on urban interference and field-size. The list of factors was far from exhaustive, but the choice was restricted for three reasons:

  (i) It is not possible to select constructs which cannot differentiate between elements.
 (ii) Constructs are confined to what the farmer can visually perceive.
(iii) Farmers are prepared to spend only a limited amount of time on completing the grid.

Upon completion of the 35 grids, by allocating scores out of 10, two sets of results were analysed. First, an averaged grid of the total sample was obtained and analysed by correlation and principal components techniques. Secondly, groups of grids were analysed in the same way. Farmers were divided into groups on the basis of structural, economic and social factors and averaged grids were calculated and compared. Correlation analysis of the single averaged grid revealed a definite relationship between the physical state of the farm and the personal factors of the farmers; attitude was shown to have an important influence on farmers' decision behaviour. Farmers thought to have the right attitude towards their farming system were perceived to have a high level of maintenance (+ 0.87), minimum urban interference (+ 0.86) and a good deal of experience (+ 0.83). The relationship between attitude and urban interference is an interesting one, given the location of the study area in the rural–urban fringe of Coventry, and will be further discussed in Chapter 8.

A more detailed insight into the relationship between elements and constructs was afforded by principal components analysis. Component 1 related to a best farm–relative's or friend's farm axis and component loadings indicated that the best farm had a sound physical base for farming, including high positive loadings for good soil quality (+ 0.84), low fertiliser requirements (+ 0.81), good field size (+ 0.77) and low levels of urban interference (+ 0.74). Other factors considered to be important on the best farm were well-organised marketing facilities (+ 0.96), quality labour (+ 0.96) and a correct attitude towards farming (+ 0.56). Negative loadings, relating to a relative's or friend's farm, were notably absent from component 1.

Due to the small size of the study area, it was not possible to draw regional comparisons between farmers. Instead, comparisons were made between groups of farmers. The 35 farmers were divided into groups in two different ways. First, a simple distinction was made between farmers according to their age, education and type of farming practised, whether arable or pastoral. Secondly, a more objective grouping procedure, using Ward's (1963) method of clustering, was undertaken, based on a total of 10 farm and farmer characteristics. Whilst primarily concerned with the objective groupings, the division of farmers on the basis of age and education produced some interesting results. Correlation analysis revealed that the younger farmers had a more physical-deterministic view of their farming operations than the older farmers, who placed far more importance on experience. Attitudes of the more educated farmers were affected by urban interference, which in turn was related to high levels of fragmentation. Levels of maintenance were shown to be related to machinery, marketing facilities, experience and attitude. Therefore, increased levels of maintenance were seen in the purchase of new machinery, which conflicted with the results of the less-educated farmers, who were reluctant to adopt new machinery and methods. These farmers considered that, with the right attitudes and experience, the essential features of farming were good labour supplies, well-drained land and non-fragmented holdings.

The objective grouping of farmers produced four groups, the characteristics of which are summarised in Table 3.6. These groups had a random spatial distribution and were not concentrated in particular parishes. The four averaged grids were first subjected to correlation analysis. In each case, results showed a high degree of relationship between a large number of the constructs, suggesting that all farmers had a good knowledge of, and a detailed approach to, agricultural decision-making. Separate principal components analyses were then conducted on the four groups of results, with attention focused upon component 1 in each case. Results for the four farmer groups are presented in Table 3.7.

Table 3.6
Objective groupings of mid-Warwickshire urban-fringe farmers

Group number	Number of farmers	Distinguishing characteristics
1	9	Young, well-educated and full-time farmers. All farms over 150 ha. Primarily *arable*, with some pasture and dairy cattle.
2	8	Farmers with wide age range, but little education. Half are part-time, and all farms under 150 ha. Essentially *livestock*, with little arable.
3	5	All farmers over 45 years of age, but all received college education. Farms below 150 ha. (3 < 50 ha.). Primarily concerned with *horticulture*, but one with beef.
4	13	Older, non-educated farmers, with farms between 50 and 400 ha. Full-time farms with *mixed agriculture*.

Source: Ilbery and Hornby (1983 p. 81).

Component 1 for the first group of farmers, who were young, well-educated and running large, full-time, primarily arable farms, relates to a best farm–another farm axis. Loadings are all positive and relate to the best farm, which was perceived to have a favourable farm and field size, with a land surface that was devoid of large stones. Low fertiliser requirements, good quality labour and low transport costs were thought to be important economic factors, just as experience and the correct attitude towards farming were important socio-personal considerations.

Half of the eight farmers in group 2 were part-time and all ran relatively small farms (less that 150 ha.) dominated by livestock enterprises. Organised around a relative's or friend's farm–worst farm axis, component 1 indicated a salience of constructs relating to a relative's or friend's farm. Factors thought to

Table 3.7
Principal components analysis of the four mid-Warwickshire farmer groups
(Component loadings for first component only)

Constructs	Farmer Groups			
	1	2	3	4
1. Farm-size	0.9318	0.3673	0.5499	0.7909
2. Field size	0.9189	0.4590	0.5866	0.7146
3. Soil quality	0.5734	0.7657	0.8422	0.9384
4. Slopes	0.0631	0.3026	0.3640	0.9333
5. Drainage	0.2988	0.8487	0.2810	0.6595
6. Land surface	0.7687	0.7411	0.9068	0.0676
7. Fragmentation	0.3885	0.2620	0.9274	0.5925
8. Urban interference	0.4090	0.1915	0.6646	0.2182
9. Fertiliser requirements	0.8188	0.4061	0.1864	0.2617
10. Labour quality	.0.9441	0.8235	0.0199	0.7021
11. Transport costs	0.8469	0.7468	0.7352	0.4066
12. Machinery	0.6108	0.8621	0.3825	0.8339
13. Marketing	0.2384	0.8434	0.1296	0.5970
14. Level of maintenance	0.1834	0.5914	0.8030	0.7200
15. Investment	0.4084	0.4596	0.4974	0.7553
16. Experience	0.7099	0.6620	0.3620	0.8685
17. Attitude	0.5508	0.7581	0.5473	0.8813
Percentage of total variance	39.77	40.16	33.86	47.79
Elements	*Component scores*			
1. Best farm	1.5617	0.2994	0.1643	0.3830
2. Worst farm	−0.2872	−1.8230	−0.9050	−1.7182
3. Another farm	−1.1974	−0.2758	1.3539	0.6532
4. Relative's or friend's farm	−0.7529	1.0590	−0.6067	0.3587
5. Neighbour's farm	−0.0104	0.1500	−1.0559	0.7368
6. Own farm	0.6863	0.5903	0.3547	0.8929

Source: Ilbery and Hornby (1983 p. 83).

be important on such a farm included superior drainage, good soils, quality labour, well-organised marketing and attitude.

Group 3 contained five farms, four of which were under 50 ha. in size and important for horticultural crops; all five farmers had received a college education. Component 1 related to a neighbour's farm–another farm axis, with the best farm approximating the latter. This farm was perceived to be little affected by fragmentation, stone-ridden land and urban interference, and in the minds of the five farmers, attitude and experience were unimportant on the best farm.

The final group contained 13 farms of mixed sizes and land-uses, run by comparatively old and uneducated farmers. An own farm–another farm axis was emphasized in component 1, with the former being characterised by good soils, land free of steep slopes, the right attitude and experience; economic factors were notably absent. Therefore, whilst the farmers of mid-Warwickshire were influenced by a fairly uniform set of physical conditions, results of the principal components analyses clearly demonstrated the diverging preceptions of different groups of farmers. In each group a different farm axis was identified and contrasting factors were elicited. This complexity needs to be further explored if one is going to obtain a more realistic explanation of decision-making processes and land-use patterns.

A detailed discussion of the Warwickshire results has been presented because of the lack of real-world applications of repertory grid procedures in agricultural geography. It is hoped that the study goes some way towards substantiating the remarks made by Townsend (1977 p. 452): 'it is possible that the repertory grid deserves in geography the role it has in psychiatry and psychology: that of a well-tried tool in both theoretical and substantive research'.

3.5 Point score analysis

An alternative and more simply devised method of analysing the importance attached by the farmers themselves to various factors affecting their decision behaviour is the technique of point score analysis, used by Van der Vliet (1972) and Henderson and Ilbery (1974) and outlined in detail by Ilbery (1977). There are notable similarities with the repertory grid system, for using point score analysis farmers are asked whether, in their opinion, each factor in a pre-selected and standardised list of decision-making factors is in general relevant, and whether it has influenced the choice of major enterprises or a decision to continue certain enterprises. The factors are presented to the farmers in a random order and if they are believed to be relevant, the farmers are asked to indicate how important they are—on a graduated scale from 1, for not really important, to 4, for essential—in influencing their decision to adopt the enterprise(s) in question. Alternatively, a value out of 10 could be given to each factor, although this is less successful with farmers.

Any such analysis of agricultural decision-making is governed by the initial selection of factors for study. Therefore, much attention needs to be paid to selecting a representative and well-balanced set of factors, as suggested in Table 3.8. The factors are grouped under three sub-headings to allow the *relative* importance of each to be measured: physical, economic and socio-personal. Although the choice of factors in the list is in itself subjective, the aim is to cover a wide spectrum of influencing factors. The division between the three groups is also necessarily arbitrary as much overlap exists within and between the classes, just as some of the factors are interrelated. However, one is dealing with farmers' perceptions and it is possible to categorise the factors into predominantly physical, economic or socio-personal groups. The technique allows

Table 3.8
*An inventory of possible factors affecting the decision-making
process in agriculture*

A. Socio-personal

  1. Personal preference
  2. Proven type of farming in area
  3. Agricultural training
  4. Personal experience
  5. Free time
  6. Prior knowledge of enterprise
  7. Personal risk
  8. Enterprise already established by previous occupier
  9. Others

B. Economic

  1. Market/demand
  2. Income
  3. Profits
  4. Under-used land available
  5. Labour
  6. Capital
  7. Transport costs
  8. Buildings/machinery
  9. Policy of co-operative
 10. Government policy
 11. Others

C. Physical

  1. Soil type
  2. Soil drainage
  3. Degree and aspect of slope
  4. Weather uncertainty
  5. Amount of rainfall
  6. Frequency of frosts
  7. Temperature variations
  8. Size of fields
  9. Others

Source: Ilbery (1977 p. 68).

for the list of factors to be modified, depending on the type of farming being analysed, and other factors to be added by the farmers themselves.

The overall importance of each factor can be measured by totalling the point scores for all the farmers interviewed, for each factor in turn. From this the factors can be ranked in order of importance to the decision-making process. Each factor will have a maximum possible score, depending on the number of farmers involved, and three indices can be calculated. Following Van der Vliet (1972) these are:

  (i) Percentage applicability (% A). The number of cases where the factor applied expressed as a percentage of the total number of cases investigated.

  (ii) Total percentage (% T). The total score, expressed as a percentage of the maximum possible score for all cases investigated.

  (iii) Percentage importance (% I). The total score, expressed as a percentage of the maximum possible score for those cases where the factor was applicable.

Further statistical analysis of this information is possible. The degree of inter-relationship between the factors can be tested using the Chi-squared test, affording a greater depth of understanding of the decision-making process, and the farmers can be grouped according to their degree of similarity in relation to the perception of decision-making factors. This classification of 'farmer types' can be achieved using Wishart's (1969) algorithm as the criterion for grouping. By taking the analysis a stage further and relating farmers' perceptions to their socio-personal characteristics, such as age, education, status and training, and to the type of farming practised, the complexities of farmer decision behaviour can begin to be unravelled.

Results of studies so far undertaken (Van der Vliet, 1972; Henderson and Ilbery, 1974; Ilbery, 1979 and 1983b), using the technique of point score analysis, indicate that the main aim of farmers is to obtain a secure and stable farm business; this above all else appears to be the dominant factor in the decision-making process, consisting of socio-personal considerations as well as economic and physical considerations. Once the essential requirements for the achievement of security are achieved, farmers appear to be more influenced by social and personal factors, choosing an enterprise system which gives most satisfaction.

The technique of point score analysis was used in a detailed study of 112 farmers in north-east Oxfordshire (Ilbery, 1979). Inter-farm differences in land-use were found to be considerable, but it was felt that these could not be attributed to variations in the physical landscape. Farmers in north-east Oxfordshire (Fig. 3.5) are subject to a broadly homogeneous physical environment which allows a wide choice of possible enterprise types. The physical uniformity is considerably enhanced by the presence of a number of superficial deposits; as Martin and Steel (1954 p. 29) remarked for the area 'the influence of the drift on the surface is remarkable'. This is confirmed by a physiographic map of the Oxford region, prepared by the Soil Science Laboratory, Oxford, in collaboration with the Military Engineering Experimental Establishment, which places almost the entire study area within its category 13 f (Ilbery, 1977). Category 13 f is described as dip-slope plateau with level to gently sloping, even topography characterised by free drainage, which allows easy management of agricultural land. Consequently, the *relative* importance of economic and socio-personal factors in the decision-making process was examined, in relation to the two main enterprises on each farm. Variations in farmer decision behaviour were thought to be important in accounting for the spatial patterns of agricultural land-use.

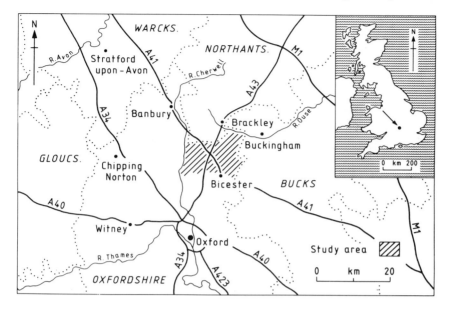

Fig. 3.5 North-east Oxfordshire: general location map

Results of the point score analysis for 19 economic and socio-personal factors are shown in Table 3.9. The final ranking of factors indicates that the three most important are of an economic nature; this is to be expected given the essentially commercial nature of farming, as far as the leading enterprises are concerned. All farmers dependent on farming for a living are necessarily influenced by such factors as income, profits and market/demand, in order to maintain the way of life to which they are accustomed. However, the next four most highly-ranked factors are of a socio-personal nature. Experience, personal preference, free time and risk avoidance emerged as major factors affecting the decision-making behaviour of farmers in north-east Oxfordshire. Indeed, six of the first eleven ranked factors have socio-personal connotations and that is without considering subsidiary enterprises in the farm system. This helps to verify the hypothesis that variations in farmers' attitudes are considerable and justify the need for more work on the effects of farmers' motives on choice of enterprise types.

In order to demonstrate the complexity and individuality of the decision-making process, the farmers of north-east Oxfordshire were classified according to their degree of similarity in relation to the nineteen decision-making factors listed in Table 3.9, farm-size and eight socio-personal characteristics of the farmers, including age, education, status and when they thought they would stop farming. The typology produced eight 'farmer types', varying in size from three to 35 farmers, with each group demonstrating the importance of different factors (Table 3.10). Once again, marked farm-to-farm variations emerged when the

Table 3.9

*Ranking of decision-making factors in order of importance
for north-east Oxfordshire farmers*

Factor number	Factor	Total score	Rank
A. Economic factors			
1	Stable market/demand	642	1
3	Regular income	524	2
5	Under-used land available	56	18
7	Did not require much labour	332	8
9	Did not require much working capital	213	10
11	Above-average profits	523	3
13	Transport costs	138	13
15	Available buildings/machinery	164	12
17	Co-operatives	33	19
19	Government policy	74	16
B. Socio-personal factors			
2	Personal preference	363	7
4	Agricultural training	82	15
6	Enterprise already here	176	11
8	Experience	490	4
10	Proven type of farming in area	314	9
12	Free time	385	6
14	Prior knowledge of enterprise	59	17
16	Personal risk	479	5
18	Trained staff	106	14

Source: Ilbery (1979 p. 206).

resultant groups were mapped (Fig. 3.6). When these farmer types were related to 'farm types' a poor relationship emerged (Ilbery, 1979), indicating that there is no simple correlation between a farmer's perception of decision-making factors and his choice of enterprise types. This necessitated more research on the relationship between farmers' values and perceptions and the type of farming practiced. Consequently, recent work by the author has concentrated on the decision-making behaviour of farmers practising a specific type of farming: hops in the West Midlands (Ilbery, 1983b) and horticulture in the Vale of Evesham (Ilbery, 1985b).

Although detailed results for the horticultural survey are not as yet available, the initial ranking of factors makes some interesting contrasts with those obtained for the hop farmers (Table 3.11). If those factors which are not common to both hops and horticulture are excluded, such as specialised hop buildings/ machinery, verticillium wilt (hop disease), horticultural grower co-operatives and

Table 3.10

A typology of farmer types in north-east Oxfordshire

Group number	Number of farmers	Distinguishing characteristics
1	3	Preference more important than income. Full-time farmers who consider free time and prior knowledge to be important factors.
2	23	Income more important than preference. Full-time farmers, over 35 years of age, who consider prior knowledge to be irrelevant.
3	35	Full-time, mainly small-scale farmers. Market/demand, income and free-time important factors.
4	4	Three of the four less than 45 years of age. Considerable importance attached to practical training and government policy.
5	21	Large-scale farmers, received above-average education for area. Market/demand considered essential by all but not one considered capital to be essential.
6	12	Full-time farmers, with younger element well represented. Obtained good practical training. Free time an irrelevant factor.
7	8	Part-time farmers over 55 years of age. Free time an important factor, but income not really important.
8	6	Group of varying ages. The only farmers in area who considered co-operatives to be an important factor.

Source: Ilbery (1979 p. 207).

transport costs (hop growers pay standardised cost for transporting their hops, irrespective of distance from warehouses), notable differences in the ranking of certain factors are apparent. For the horticultural growers, the socio-personal factors of experience and personal preference ranked first and third in the list of decision-making factors. Along with the second ranked factors of drainage, these three have a total point score far in excess of the remaining factors, emphasising their considerable dominance in the horticultural structure of the area. Whilst drainage is also important to the hop farmers, experience and personal preference ranked far lower, at seventh and eleventh respectively.

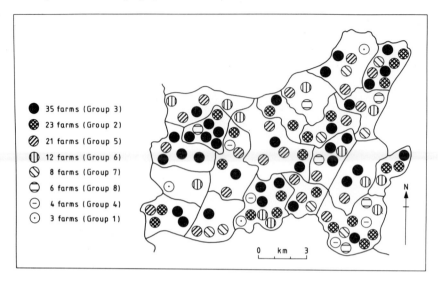

Fig. 3.6   Classification of farmers in north-east Oxfordshire on the basis of
28 decision-making factors (Ilbery, 1979, p. 208)

Certain differences in the perception of the importance of physical and economic factors also occurred. With drainage and soil type important to both groups
of farmers, it is noticeable that the volume of water supply, temperature (growing
season) and frequency of frosts are more important considerations to the horti-
culturalists than to the hop farmers. These differences relate to the nature of the
two types of farming, with horticulture in the Vale renowned for its early season
produce and being dependent on good temperatures and irrigation systems and
avoiding frost pockets. Similar conclusions can be drawn for the differences in
ranking of certain economic factors. Both crops are capital-intensive and hence
the importance of this factor; they are also labour-intensive, but hop farming is
much more dependent upon a skilled labour supply than horticulture and this is
the reason for the large difference between the two groups in terms of the
perceived importance of this factor. Size of farm is not a highly ranked factor
for either type of farming, although it plays a more significant role in the Vale of
Evesham and relates in part to levels of fragmentation (Ilbery, 1984c). On the
other hand, a stable market/demand is a vital consideration to the hop farmers,
many of whom would be forced out of business without the stabilising effects of
the HMB (Ilbery, 1984a and b). The final contrast concerns the role of distance
as an influencing factor. In both examples it ranks fairly lowly, although proximity to the market is of more significance to the horticultural farmers than
distance to the headquarters of the HMB is to the hop farmers.

Multivariate analyses of the two sets of data demonstrated considerable
variability amongst each of these relatively homogeneous groups of farmers,
with cluster analysis (Ward, 1963) producing 9 groups of hop farmers and 7

Table 3.11

Ranking of decision-making factors by hop farmers and horticultural growers

Hops (127 farmers)	Score	*Horticulture* (205 farmers)	Score
1. Buildings/machinery	440	1. Experience	710
2. Stable market/demand	423	2. Drainage	608
3. Drainage	416	3. Personal preference	507
4. Soil type	396	4. Soil type	459
5. Skilled labour supply	387	5. Volume of water supply	459
6. Available capital	386	6. Temperature	457
7. Experience	362	7. Available capital	453
8. Regular income	356	8. Rainfall	440
9. Verticillium wilt	341	9. Frequency of frosts	439
10. Shelter	337	10. Size of farm	430
11. Personal preference	330	11. Transport costs	429
12. 25–35 inches rainfall	287	12. Regular income	425
13. Height of water table	286	13. Stable market/demand	423
14. Volume of water supply	285	14. Proximity of main markets	370
15. Temperature	284	15. Level land	365
16. Area tradition	247	16. Shelter	257
17. Level land	190	17. Low levels of risk	337
18. Family tradition	182	18. Area tradition	331
19. Frequency of frosts	172	19. Height of water table	310
20. Agricultural training	172	20. Government policy	282
21. Size of farm	53	21. Family tradition	260
22. Free time	45	22. Grower co-operatives	219
23. Low levels of risk	31	23. Skilled labour supply	215
24. Distance from HMB	20	24. Horticultural training	200
		25. Free time	197

Source: Author's surveys.

groups of horticultural growers. Clearly, much more work is required on the decision behaviour of farmers practising different farm types.

This chapter has attempted to provide a review of some of the techniques used to examine the decision-making process in agriculture and its effects on spatial patterns of agricultural land-use. The differences between normative/ mathematical and behavioural/descriptive approaches are quite marked and there have been few attempts to bridge the gap. However, Hayter (1975) has suggested that a Bayesian approach to decision-making could provide the necessary link because it takes account of an individual's subjective feelings and perceptions within a normative framework. The Bayesian model is based on the use of subjective probabilities in choice behaviour, derived from hunches, memory and judgement, presented in the form of a decision tree. Its subjective probability framework provides 'a complementary but more normative model of the effect of uncertainty on decision-making than the more behavioural path based upon subjective generalisations made by the farmer' (Hayter, 1975 p. 95). However, the Bayesian model awaits rigorous empirical testing in geography, although Hart (1980) has similarly proposed the linking of economic and behavioural approaches to agriculural location by the use of conditional probabilities. Future attempts to incorporate both economic and behavioural viewpoints into land-use models could well follow this methodology.

DIFFUSION OF AGRICULTURAL INNOVATIONS

4.1 General characteristics

One important aspect of agricultural decision-making concerns the diffusion or spread of innovations, their adoption or non-adoption and resultant effects on patterns of land-use. Indeed, a major reason for the complex and dynamic nature of farming patterns is the uneven rate of acceptance of new ideas, techniques and products. Not all members of a group of potential adopters adopt simultaneously, and some never adopt.

That diffusion is an integral element of the evolution of the agricultural landscape has been long recognised, dating from the work of cultural geographers of the early twentieth century (L. Brown, 1981). By the late 1960s, innovation diffusion research had become prominent in the establishment of the behavioural approach in geography. It was one of the first areas of geographic inquiry to focus upon the role of information in human decision-making (M. Brown, 1981). In more recent years emphasis has again changed, from behavioural to structural and radical, demonstrating the ability of diffusion studies to accommodate continued developments in geographical methodology and philosophy.

In reviewing the links between decision-making and innovations, Jones (1975) provided a useful platform from which to examine agricultural diffusions. Eight important generalisations were isolated:

  (i) The creation of new knowledge and practices largely occurs outside farms. Very few farmers are inventors of new practices.

 (ii) A large number of channels of communication exist to inform and advise farmers on new innovations, ranging from salesmen to government advisory services. However, farmers' use of and receptivity to them varies widely.

(iii) Individual farmers are in a weak marketing position (Chapter 6) and so tend not to conceal ideas from one another. Consequently, inter-personal contact between farmers can be an important channel of information. Yet, farmers in a region are far from uniform and much diversity exists in terms of farm type, scale of operation and farmer characteristics.

 (iv) New information and innovations take time to be adopted by the farming community and some never are.

  (v) The need to become informed about, and to consider innovative items, arises from farmers' motivations and problems. Once again these vary considerably, reflecting differing perceptions among farmers of the qualities and characteristics of new ideas.

 (vi) The possibility of rejection or non-adoption must be part of any model which aims to be descriptive of a farmer's decision-making.

(vii) The alternatives open to a farmer are much wider than the simple accept-ance or rejection of an idea. Courses of action available are related to the amount and quality of knowledge possessed by farmers, which varies enormously.

(viii) Any new information is surrounded by uncertainty and farmers will look for a satisfactory solution among possible alternatives. An important com-ponent of the decision-making process in this context is the variation in socio-personal characteristics of the farmers.

These statements suggest that the diffusion of agricultural innovations is related to the receipt and acceptance or rejection of information, which in turn reflects a wide range of behavioural, psychological and economic characteristics of individual farmers. This is somewhat paradoxical as the role of information in shaping the agricultural landscape has been little examined by geographers. As Holt (1970) remarked, the topic is almost too big, too vague and too important to think about constructively. Yet, one reason for the spatial variation in land-use is that farmers vary in their willingness, ability and opportunity to use information (Found, 1971). Fletcher (1983) addressed this problem with a survey of six information flows in North Wales and found that a considerable volume of information was provided by official organisations. However, this was on a discriminatory basis, primarily for dairy units in excess of 120 ha. Good use was made of ADAS information and the mass media, but commercial firms, marketing bodies and unions were grossly underutilised. Lowland areas emerged as regions of communicative opportunity, whereas the hills constituted areas of deprivation.

There are two major groups of information sources available to the farmer (Morgan and Munton, 1971): first, those *external* to the agricultural community, including the mass media, advisory services and research centres; and secondly, those *internal* to the community, based largely on inter-personal contact between farmers. It is doubtful whether the former are complete enough to develop optimal patterns of land-use on individual farms. However, they do make the farmer *aware* of information, even if personal contact is more important in effecting the *use* of information. The distinction between awareness and use of information is an important one as the description and explanation of innovation diffusion is dependent upon it.

Diffusion research has demonstrated a close relationship between the use of information and certain farmer characteristics (Jones, 1963). For example, the more educated farmers seek and use new information to a greater degree than the less educated and thus tend to be early adopters of innovations. In contrast, older farmers, who often run small, owner-occupied farms, seek new information less, reflecting a more routine habit and pattern of behaviour. In a similar vein, the more 'urban' farmers are early adopters, possibly due to superior com-munication links. This suggests that location is an important variable in the diffusion process, even though spatial variations in the spread of information have attracted little research effort. One noted exception is Brunn and Raitz's

(1978) study of inter-regional contrasts in farm magazine publications in the USA.

Commenting upon the lack of knowledge about the role of information, Brunn and Raitz vigorously demonstrated its importance: 'understanding the amount, type and quality of information available to farmers for decision-making is the key to understanding how the geography of agriculture is created, and how patterns of production might be reinforced or altered' (p. 277). With a rapid increase in farm-size and the productivity of large farms in the USA, the authors stated that farm magazines are the most important source of information for farmers. Three hundred and seventy-eight major farm magazines were identified and classified into 19 specific categories (Table 4.1). These are published in 47 states (Alaska, Hawaii and Rhode Island are excluded) and in 232 different cities and towns. On a regional basis, the largest number of magazines are published in the Mid-West. However, an important distinction needs to be made between general and specialised magazines. The former tend to be published in the large cities of the north and east, whereas the latter are located within the region which they seek to serve; for example, magazines on fruit and vegetables are published in, or immediately adjacent to, the major growing area of California, Florida, Michigan and Ohio.

Brunn and Raitz continued by identifying two significant changes in farm

Table 4.1

Major farm magazines by type in the USA

Dairy cattle	46
Beef cattle	45
National farm organisations	38
Fruit, nut, and vegetable	32
Horse	29
General livestock	25
Poultry and poultry products	21
Field crops	20
Feed and grain	17
Specialised	16
Farm implement and supply	14
General horticulture and nursery	13
Swine	13
Sheep, goats, and products	12
Floriculture	10
Chemical and fertiliser	8
Agribusiness and large-scale farming	7
Specialised livestock	7
Farm co-operative	5
Total	378

Source: Brunn and Raitz (1978 p. 281).

magazines over the past twenty years, both of which are a result of greater specialisation in agriculture and regional shifts in production patterns; first, the increase in the number of specialised magazines; and secondly, the appearance of new magazines oriented to the growth and changes in agriculture in the south and far west. In their conclusion, the authors called for much more work on the role of farm magazines in the evolving structure of agriculture and in altering crop and livestock patterns.

Whilst information sources have received limited attention in agricultural geography, the diffusion of actual innovations has been researched continuously, with the voluminous and expanding literature aptly synthesised in successive reviews (Jones, 1963 and 1967; Brown and Moore, 1969; Rogers and Shoemaker, 1971; Blaikie, 1978; L. Brown, 1981). The agricultural geography of different areas has been affected by the spread of new crops, technology and special diseases; this can be demonstrated with brief reference to selected studies of contemporary Great Britain. Crop and animal diseases can have fundamental effects on the nature of the agricultural landscape. The latter would include outbreaks of foot and mouth (cattle), swine vesicular (pigs) and fowl pest (poultry). Gilg (1973) examined in detail the geographical consequences of the 1970-1 fowl pest attack in England. Between August 1970 and June 1971 there were 6,500 outbreaks of the disease, and the origins of the epidemic were traced to a district in Essex which had a heavy poultry population. From here the disease spread rapidly outwards over the landscape in the form of a wave, generated by local movements of all kinds.

With regards to specific crops in Great Britain, the 1970s witnessed a growth and geographical spread of maize (Tarrant, 1975) and oil-seed rape (Wrathall, 1978), as well as a renaissance of viticulture (Ilbery, 1983d). Maize production in England increased by 440 per cent in just three years, from 1,434 ha. in 1970 to 7,770 ha. in 1973. Used primarily as a silage crop and to a lesser extent as a grain crop, the quick adoption of maize was due to the creation of new varieties especially suited to the climate of parts of the United Kingdom and to the rapid rise in the price of feedstuffs (Tarrant, 1975). The growth and spatial distribution of the maize crop is portrayed in Fig. 4.1, which shows total area in each county and the percentage destined for grain maize. Maize grown for silage is found in a triangular area, from Devon to Yorkshire and Essex, whereas grain maize is more confined to the south-east.

Data from a small sample of farmers growing maize suggested that the diffusion process relied heavily upon transfers of information between farmers, but with other factors of considerable importance too, notably the weather and the relative success of the crop in previous seasons. The 36 farmers interviewed were members of the Maize Development Association (MDA) and in terms of adoption, 10 said that other farmers were the source of persuasion, 6 quoted the MDA, 6 trade and farmer journals, 4 grain merchants and 2 ADAS. Five farmers had personally visited Europe or the USA and adapted as a result. These farmers are typical of the pioneer status of early adopters, being relatively mobile and

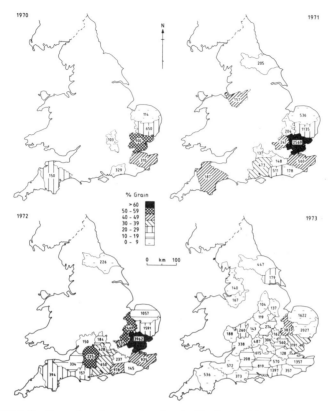

Fig. 4.1   Distribution of maize production in England, 1970–3 (Tarrant, 1975 p. 177)

coming from the wealthy section of the farming population. In turn, 23 of the interviewees had influenced other farmers to adopt, often over considerable distances. According to Tarrant, the distribution of maize had two features common to all innovations: first, the geographical spread over time from the most suitable areas to the less favoured, while the original areas consolidated their position; and secondly, the considerable early variation in the annual pattern of adoption, which was compounded by cyclic fluctuations typical of agricultural production.

More dramatic than maize has been the 'yellow revolution' of British arable fields. Oil-seed rape experienced an eleven-fold increase in area in seven years, from 4,004 ha. in 1970 to 47,808 ha. in 1976 (Wrathall, 1978). By 1981 this figure had risen to 124,838 ha.; representing a phenomenal increase of 3,000 per cent in little more than a decade. The importance of oil-seed rape as a cash crop emerged with Britain's entry into the EEC and the sharp rise in world commodity prices in 1972–4. As Wrathall explained, a large deficiency in vegetable oils and protein meal in Western Europe encouraged the EEC Agricultural

Commission to set persuasive target prices in order to make rape-growing attractive to farmers. In addition, the Commission decided to pay a special support
price to processors when, and if, the world price falls below the target price.

Rape-seed requires a soil with a pH of not less than 6 and grows best on heavy,
moisture-retaining· but not waterlogged, soils. The main area of production to
emerge is a broad belt stretching from the Solent to the Humber (Fig. 4.2), with
the heaviest concentration in East Anglia and Humberside. Until 1975, Hampshire
headed the list of producers, reflecting the interest of a small group of farmers
who were the innovators in the development of the crop (Wrathall, 1978). In
1976, eight counties grew over 2,500 ha., with Northamptonshire the largest
producer at 5,326 ha. By 1981, these figures had been completely transformed:
there were 16 counties growing more than 2,500 ha., 6 of which produced over
7,350 ha. Lincolnshire emerged as a clear leader, with 17,696 ha., to be followed
by Humberside with 11,765 ha.

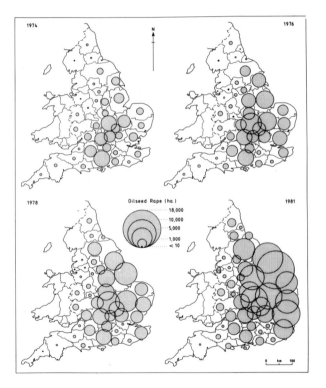

Fig. 4.2   Distribution of oil seed rape in England, 1974–81

Oil-seed rape improves the structure and fertility of the soil, ready for the
subsequent cereal crop. It is this association with cereals as a break crop which
suggests that rape has an optimistic future in Britain. However, its continued

success is dependent upon EEC oil-seed prices and to a lesser extent on the weather and diseases.

Although looked upon with a certain amount of incredulity, the commercial production of 'English' wine flourished in the 1970s. From a total of 5 vineyards before 1970, there are now estimated to be over 220 commercial vineyards, covering up to 1,000 acres (405 ha.). In 1983, wine production exceeded one million bottles. The fickle climate, together with the geographical position of most of Britain north of the 51°N theoretical northern limit for vines, makes this growth difficult to understand and explain (Ilbery, 1983d). One can trace the beginnings of the post-war renaissance back to certain innovative individuals. Barrington-Brock and Hyams established vineyards in Surrey and Kent between 1946 and 1948 and the former was responsible for the Viticultural Research Station at Oxted. In 1952, Sir Guy Salisbury Jones set up the first commercial vineyard on a three-acre site in Hambledon, Hampshire. From these initial actions the new wine industry 'took off' and by 1973 there were 64 vineyards. A further 66 were added by 1977 and in 1980 there were 220 commercial vineyards in England and Wales. Figure 4.3 highlights the growth and distribution of viticulture since 1973 and in particular its concentration in the south-east and East Anglia. Five counties—Kent, East Sussex, Hampshire, Essex and Suffolk—accounted for 40 per cent of all vineyards and 46 per cent of the total area of vines in 1980. Also of interest is the increase in vine-growing counties, from 19 in 1973 to 31 in 1980, and the corresponding movement westwards and northwards. The margins of vine cultivation and the location of specific vineyard sites

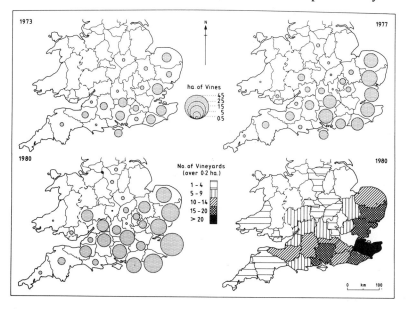

Fig. 4.3   The growth in vine-growing areas in England and Wales, 1973–80 (Ilbery, 1983d p. 343)

are determined largely by physical factors. Only two commercial vineyards are found north of 53°N and all but one are within the 16°N July isotherm. Indeed, very few vineyards are found north of a line drawn from the Wash to the Severn (the 'Wine' line), with the exception of those located on the terraces of the Severn in Herefordshire. The vine would appear to prefer the more mature soils associated with Jurassic/chalk rocks rather than the younger boulder clay and stagnogley soils of much of upland Britain.

Despite the importance of physical controls, the growth and distribution of viticulture reflects various human factors. Wine drinking has become more readily accepted and is sold in public houses and drunk by people of all classes. The increase in demand is in part related to the popular press, which discovered 'English' wine in the mid-1970s and gave it enthusiastic publicity. Two kinds of people, with the necessary labour-intensive attitude, were drawn to it: the retired, and young couples of varied backgrounds. Less than 50 per cent of those involved are farmers and nearly 80 per cent of the vineyards are less than 2 ha. in size. Industrialists have also become attracted to the vine and McAlpine owns the largest vineyard (13 ha.) in England, at Lamberhurst in Kent, and Ready Mix Concrete Ltd. have planted vineyards of 2 ha. and 8 ha. in Ripley, Surrey and at Eversley, Hampshire respectively.

Two other factors have been dominant in the growth of viticulture: first, the development of new grape varieties, which are more disease-resistant and suited to English conditions; and secondly, the formation of the English Vineyards Association (EVA) in 1967, to cater for the interests of commercial and amateur vinegrowers. In particular, the EVA represents its members in all negotiations with the government, EEC, MAFF and Wine Standards Board; promotes the image of English wine through the press, radio and television; helps members with problems concerning wine; and sets standards of quality for English wine.

The major impediment to continued growth, apart from climatic conditions, is government indifference. As well as being taxed at source, wine is taxed more heavily than beer, and 'British' or 'Made' wines (from imported grape juices) have fiscal preference over 'English' wines, paying 43p tax per bottle as against 67p. Also, by being classified as non-agricultural, wine processors have to pay normal rates on business premises and are not eligible for EEC grants and loans.

In each of these examples, a series of waves emanating from some central point can be identified. However, a proper explanation of the patterns can only be obtained by examining the underlying processes and it is here where the approaches developed by geographers have varied over time. For example, information channels and inter-farmer contact in particular would appear to play an important role in the diffusion process. This source dominated early thinking and forms the basis of discussion in the next section.

4.2 The adoption perspective

The traditional and most completely developed approach to diffusion studies in geography focuses upon the processes by which adoption occurs, or the demand aspect of diffusion. Emphasis is placed on the role of communications in the adoption process and the individual decision-maker as an entrepreneur (Blaikie, 1978). This approach has been synthesized by Rogers and Shoemaker (1971) and is represented in geography by the ideas of Hagerstrand (1952, 1953 and 1967). Hagerstrand's work can be divided into two distinct parts: first, an early emphasis on diffusion patterns; and secondly, a change in direction to focus attention on generative processes. From his early investigations into such technical innovations as grazing improvement subsidies and bovine tuberculosis controls, Hagerstrand (1952) identified three empirical regularities of diffusion (Fig. 4.4):

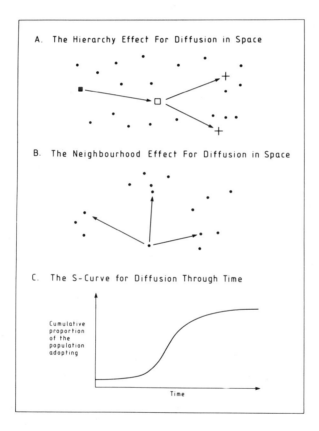

Fig. 4.4   Empirical regularities in diffusion

(i) *The hierarchical effect*, or tendency for individuals in large places to adopt earlier than people in places further down the hierarchy.
(ii) *The neighbourhood effect*, or tendency for diffusion to be strongly influenced by the friction of distance. Therefore, within the hinterland of a single urban centre, diffusion is expected to proceed in a wave-like fashion

outwards, first hitting farmers in the rural–urban fringe rather than in purely rural areas. A similar pattern is expected in diffusion among a rural population. Various studies, at different geographical scales, have been concerned with the neighbourhood effect, including Griliches (1957) diffusion of hybrid corn in the USA and Hagerstrand's (1967) bovine TB control in Sweden.

(iii) *The logistic effect*, or the tendency of the cumulative level of adoption over time to approximate an S-shaped curve. The actual shape of this curve depends on the nature of the innovation and the degree of resistance expressed by potential adopters (Tarrant, 1974).

Whilst geographers have searched for such spatial regularities in diffusion patterns, they do not always exist. Consequently, a fourth possible category is the *random effect*, which was demonstrated among others by Hanham (1973) in the diffusion pattern of artificial insemination among a sample of Swedish farmers.

The second element of Hagerstrand's work came with the publication in 1953 of his Ph.D. thesis 'Innovation diffusion as a spatial process' (translated by Pred in 1967). He conceptualised the adoption of innovations as the outcome of a learning or communications process. This implies that factors related to the effective flow of information are very important and that a 'fundamental step in examining the process of diffusion is identification of the spatial characteristics of flows and resistances to adoption' (L. Brown, 1981 p. 19). Interpersonal information flows, especially face-to-face communications, were considered to be most effective in the learning process, although messages from the mass media played a certain role. Spatially, the circulation of information reflects networks of social communications, which differ between individuals and are characterised by biases and distortions from various social and physical resistances.

To model this conceptualisation, Hagerstrand used a stochastic or Monte Carlo simulation, in which he developed the idea of a grid of probabilities known as the mean information field (MIF). Two main assumptions were made about the spatial structure of this field (M. Brown, 1981): the average frequency of contact between any two locations is the same for all locations separated by an equal distance; and the expected frequency of contact is higher for nearer location than for more distant ones.

In the actual model, diffusion impulses were transmitted by interpersonal communication only and the frequency of contact was determined by the distance separating individuals. Adoption took place after a specified number of messages were received; this varied according to the individual's resistance to adoption. Time was treated not as a continuous process but in discrete units of equal interval and each past adopter sent a message in every time interval (L. Brown, 1981). Unless barriers intervened, the actual destination of each message was dependent on the probability of contact between teller and potential receiver, as determined by the MIF. Random numbers were used to determine which 'cell' in the MIF was to receive the message. If this message passed over a water, mountain or forest barrier it was lost. The procedure was repeated for every adopter and for every time interval. It was possible for a past adopter to receive a message but in such a case it was once more lost and not repeated. Similarly, a non-adopter might be willing to adopt after receiving one message, in which case it was stored until sufficient messages were accumulated to enable him to overcome his resistance to adoption.

Therefore, the model was able to produce a series of maps depicting the spatial distribution of the adoption of innovations over time. The pattern at each point in time is dependent on the pattern generated for the preceding time period and so a person cannot learn about an innovation except from individuals who have already adopted it. Hagerstrand (1967) compared his simulated diffusions with the actual spread of the Swedish farm subsidy scheme and tuberculin-tested dairy herds, and obtained a close approximation. This heralded the beginning of a flood of empirical studies, well summarised by L. Brown (1968) and Rogers and Shoemaker (1971), on the diffusion of innovations and other diffusion-like situations. Of these, the most often quoted example is Bowden's (1965) work on the adoption of pump irrigation in Colorado. Bowden created a circular MIF based on two communication fields: first, the distance travelled to attend a local free barbecue in Yuma; and secondly, long-distance (regional) telephone calls from Yuma. He also assumed that a township would be withdrawn from the Hagerstrand-type simulation when it reached a ceiling of sixteen wells. The closeness of fit between simulated and real diffusion patterns was quite good, enabling Bowden to predict likely future adoptions and the rate of depletion of groundwater resources. Similar applications were carried out by Misra (1969), on the diffusion of agricultural innovations in Mysore, India, and by Johansen (1971) on the diffusion of strip cropping in south-western Wisconsin. Strip cropping was developed to prevent soil erosion and conserve soil structure and moisture on hilly or sloping land. Its adoption, from the late 1930s onwards, appeared to spread from the Coon Valley experimental station. In an attempt to simulate the pattern of adoption, Johansen (1971) used Hagerstrand's Monte Carlo technique, modified to account for the influence of major community centres on communication patterns among farmers. Therefore, rather than assuming a random spread of information over a homogeneous plain of potential adopters, information flow was considered to be structured through 'channels of community, neighbourhood and social group interaction within the service area of a dominant centre' (Johansen, 1971 p. 672).

Five simulations were run, each with 30 generations and for both the regular Hagerstrand model and the modified version. The former consistently under-represented the actual pattern of adopters and Johansen attributed this to the policy of the Soil Conservation Service to introduce strip cropping into communities outside the original area of adoption. A much better 'fit' was provided by the modified model, although some 'cells' were overcorrected, especially in later years. Johansen concluded that a more plausible explanation of the diffusion process would be obtained by including the social structure of an area and its communication channels in the Hagerstrand model.

An important empirical regularity in these and other examples of agricultural diffusions is the logistic curve of adopters. Rogers (1962) plotted this curve as a normal distribution of the number of adopters with time (Fig. 4.5). From this he was able to divide adopters into five categories, ranging from innovators through to laggards, which is now commonly accepted in diffusion studies. This inevitably led to a comparison of the different groups of adopters, with significant differences in the economic, social, locational and demographic characteristics of each group being revealed. Based on the findings from several British studies, and confirmed by many studies in other countries, Jones (1975) was able to succinctly summarise the characteristics of farmers in the five categories of adoption (Table 4.2). It is clear from this table that the importance of information sources differs across adopter subgroups. For example, Rogers and Shoemaker (1971) stated that innovators and early adopters have more diffusion agency and social system interaction than late adopters and tend to use a greater variety of information sources. On the other hand, laggards rely heavily upon social interaction and adopt primarily as a result of information from existing adopters.

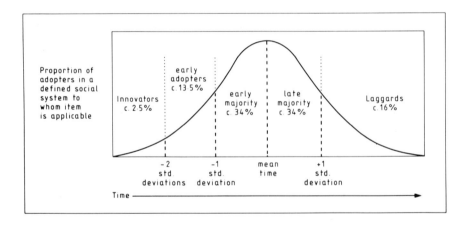

Fig. 4.5   Categories of adopters and the normal diffusion curve (Jones, 1975 p. 40)

This type of study can be viewed as behavioural in that it is primarily concerned with the process by which individuals come to know about and accept innovations, and it recognises individual differences in these processes (M. Brown, 1981). By concentrating on the characteristics of the decision-makers in particular and on other situational factors affecting the diffusion process, various correlates of innovativeness can be identified. These have again been synthesized by Jones (1975) and are self-explanatory (Fig. 4.6). The complexity of processes at work is clearly portrayed in that many of the factors associated with a relatively high level of innovativeness among farmers, are interrelated.

Table 4.2

Characteristics of farmers in the five adoption categories

Adopter category	Personal characteristics	Salient values and social relationships	Communication behaviour
Innovators	Highest social status; largest and most specialised operations; wealthy; often young; well educated; often experience in non-farming environment.	'Venturesome'; willing to accept risks; some opinion leadership; cosmopolite.	Closest contact with scientific information sources; interaction with other innovators; relatively greatest use of impersonal channels of information.
Early adopters	High social status; often large and specialised operations.	'Respected'; regarded by many others in the community as a model and an influential; greatest opinion leadership of any adopter category in most communities.	Greatest contact with local change agents (including extension or advisory services, commercial technical advisers, etc.); competent users of mass media.
Early majority	Above-average social status; average-sized operations.	'Deliberate'; willing to consider new ideas only after peers have adopted; some opinion leadership.	Considerable contact with change agents and early adopters; receive mass media.
Late majority	Below-average social status; small operations; little special-isation; relatively low income.	'Sceptical'; overwhelming pressure from peers needed before adoption occurs; little opinion leadership.	Interaction with peers who are mainly early or late majority; less use of mass media.
Laggards	Little specialisation; lowest social status; smallest operations; lowest income; often oldest.	'Traditional'; oriented towards the past; avoid risks; little if any opinion leadership; almost isolated socially.	Neighbours, friends, and relatives with similar values are main information source; suspicious of change agents.

Source: Jones (1975 p. 42).

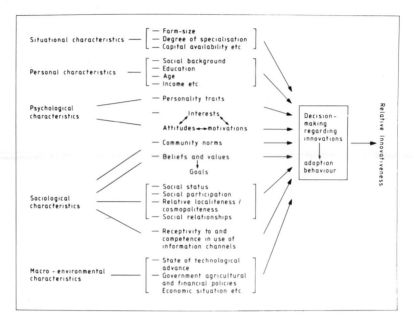

Fig. 4.6   Factors affecting the diffusion of innovations among farmers (Jones, 1975 p. 42)

Whilst the adoption perspective in general and Hagerstrand's work in particular represent the most completely developed approach to diffusion studies, their reliance upon personal information flows and characteristics of the individual decision-maker has been criticised by the more recent geographical literature on innovation diffusion. Criticisms are numerous and wide-ranging and include the following:

(i) Tarrant (1974) has warned of the dangers of using models to simulate diffusion processes. The subdivision of a continuous process into separate stages is unrealistic and it is difficult to assess the amount learnt about processes purely from a simulation exercise. Inputs into a model can be modified in order to obtain the correct results, but for totally the wrong reasons.

(ii) Hagerstrand's work, which has often been misused by subsequent workers' attempts to develop a general diffusion model for rural areas, was developed before recent advances in transport and communications. Thus, distance and distance–decay effects, fundamental to the neighbourhood effect, may have lost some of their prominence relative to other influencing factors.

(iii) Although Hagerstrand viewed adoption as a learning process, he did not interview those individuals whose behaviour was being modelled to determine the importance and role of information flows (M. Brown, 1981). Correspondence between simulated and actual patterns is not sufficient to

warrant acceptance of the proposed behavioural processes. Such instrumentalism has been discussed by Agnew (1979), who was critical of the use
of predictive models of innovation diffusion.

(iv) The use of time of adoption as a surrogate measure to classify people as
innovators, early adopters, late adopters or laggards is not without its problems. Diffusion workers have rarely made the important distinction as to
whether potential adopters obtain information by seeking it or by merely
receiving it without solicitation (L. Brown, 1981). For example, innovators
and early adopters are not necessarily less resistant to change, in general.
They may simply have received more promotional communications as a
result of some diffusion agency's market segmentation policy (M. Brown,
1981).

(v) Despite the context of the adoption perspective, there still remains the
problem of identifying in the real world how far adoption patterns can be
explained by patterns of information circulation and how far by the characteristics of the adopter himself (Blaikie, 1978). For example, it is difficult
to decide how much a pattern of adoption is due to information variables
and how much to structural variables such as farm-size, availability of capital
and access to credit. In a study of information networks in southern
Morocco, Blaikie (1973) found the latter to be more important causal
factors in the adoption of new agricultural practices. Similarly, Garst (1974)
demonstrated the greater significance of infrastructural over information
variables in the diffusion of new crops in Kenya. Lack of information is not
necessarily the reason for non-adoption and it would appear that the adoption perspective overplayed the role of information in innovation diffusion.

(vi) The adoption perspective, with its assumption of an equal opportunity to
adopt, ignores processes other than those pertaining to behavioural variables.
As L. Brown (1975) commented, the adoption of innovations by individuals
or households is the third stage of the diffusion process. Prior to adoption,
diffusion agencies are established through which the innovation will be distributed to the population. Each agency also implements a strategy to induce
adoption among the population in its service area. These two initial stages
demostrate that the opportunity to adopt is far from equal, and highlight
the need for more emphasis on supply rather than demand aspects of diffusion. This forms the focus of attention in the next section.

4.3 The market and infrastructure perspective

Lawrence Brown is primarily responsible for articulating the role of supply factors in the diffusion process and much of this section is based upon his work.
The nub of his thesis is that individual choice behaviour is constrained by government and private institutions, thus shifting the focus of attention away from the
adopter and towards the *diffusion agency*. This agency can be defined as 'the
public or private sector through which an innovation is distributed or made

available to the population at large' (L. Brown, 1981 p. 50). The definition is broad enough to include retail and wholesale outlets, government agencies and non-profit organisations.

Therefore, the first stage in the diffusion process is the establishment of diffusion agencies. These may be initiated by a single propogator (or several working together), as in a multiple-facility location problem, or by many propagators working independently. They may have existed prior to the diffusion process or be newly established for the innovation. Whichever is the case, their location(s) help to determine where and when the innovation will be available, and provide the general outline of the spatial pattern of diffusion.

In the second stage, each diffusion agency develops and implements a *stategy* to promote adoption in its market or service area (L. Brown, 1981). This strategy involves numerous activities, although four are particularly relevant to the spatial pattern of diffusion (M. Brown, 1981):

(i) *Infrastructure provision*, including institutional and other structures which enable or enhance the use of an innovation.

(ii) *Pricing*, including its level and spatial variation.

(iii) *Promotional communications*, which vary according to source, channel, content and receiver.

(iv) *Market selection and segmentation*, including different market strategies for different market segments.

These four aspects can in turn be related to both objective and subjective attributes of an innovation (M. Brown, 1977). In particular, infrastructure provision and pricing affect objective attributes of an innovation, while market selection and segmentation and promotional communications primarily affect the potential adopter's belief about, and evaluation of, these attributes, or the subjective attributes of the innovation. This is diagrammatically portrayed in Fig. 4.7, which also illustrates the way in which the diffusion agency strategy complements the adoption perspective. More information on this relationship will be provided towards the end of the section.

A further twofold typology is normally made before embarking upon empirical case studies. Innovations can be classified as either infrastructure constrained or infrastructure independent (L. Brown, 1975). The former relate to infrastructure provision and pricing and thus to objective attributes of an innovation, whilst the latter involve promotional communications and market selection and segmentation, and subjective attributes.

Both types of innovation can have a marked impact on patterns of agricultural land-use. The importance of infrastructure-constrained innovations was demonstrated by numerous case-studies in the early 1970s, as listed by L. Brown (1981). These included.

(i) Artificial insemination in southern Sweden (Hanham, 1973), involving a technical service infrastructure maintained by a government diffusion agency.

(ii) Ammonia fertiliser in the Corn Belt (Erickson, 1973), involving a storage and distribution infrastructure maintained by private enterprise.

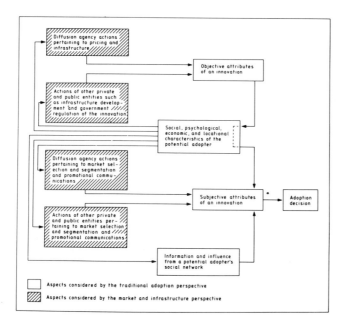

Fig. 4.7   The interface between diffusion agency actions and adoption behaviour (L. Brown, 1981 p. 103)

(iii) Hybrid grain corn in Quebec (Smith, 1974), involving an infrastructure of marketing and processing sites.

(iv) Various agricultural innovations in Kenya (Garst, 1974), which involved an infrastructure of marketing sites, collection systems and price and production controls maintained by both entrepreneurial diffusion agencies and government institutions. This last example will be further developed in section 4.4.

With regards to infrastructure-independent innovations, adoption will be bounded only by the limit of the diffusion agency's service areas and 'will in general be uniform but comprised of randomly distributed clusters of adopters reflecting interpersonal information flows', (L. Brown, 1981 p. 127). Examples from the literature include De Temple's (1971) work on 2,4D seed spray around Collins; Iowa and Harvestore feed systems in north-east Iowa; and studies by M. Brown, Maxson and L. Brown (1977), M. Brown (1980) and L. Brown (1981) on various agricultural innovations in south-eastern Ohio.

M. Brown (1980) and L. Brown (1981) analysed the diffusion of four agricultural innovations in a four-county area of eastern Ohio, two of which were infrastructure-constrained (Pro-las and custom-blended fertiliser) and two infrastructure-independent ('No-till farming' and the 'Ohio Production Testing Programme'). One from each category will be used to illustrate the main effects of diffusion agency strategy.

Custom-blended fertiliser was introduced into four counties of eastern Ohio in 1971 by the Belmont County Farm Bureau. It is a fertiliser mixed individually to match the soil characteristics of each farm and was distributed from the Farm Bureau's blend plant in Quaker city via the transportation infrastructure. The cost of custom-blended fertiliser varied according to the location of the farmer, and was either transported by the purchaser or delivered at a cost per ton mile. With a distance-related delivery price, the spatial distribution of adopters did not affect profits associated with the innovation. Consequently, the Farm Bureau promoted its product throughout the four county market area, relying mainly upon the mass media.

The product was adopted in a fairly linear fashion between 1971 and 1974 and had a wide spatial distribution. However, a distinct cluster of adopters around the Quaker city blend plant was apparent, with a scattering in peripheral areas. Clustering appeared to occur more towards the end of the study period, as confirmed by a decreasing R-statistic for each of the four years examined, and suggested that the diffusion pattern became more rational over time. This distance–decay pattern of adoption is not surprising given the pricing policies adopted for custom-blended fertiliser by the Bureau. With such a policy, there was little need to spatially segment the market or to personalise promotional communications.

The diffusion of no-till farming in the four-county area was independent of major infrastructure and pricing effects. Therefore, the impact of diffusion agencies upon diffusion patterns occurred largely through promotional communications and market segmentation policies. No-till farming, a method of planting corn and forage crops without ploughing, was developed in the late 1960s and concurrently introduced in Ohio. Its spread involved numerous private and public agencies, including 'no-till planter dealers, the Chevron Chemical and Geigy Companies who supply the herbicides, farm supply dealers who sell the herbicides locally, the Co-operative Extension Service, the Soil Conservation Service and other government agencies' (L. Brown, 1981 p. 134).

Each of these diffusion agents undertook promotional communications, through a wide range of information channels, from the mass media and farm journals to local demonstrations and personal contact with farmers. The costs of the innovation were high, at over $4,000 for a no-till planter, but uniform throughout the area. As a result, there was a tendency to bias promotional campaigns towards the richer and primarily arable farmers. In the same vein, the Co-operative Extension Service directed their promotional efforts towards opinion leaders (wealthier, better-educated farmers with larger farms) who it was hoped would transmit the ideas to the wider farming population. Assuming a random distribution of large, mainly arable, farms, one would not expect a spatial clustering of adopters, as was the case with custom-blended fertiliser.

The overall trend in no-till farming usage between 1971 and 1974 was one of constant annual growth, with expected seasonal spurts at the time of corn planting. Adoption was slower than for custom-blended fertiliser and can be explained in part by the cost of the innovation. Spatially, small localised clusters of adopters were spread throughout the study area, except in the cattle-dominated Monroe county. The essentially random pattern, confirmed by the R-statistic, was related to the dispersed nature of the diffusion agencies themselves and the lack of infrastructure constraints.

Therefore, the infrastructure-constrained/independent dichotomy is useful when analysing the spatial pattern of diffusion. The study also showed that in the case of the infrastructure-independent, no-till farming, there was a systematic segmentation of the market on the basis of socio-economic characteristics. This was confirmed by the fact that receivers of information about the innovation and early adopters had significantly larger farms, farm incomes, family incomes and areas devoted to corn.

These findings have a broader implication too because they help to overcome the criticism that the market and infrastructure perspective has, by concentrating on the actions of diffusion agencies and other institutions, ignored behavioural aspects of the adoption decision. Figure 4.7 illustrates the manner in which the diffusion agency strategy interfaces with adoption behaviour. As M. Brown (1981 pp. 130–1) remarks, 'the activities of the diffusion agency are seen as influencing the subjective attributes of an innovation, and therefore adoption, both by altering objective attributes such as pricing and infrastructures, and by disseminating promotional communications which primarily affect the potential adopter's beliefs about, and evaluation of, these attributes'. The links between adoption and market and infrastructure-perspectives have received little attention, although work by L. Brown and Lentnek (1973) and M. Brown (1980) was moulded in this kind of explanatory framework. The former developed a model that integrated both information and market factors in an attempt to explain the changeover from traditional to commercial dairying in the state of Aguascalientes, Mexico, between 1958 and 1968. Based on a spatially stratified, 0.5 per cent random sample of the rural farm household population of Aguascalientes, and a systematic sample of one out of every three Nestlé Corporation suppliers of raw milk during 1968 along selected routes (Fig. 4.8), it was possible to compare the characteristics of adopters with those of non-adopters.

Nestlé Corporation established a collection depot in Pabellon, just north of Aguascalientes, in 1958, in order to expand its supply region and satisfy rising demands for powdered milk. Between 1958 and 1968, Nestlé helped to create an ideal economic environment for commercial dairying. This was related to various factors:

(i) The company opened new milk collection routes out of Pabellon and encouraged modern practices of dairying among the farmers.

(ii) They bore all transport costs and provided a guaranteed, long-term market at a fixed price.

(iii) They provided free technical advice and necessary inputs like feed supplements at company cost.

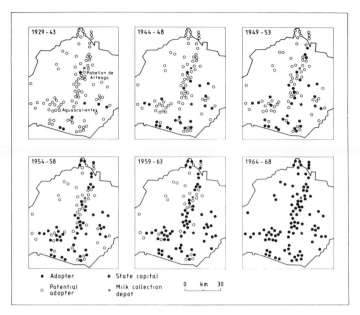

Fig. 4.8   Adoption of commercial dairying in the state of Aguascalientes, Mexico, 1929–68 (L. Brown and Lentnek, 1973 p. 282)

(iv) Physical conditions in the area were suitable for milk production and land tenure was relatively secure.

(v) A weekly cash flow from dairy farming reduced problems related to the capitalisation of adoption. Also, most farmers already had cattle for domestic milk production and these were used to begin commercial production.

(vi) The return to investment in dairying was more than five times that for corn and beans, the major alternatives.

Despite these conditions, commercial dairying in the area had reached only a small proportion of the farmers by 1968. This led Brown and Lentnek (1973) to hypothesise that factors of a non-economic nature were important in the adoption process. Consequently, 20 variables relating to the farmer and the adoption of commercial dairying in the Pabellon supply shed were subjected to principal components analysis and stepwise regression. In distinguishing adopters from non-adopters, it was shown that age and age-related characteristics were related to adoption, but that these were limited by a potential adopter's access to the market and information about the innovation. Three broad findings were presented from their empirical analyses (p. 291):

(i) The supply shed expanded in a spatially sequential fashion such that accessibility to the market and information was a major filter in defining potential adopters.

(ii) Within the supply shed factors related to age were the major determinant of adoption.

(iii) To meet increased demand, the collector extended transport routes to include areas previously untapped, as well as undertaking to persuade non-adopters within the existing supply shed.

The study by Brown and Lentnek (1973), whilst combining both information and market factors, is also important in that it provides a link with the third perspective to be developed in diffusion studies—the development perspective.

4.4 Development and radical perspectives

A third major strand of diffusion research is concerned with the impact and consequences of innovation diffusion on economic development and on individual and societal welfare (Goss, 1979). L. Brown (1981) suggests this is a logical extension of the market and infrastructure perspective, in so far as it stresses the importance of access to resources and public infrastructure in innovation diffusion. As a consequence, the development perspective questions the idea of adoption being a learning process in which individuals gain information predominantly through social communications. A radical viewpoint is sometimes incorporated, as it is felt that innovation adoption cannot be understood without consideration of the social, economic and political conditions that operate independently of the individual. Space is what the political economy makes it and Blaikie (1978) emphasised the need for a resource theory of innovation, where individual access to the means of production, the state of the market and related infrastructure, and the resources provided by government and private institutions, are included.

The development and radical perspectives have been particularly forceful in demonstrating that innovation diffusion is not always beneficial and is typically more advantageous to some people than others, thus widening regional disparities (M. Brown, 1981). This conflicts with the adoption perspective, which viewed diffusion as leading to social change and enabling traditional societies to become modern and cosmopolite (Rogers and Shoemaker, 1971). Various studies in this latter vein were conducted in Third World settings, including Menanteau-Horta (1967), Hanneman *et al.* (1969) and Garst (1973) on agricultural innovations in Chile, Colombia and Kenya respectively, and Wilbanks (1972) and Mayfield and Yapa (1974) on innovations in rural India.

In a rare application of the market and infrastructure perspective in a Third World context, Garst (1974) analysed the spatial diffusion of six crop and livestock innovations in the Kisii district of Kenya. The objective of his work was to 'determine the facilitating and constraining factors' of the diffusion process and to 'examine the role of social characteristics and communications media' (p. 300). Garst used a two-stage sampling procedure to gather his data: first, 1,935 interviews (5 per cent sample) were conducted in 93 randomly-located clusters to determine if and when the farmer adopted each innovation; and secondly, 485 in-depth interviews (25 per cent sample of the first sample) were conducted and aggregated to the 93 original sampling areas for purposes of analysis.

The adoption trends over time for the six innovations are shown in Fig. 4.9. As coffee was the first crop to be introduced, as well as exhibiting the classic S-shaped curve, it will be used as a case example. The first coffee 'plot' was planted by a European resident in 1921, but it was not until 1935 that Africans were allowed to plant coffee with no restrictions. In 1940, coffee was grown in three separate places (Fig. 4.10), although it did not spread eastwards until the early 1950s. By 1956 it had advanced to its maximum eastern position and in the next 15 years it continued to increase in intensity within the adopted area. Two factors restricted further eastern movement: first, there was a lack of coffee-processing factories in the east; and secondly, tea and pyrethrum were economically attractive alternatives.

With its 65 factories, the Kisii Farmers Co-operative Union processed and marketed the coffee. Since the only means of transport available to the farmers was head portage, the distance to the market had to be very short. Before the

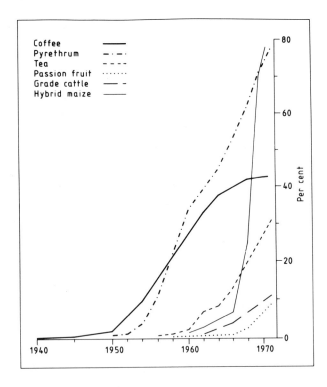

Fig. 4.9   Adoption growth curves for six agricultural innovations in the Kisii district of Kenya (Garst, 1974 p. 303)

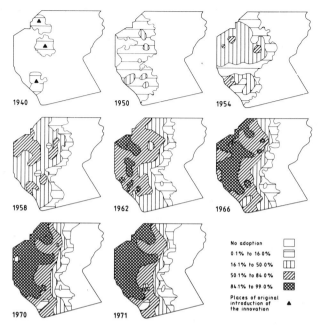

Fig. 4.10   The diffusion of coffee in the Kisii district of Kenya (Garst, 1974 p. 302)

Union would agree to build a new factory, a sufficient amount of production, at greater than normal head portage distance, was required. Although initially built as a response to previous adoption, a new factory acted as an incentive for others to begin growing coffee. Therefore, processing and marketing facilities had little effect on initial adopters (innovators), but a considerable influence on later adopters.

Analysis of the data from the 485 interviews established that the east–west directional contrast in coffee production reflected spatial variations in the location of processing and marketing facilities and that these were more import-ant than 'cosmopolitan' factors (active/passive) in the diffusion process. With each of the six innovations having its own set of starting points, Garst (1974) concluded that ecological, infrastructure and market controls, rather than receptivity on the part of potential adopters, were the important factors of innovation diffusion among the Gusii of Kisii.

Therefore, the development perspective stresses the importance of constraints to adoption and suggests that non-adoption is not the result of a lack of inno-vativeness but a consequence of differential access to resources, such as information, capital, education and public infrastructure and facilities. This was pursued by Yapa and Mayfield (1978) in a study of the relative importance of personal, information and resource factors in non-adoption in the state of Karnataka, India. Data were obtained for two groups of peasant farmers: first,

151 farmers who had adopted a new variety of hybrid maize; and secondly, 61 who had not. The sample was taken from 34 villages to the north of Bangalore, with each village as far as possible including both adopters and non-adopters.

To distinguish between the two groups, 29 discriminating variables were used, with 6 relating to personal characteristics of the farmer (biographical), 16 to aspects of communications (communications) and 7 describing access to agricultural inputs and resources (resources). Discriminant analyses on the three sets showed that biographical data were able correctly to classify 60 per cent of subjects as adopters or non-adopters; communications data could classify 64 per cent properly; and resources data could classify 74 per cent correctly. From this the authors were able to imply that political economy considerations of access to resources were more closely related to adoption behaviour than communications. In particular, differential access to land or security of tenure, capital and inputs like seed, fertiliser and water were important in distinguishing adopters from non-adopters. These were especially critical for smaller-scale farmers. Non-adoption was not a 'passive state caused by apathy or resistance' but 'an active state arising out of the structural arrangements of the economy' (Yapa and Mayfield, 1978 pp. 148-9).

Similar conclusions were reached by Havens and Flinn (1975) in their study of the diffusion of new coffee-producing technology in Colombia. Unequal access to financial assistance, rather than farmer characteristics, was the main distinguishing feature between adopters and non-adopters. Lack of adoption was partially due to 'perceived or real institutional blocks to credit availability' (p. 478). The larger-scale and more-educated farmers had greater access to credit, whereas the smaller-scale non-adopters had little collateral and so often did not bother asking for credit. This study presented clear evidence of the diffusion of agricultural technology being affected by an institutional constraint.

These studies help to highlight the need for more emphasis to be placed upon the constraints and consequences of innovation diffusion. Both distributional effects and unanticipated consequences warrant further attention, and diffusion theory and its application needs to be reassessed, especially in Third World contexts (Goss, 1979). However, in line with other perspectives the development perspective has progressed rather independently, with little cross-referencing. As a result, it can be criticised for a lack of insight into the relative importance of behavioural and other variables in different types of diffusion (M. Brown, 1981). The complementary nature of the different perspectives needs to be emphasised, for as Blaikie (1978 p. 274) commented, 'it is only when information, resources and personal attributes (correlates of innovativeness) together coincide in a decision-maker that innovation will occur'.

In an attempt to incorporate aspects of the behavioural, market, infrastructure and institutional concerns into diffusion theory, M. Brown (1981) advocated a greater focus of attention on human cognitive processes, including the development of attitudes and the role of personal constructs in decision-making processes. Although information and personal construct theories have not been applied to diffusion processes, M. Brown (1980) compared a set of psychological variables pertaining to an individual's attitudes toward adoption with a set of socio-economic and locational variables, in an attempt to discriminate between adopters and non-adopters.

The diffusion of five agricultural innovations in Appalachian Ohio formed the framework for study and 597 farm operators were examined by means of canonical correlation analysis and discriminant-function analysis. Results demonstrated that attitudinal variables were superior to the social-categories variables in their ability to discriminate between adopters and non-adopters. 'On the average, the social-categories variables were able to classify 62.5 per cent of the respondents correctly, whereas the smaller number of attitudinal variables could properly identify 73.2 per cent' (M. Brown, 1980 p. 181). When used in conjunction, attitudinal and social categories variables successfully classified 77.4 per cent of the cases—4.2 per cent more than with attitudes alone. Therefore, each set of variables explained some unique as well as common aspects of adoption behaviour, but attitudes contributed more.

Whilst this study by M. Brown (1980) underlied the importance of attitude or choice variables in the USA, it has already been shown how research by Havens and Flinn (1975) and Yapa and Mayfield (1978) highlighted the role of resource or constraining factors in the adoption of agricultural innovations in Colombia and India respectively. Such inconsistencies can be interpreted as support for the radical thesis that different causal explanations are required for innovation diffusion within different social, political and economic relations (M. Brown, 1981). A more integrated approach, employing aspects of all three perspectives discussed in this chapter, would seem appropriate, especially if it allowed the relative importance of behavioural and other processes in different diffusions, to be assessed.

5

ECONOMIC PRINCIPLES AND AGRICULTURE

The previous three chapters have demonstrated how behaviour is constrained by the economic environment of farming. As agriculture is primarily an economic activity, governed by the laws of supply and demand, there is a need for a more systematic understanding of economic considerations. However, the economic environment is 'filtered' by the farmer before he reacts to it. With farmers responding in different ways to perceived or actual changes in economic influences, a complex mosaic of farming types is created.

Location is a central concept, as the importance of economic factors varies spatially. For example, the impact of technological change in agriculture will not be felt simultaneously in different places (Ritson, 1977) and can only be understood by studying the decision-making behaviour of farmers. An investigation of the way in which decisions are taken and the objectives which motivate farmers will help provide a better understanding of the role of economic factors in agricultural land-use patterns.

This chapter will begin by providing an abstract outline of the different sets of economic relationships which affect individual farms, before developing the spatial aspects of post-war agricultural trends in the Western world in more detail. In particular, attention will be focused upon economies of scale, agglomeration and specialisation of production, with behavioural overtones being included where necessary.

5.1 Economic relationships and the farm system

Following Hurst (1974), two sets of economic relationships interact to determine the farm system: supply and demand, and factors of production. Price–cost relations represent one of the major determinants of production and consumption levels within an economy, and help to determine a farmer's choice of what and how much to produce. The supply of agricultural commodities depends upon the satisfaction of demand, which is expressed in the market (population X standard of living). Therefore, supply and demand govern prices and in turn are affected by them.

Three simple laws are applicable:
 (i) With a constant supply, the higher the demand the higher the price.
 (ii) With a constant demand, the larger the supply the lower the price.
 (iii) In a perfect market, one gets an oscillation of prices around an equilibrium price (where supply and demand curves intersect).
This supply–demand–price syndrome affects, and is affected by, location. The

volume of demand at any location is related to variations in the geographical pattern of transfer costs at that location and to variations in the factors of production. Similarly, the pattern of food demand is affected by spatial differences in such factors as culture, tradition, tastes, size of population, incomes, prices of products and climate. Thus, the pattern and 'extent' of agricultural production reflect these interrelationships, with market demand the vital factor. For example, the high demand for animal foods in the Western world has led to livestock products accounting for two-thirds of the value of farm production (Grigg, 1984); in turn there animals are increasingly being fed on grains rather than pasture. The margins of cultivation (Chapter 1) may also change as production expands in response to continued population and economic growth; these margins are often pushed well beyond physically-defined limits to agricultural production (Parry, 1976).

An important concept affecting all farmers is elasticity of supply and demand, or the size of relative changes in supply and demand consequent upon price alterations. Two possibilities present themselves: first, supply and demand are said to be *elastic* when a change in price brings about a more than proportional change in supply and demand; and secondly, they are *inelastic* when a change in price brings about a less-than-proportional change in supply or demand.

The supply of agricultural commodities is relatively inelastic because major inputs, like productive land, are fairly limited. However, many interlinked factors can create a change in the supply of an agricultural good. Unplanned variations in supply occur as a result of unpredictable forces, often of a physical nature. These uncontrollable influences vary spatially, as do the farmers' reactions to them, causing supply to vary between farms, regions and countries. Technological change can lead to an increase in supply through the widespread use of mechanisation, herbicides, fertilisers and new, disease-resistant crop varieties. As a generalisation, the impact of technological change will be felt first on the larger and more capital-intensive farms. This in turn will help to perpetuate the trend towards fewer and larger farms producing more and more food; just 10 per cent of farms account for 50 per cent of the food produced in Britain (Norton-Taylor, 1982). Other factors initiating a change in supply include the price of inputs and other products, the number of producers involved and producer expectations of future trends.

In a similar fashion, the demand for many agricultural items is price inelastic. This is because relatively fixed quantities of basic foods, such as milk, eggs, butter, bread, potatoes and cheese, are always required by consumers. However, to the individual farmer demand may appear to be elastic; he has no real influence on the price as he produces such a small part of total supply. By producing more, the farmer perceives that his income will accordingly increase. But here lies the danger, for if all farmers attempt to do this a very large surplus may occur. Such overproduction would have an adverse effect on the price and farmers' incomes would fall. With so many producers in agriculture, the individual farmer is in a weak marketing position and this necessitates some general control on agricultural production, which is usually government backed (Chapter 6).

Turning attention to factors of production, land, labour and capital can be described as inputs into the farm system. As most decisions concerning the use of these factors are taken by individual farmers, management is often added as a fourth factor. All agricultural systems, from subsistence to highly commercialised, are dependent on land and labour, but capital is often lacking in peasant economies. The relative importance of land and labour is declining in many commercial farming systems, whereas capital investment and management skills are of increasing significance with the development of agribusiness and vertical integration in agriculture (Chapter 7).

The geographical importance of factors of production is well summarised by Morgan and Munton (1971 pp. 46-7): the presence or absence, quality and price of each factor of production varies spatially, affecting the relationships between them and their deployment on individual farms'. As the authors rightly point out, these patterns are dynamic because capital and labour are geographically mobile. The important elements of each factor of production will now be discussed.

1. Land

This is a peculiar factor of production because each unit of land is locationally unique and total supply is more or less fixed (Ritson, 1977). However, the use to which land is put is flexible and open to many competing agricultural interests. This flexibility appears to be declining as rotation and patterns of mixed farming are being replaced by increased regional specialisation (Bowler, 1981a). Therefore, land is not a homogeneous factor of production and its use varies spatially according to numerous factors, including:

Land quality. The production potential of land varies according to spatial differences in its physical, chemical and biological properties. This is clearly portrayed in the MAFF's (1968) land capability maps where land is classified into five grades according to the physical limitations imposed on agriculture. Based on soil, relief and climatic characteristics, grade 1 land, for example, is most suited to agricultural production. Part of this classification has been reproduced for Hereford and Worcestershire (Fig. 5.1 (*a*)) and shows the extent and complexity of spatial variability in land quality, which will, at least in part, be reflected in the land-use patterns of the area. A similar exercise has been carried out by the Soil Survey of England and Wales in its production of land-use capability maps. Following the work of Bibby and Mackney (1969), land has been graded into seven classes according to its potential and the severity of physical limitations to crop growth. Grades one to four comprise land suited to cultivation and these too have been reproduced for Hereford and Worcestershire

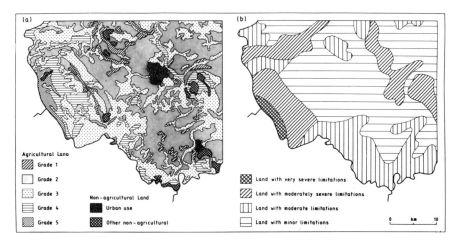

Fig. 5.1   Land quality variations in Hereford and Worcestershire: (*a*) Land capability (MAFF, 1968); (*b*) Land-use capability (Soil Survey of England and Wales, 1977)

(Fig. 5.1 (*b*)). Whilst not so complex as the land capability map of the county, marked variations in land quality occur within relatively small areas.

Land prices. The price of agricultural land in most advanced economies has increased considerably during the last two decades. In the USA, land values have risen by nearly 700 per cent, from $33 per hectare in 1960 to $260 in 1981. However, the pattern of land prices varies noticeably between the individual states (Fig. 5.2) and, with the exception of California, the highest land values are found in the eastern states, which are characterised by smaller farm sizes and, importantly, greater rates of urbanisation. Prices reach a peak in Illinois and the contiguous coastal states of Maryland, New Jersey, Connecticut and Rhode Island.

A similar trend is apparent in the United Kingdom, where land prices have risen from an average of £570 per hectare in 1969 to over £2,970 in 1980. Reasons for this marked increase, especially in the early part of the 1970s, are numerous and range from a need to increase farm-size, in order to keep pace with technological change and obtain economies of scale, to speculation in the land market by institutional buyers (Munton, 1976) and non-economic desires to own land for a feeling of social responsibility and a sense of inheritance (Denman, 1965). Consequences of this trend include the increased intensification of production, as farmers attempt to maintain the same profit margins during the post-war 'price–cost squeeze' (Bowler, 1981), and the spread of the more profitable cereal enterprises westwards. Once again, land prices are not spatially uniform and are highest in areas of better quality land and in the rural–urban fringe (Chapter 8).

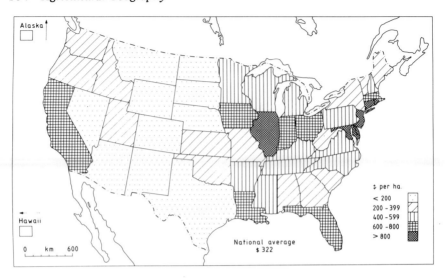

Fig. 5.2   The value of agricultural land and buildings in the USA, 1981.

Land tenure. Systems of land tenure vary enormously between regions and countries, having fundamental effects on farm-size structure, land fragmentation, and ultimately, land-use patterns. Hurst (1974) classified the land-tenure systems of the world into four main types: communal tenure, latifundia, freehold and tenancy. In the Western world, the main contrast in tenure is between owner-occupancy and tenancy. The dominant trend is one of increased land ownership. At the beginning of the twentieth century only 12 per cent of UK farms were owner-occupied; by 1980 the figure stood at 66 per cent (Haines, 1982). Similarly in the USA, 88 per cent of all farms were wholly or partly owner-occupied in 1980. Agriculture is becoming a closed industry with entry either difficult or impossible, unless large sums of capital are available; the traditional agricultural ladder is now of little relevance. By nature, farmers are highly independent with a strong desire to be their own masters. Ownership confers greater freedom of choice upon the farmer than tenancy, even though the latter may carry greater profits. This only helps to reinforce the importance of non-economic motives in the purchase of agricultural land (Morgan and Munton, 1971).

Tenant farmers often work within a different decision-making milieu and, although management policies may be similar, the choice of enterprise can be restricted by tenancy agreements. For example, dairying is practised on many rented farms because of clauses in the contract, just as hops are produced on certain farms in Hereford and Worcestershire for this reason alone (Ilbery, 1982). One form of tenure which could increase in popularity with reduced profit margins in farming is sale and leaseback (Haines, 1982). Under such a system, the farmer sells his land, possibly to an institutional buyer, on the understanding that he can continue to farm it for a specified time period. This has been especially common in parts of eastern England (Munton, 1977). The longer the specified time, the more willing the farmer may be to invest his new source of capital in the farm. As Haines explains, sale and leaseback would become an attractive form of tenure if a wealth tax was introduced.

Land location. Spatial variations in agricultural land-use results in part from the location of farmland in relation to both factor and product markets. The price of inputs and outputs may rise with increasing distance between farmstead and the market. This formed the basis of von Thünen's theory of agricultural location, where land-use became differentiated in relation to the market. Land distant from the market might be used less intensively or not be brought into cultivation at all; this is known as the extensive margin of cultivation. In reality, Ritson (1977) has shown that the importance of land location in relation to the market has been reduced. This is due, amongst many things, to the relative fall in transport costs compared with other production costs.

2. Labour

Although the size of the agricultural labour force is declining in the Western world, labour productivity is increasing, due mainly to the substitution of machinery for men. The level of labour inputs depends on various interrelated factors, including its cost and availability, land quality, the desire to obtain a particular level of output and the type of farm system practised. In relation to this last factor, labour requirements vary enormously for different land-use types, from 2,700 SMDs per hectare for crops under glass or sheds, to 0.04 SMDs per head for egg-laying chickens (MAFF, 1976). An important concept in this context, with implications for management decisions, is the marginal productivity of labour, which tends to decrease with increasing inputs (Morgan and Munton, 1971). This is particularly relevant for small farms, where the farmer may obtain a lower marginal return than if he was employed on a larger farm, and in much of Third World agriculture (Morgan, 1978).

As mentioned repeatedly in this book, farming remains a traditional occupation for a majority of farmers and farm labourers. This helps to explain the fact that agricultural labour is less occupationally mobile than other forms of employment. Gasson (1968), in a mid-1960s study of farmers' sons in the English Fens, found a strong desire to avoid white-collar employment and remain on their fathers' farms, although this declined as farm-size fell. The trend seems to have continued, for a survey of hop farmers in Hereford and Worcestershire in 1980 showed that more than 60 per cent had taken over the hop unit from their fathers (Ilbery, 1983b). The immobility of agricultural labour appears most severe in areas of small, owner-occupied farms and has become a major planning problem, particularly on the European mainland. Government schemes have been introduced in countries like France and West Germany to encourage farmers to leave the land (Chapter 6).

Despite this occupational immobility, a major post-war concern in advanced economies has been the rapid drift of farm labour from the land. In England and Wales, the total agricultural labour force fell by 64 per cent in thirty years, from just under 800,000 in 1950 to 290,000 in 1980; agriculture now employs just 2.7 per cent of the working population. In the USA, numbers have fallen by the same magnitude, from 9.9 millions in 1950 to 3.7 in 1980. Reasons for this are complex and vary from area to area, but the major ones include:

(i) The low wage levels of farm workers compared to other forms of employment. Better wages in the cities attract farm labourers, especially those in the rural–urban fringe (Chapter 8) where farm wages are at their highest. Causes of low farm wages range from occupational immobility and weak trade-union activity to lower costs of living and non-monetary rewards such as a rural environment, healthy job and preference for a farm life.

(ii) Technological change in agriculture, in the form of mechanisation and specialisation, has released labour and made much farm work boring and repetitive (Morgan and Munton, 1971).

(iii) Retired labourers are not being replaced because candidates have not got the required skills, or they demand higher wages than the traditional labourer if they have.

(iv) Farm labourers often work long hours and the length of working week can vary tremendously. This is at variance with most other forms of employment and the growing affluence and leisure time of Western societies.

(v) Although more important in developing economies, under-employment of labour can occur in agriculture in the Western world. This often reflects the seasonal nature of many farming activities and is contributory to the declining farming population.

3. Capital

This is a key element in the production function of any business and in agriculture it has been replacing land and labour in importance. According to Hill and Ingersent (1977), this reflects the farmers' response to rising costs of land and labour, due to increased competition for their use, and the relative cheapness of machinery, fertilisers and other capital investments, which have remained low in price because of technological innovation and economies of scale in manufacturing. It also reflects the growth of agribusiness and vertical integration in agriculture, government policies, and contracting agreements with food companies. These bodies often provide the bulk of capital investment, which can mean a considerable saving for the farmer. In the Western world there are few problems of access to credit sources, although capital is not a completely mobile factor of production and availability can be biased towards the larger farms, which tend to be run by better educated farmers with greater knowledge of fiscal matters. Thus, whilst the scale and price of capital investment can vary spatially, improvements in communications have broadened the spatial network of credit sources (Morgan and Munton, 1971).

The main sources of capital in agriculture, apart from vertical integration and sale-leaseback schemes, are the clearing banks, the farming industry itself, insurance companies, building societies and government grants and subsidies. In Britain, there is also the Agricultural Mortgage Corporation, which was set up in 1929 when farmers experienced difficulty in raising capital and whose lending increased by 74 per cent between 1968 and 1972 alone (Hill, 1974). The size of lending activities continues to expand, and Haines (1982) has shown how the farm debt in California increased by 180 per cent between 1970 and 1979 and how in Britain in February 1980 more capital was on loan than to any other industry.

Bosanquet (1968) identified a significant difference in credit sources according to land tenure. Tenant farmers raised 64 per cent of their credit from clearing banks, compared to 40 per cent for owner-occupiers, and only 17 per cent from private sources (38 per cent for owner-occupiers). With an increase in owner-occupancy, such a distinction, along with the one between landlord and tenant capital, is of reduced relevance. Indeed, many farmers, especially the small owner-occupiers, are wary of taking credit. Some of these are in a strong financial position, because of tax concessions, grants and home production, and can finance capital from farm profits. This will affect their decision behaviour and attitude towards technological change, specialisation and choice of enterprise. For this reason, traditional farming systems are often found in close proximity to modern, capital-intensive systems.

Government has an important bearing on the pattern of capital investment in agriculture (Chapter 6). Grants and subsidies are provided and interest rates on borrowed loans may be subsidised. For example, schemes exist to assist depressed agricultural areas, as in the EEC. Following the directive on less-favoured farming areas in 1975, priority agricultural zones were delimited on the basis of three criteria:

(i) An above-EEC-average employment in agriculture.

(ii) A per capita gross domestic product below the Community average.

(iii) A below-average number of workers in manufacturing employment.

Three types of problem region were outlined from these criteria (Fig. 5.3), covering large and primarily peripheral areas of the EEC. Farmers within these areas are eligible for an annual compensatory allowance to cover increasing costs of production, paid in terms of a grant per hectare or head of livestock. Also, favourable rates of aid are available for structural modernisation and investment in non-agricultural enterprises such as tourism (Ilbery, 1981b).

4. Management

A lengthy exposition of management principles will not be given here as they have already formed the focus of earlier chapters. However, certain points need

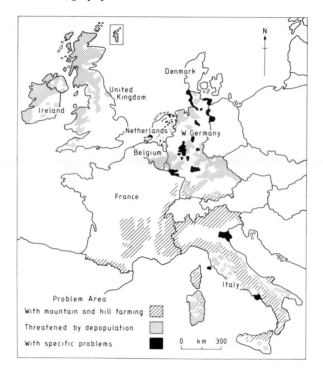

Fig. 5.3   Agricultural problem areas of the EEC (Bowler, 1976c p. 29)

to be raised in the context of this present discussion, as the allocation of land, labour and capital resources to alternative enterprises within the farm system is a major management decision. Management is the process through which the farmer makes three sets of interrelated decisions:
  (i) What to produce (types of land-use) and how much of each input or resource to commit to each enterprise.
 (ii) What output to aim for (intensity of land-use) and how to achieve it.
(iii) How the output should be marketed.
Therefore, one of the farmer's main inputs is his management skills. However, farmers do not demonstrate equal competence in exercising these skills and this can be reflected in spatial variations in land-use patterns. Once again, location may affect management decisions, as farmers in proximity to urban centres or major road networks could decide to grow crops which can be marketed directly to the consumer, via farm shops, roadside stalls and pick-your-own schemes.
   A majority of farmers are still small businessmen, largely self-financed, who derive psychic satisfaction as well as money income from farming (Hill and Ingersent, 1977). As a result, the enterprise decision often rests on personal preferences as well as on profitability. These preferences relate to two main factors (Haines, 1982): first, a farmer's conception of what constitutes an

acceptable level of profit; and secondly, his active dislike of, or enthusiasm for, particular enterprises. It is thus difficult to explain farmers' economic behaviour without reference to their motivations and attitudes, because such factors as independence, doing the work they like and belonging to the farming community affect management decisions (Gasson, 1973; Ilbery, 1983c).

On most farms the enterprise decision is an infrequent one, but risk and uncertainty remain an integral part of farm management. Farmers make production decisions with imperfect knowledge of weather conditions, prices and yields, marketing arrangements and government policy. However, the important point is that farmers' attitudes to risk avoidance vary according to numerous factors, ranging from financial reserves and the ability to borrow to the more personal circumstances of family commitments, experience, training and the enjoyment of gambling. Risk and uncertainty in agriculture present a major case for enterprise diversification, which generally leads to lower farm incomes. However, with technological change, increasing government support and a need to obtain economies of scale, the modern trend is towards specialisation of production.

5.2 Economies of scale and farm-size

The main post-war agricultural trends in developed economies, including the decline in the number of farms and farm workers, the increase in farm-size and a move towards increased concentration and specialisation, have been well documented by agricultural economists (Britton and Hill, 1975; Hill and Ingersent, 1977; Britton, 1977). These trends reflect the farmers' desire to obtain economies of scale, in order to maintain profit margins during the major price–cost squeeze of the last twenty years. Unfortunately, the spatial dimension of these changes has received scant attention from such authors, even though it is clear that there are marked areal variations in farm-size and that specialisation of production often has a distinct regional character.

Increasing farm-size is a characteristic feature of most advanced Western economies, implying a more effective use of resources. However, evidence is appearing which suggests that there is a limit to this process and that diseconomies begin to occur above a certain optimum size, which varies according to the type of farming practised. Scale economies are normally discussed in terms of farm-size. As farm-size varies enormously, from over 40,000 ha. for the collective (Sovkhoz) farms in Russia to less than 1 ha. units in the peasant economy of Java (Hurst, 1974), economies of scale represent one of the fundamental factors in the locational process. There are two kinds of scale economy: first, external economies of scale, which occur outside the individual farm but within the agricultural industry; and secondly, internal economies of scale, which occur within the individual farm. Morgan and Munton (1971) note that the distinction between the two is not always clear and depends on the scale of analysis, i.e. whether an industrial or firm viewpoint is taken. This point is demonstrated in relation to poultry production where, with an increase in the number of poultry producers, the government may provide advisory services specifically for their use. Although this would be an external economy to the individual producer, it represents an internal economy to the poultry industry generally. Irrespective of the stance adopted, it is possible that such economies will lead to regional specialisation. This in turn could encourage further economies, in the form of new infrastructure and standard transport charges to packing stations, and so leading to even greater concentration. These principles have been analysed in relation to poultry production in the East Midlands (White and Watts, 1977) and will be returned to later.

1. External economies of scale

Much attention in agricultural geography has been focused on internal economies of scale, but Morgan and Munton (1971) point to three useful examples of external economies which have had a profound impact on the spatial character of agriculture. The first is Harvey's (1963) classic study of the regional concentration of the expanding hop industry in Kent and the West Midlands in the nineteenth century. Fossilisation of the pattern in these two areas was attributed to external economies obtained from localised production, including a pool of skilled labour, specific repair and supply services, and good credit sources and marketing channels. It would appear that these advantages have been removed during the post-war period of decline (Ilbery, 1983a), but the industry remains regionally concentrated because of geographical inertia and a perceived local comparative advantage.

Secondly, concentration of horticulture in the Vale of Evesham occurred for similar reasons, following the initial physical advantages of the area and the demand and labour supply from the West Midland conurbations. Expansion of production in the area was largely unrelated to physical conditions and was associated more with external economies provided by local skilled labour, specialised local markets and the development of co-operative organisations. Once again, these advantages are less applicable today as the industry contracts in size and area and is related more to prevailing physical characteristics. The third example relates to the Milk Marketing Board, established in 1933. One of the stated objectives of the Board was to reduce the farmers' cost of transporting milk from the farm to the dairy. Thus, standard milk charges were introduced, which had the effect of providing external economies for those producers furthest removed from the dairy and centres of demand. The consequence of this was an expansion of milk production away from the major markets in the east (Chisholm, 1957; Chapter 6).

A more contemporary study demonstrating the importance of external economies of scale is White and Watt's (1977) investigation of semi-industrial poultry production in the East Midlands. Poultry producers can obtain internal economies of scale by increasing the size of their production unit. However, they all benefit from external economies provided by the packing stations, who operate a spatially uniform purchase price by paying the same price per pound for chicks of the same grade, and by covering the costs of transporting the chicks from growing plants to packing station. This has had the effect of further concentrating the expanding poultry production industry in the East Midlands, just as in the examples of expanding hop and horticultural production. However, White and Watts suggest that it is important to differentiate between corporate organisations producing chicks and individual plants. Detailed study demonstrated that the former tended towards 'economically rational patterns', by clustering around their major markets (packing stations), collecting inputs from the nearest feed mills and hatcheries and distributing output to the nearest sources. However, individual plants, which were much smaller, collected inputs and distributed produce over long distances and showed no tendency to cluster around their markets. There was little economic rationality in their resultant distribution, leading White and Watts to conclude that non-economic (behavioural) factors must have affected the spatial pattern of individual poultry plants.

2. Internal economies of scale and farm-size

Internal economies of scale can be obtained in two ways: first, by increasing farm-size; and secondly, by increasing enterprise specialisation on individual farms. Following Todd (1979), there are three types of internal economy:
   (i) *Technical*, related to mechanisation.
  (ii) *Managerial*, related to the adoption of modern farm practices.
 (iii) *Marketing*, related to farm specialisation.
Together they encourage the trend to farm enlargement. However, there are problems with the measurement of farm-size (Gregor, 1979). Land area is most commonly used, with farms of less than 20–30 ha. considered small and those over 120 ha. large. Unfortunately, this takes little account of the ratio of inputs to outputs, which vary greatly for different enterprises and goven the real 'area' of the farm. For example, 1 ha. of intensive pig or poultry production may in all senses, apart from area, be equivalent to 100 ha. of extensive arable production. Nevertheless, the alternative forms of measurement have similar problems. Standard labour inputs (SMDs), available for crops and livestock per hectare, can be used to measure the size of farm businesses (Coppock, 1971; Bowler, 1975a), but the final index is of labour intensity which naturally favours labour-intensive enterprises. Standard enterprise outputs or gross margins have also been suggested (Jackson *et al.*, 1963; Clark, 1982), but suffer from data availability problems, and the amount of capital accumulation has recently been used to examine farm-size variations in the USA (Gregor, 1982). However, this provides little more insight than variations depicted according to land area. Consequently, area remains most popular and is used as the basis for the following discussion.
    Whichever method of measurement is used, increasing farm-size is a generally

accepted trend in most advanced economies. In Western Europe, the number of farms has declined rapidly, epitomised by falls of 42 per cent in the United Kingdom between 1900 and 1980 (Haines, 1982) and 39 per cent in Denmark between 1946 and 1977 (Kampp, 1979). Similarly in North America, the number of farms in the USA fell by 63 per cent between 1930 and 1981 and in Manitoba, Canada, by 30 per cent between 1961 and 1976 alone (Todd, 1979). This trend has been accompanied by a corresponding increase in average farm-size, as demonstrated by Scotland, from 40 ha. in 1960 to 54 ha. in 1975 (Clark, 1979); England and Wales, from 25 to 57 ha. between 1900 and 1980; Denmark, from 15.2 to 22.9 ha. between 1946 and 1977 (Kampp, 1979); and the USA, from 61 ha. in 1930 to 174 ha. in 1981. In most cases, the rate of decline in the number of farms has been in inverse proportion to their size, with the losses greatest amongst the smallest holdings. Absolute gains have only occurred in the largest farm-size categories, indicative of the rising importance of scale economies in farming operations (Todd, 1979).

The main geographical significance of this trend is that there are wide variations in the spatial distribution of farm sizes which, due to the direct relationship between farm-size and enterprise type, are reflected in patterns of agricultural land-use. Figure 5.4 depicts average farm-size variations for the states of USA and immediately apparent is the marked east–west contrast. Thirteen states have an average farm-size of less than 75 ha., all concentrated in the north-east, whereas six states record average sizes of over 1,000 ha., all in the west. The pattern corresponds closely with Gregor's (1982) county-level map based on capital accumulation data, which shows an extensive spread of large-scale farming over the western half of USA. This spread is selective and most

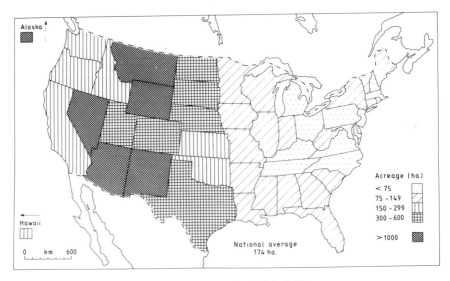

Fig. 5.4   Average farm-size variations in the USA, 1981

prominent where irrigation and a mild climate favour farming of high intensity in the south-west and where large farm-sizes permit greater productivity in the Great Plains and Intermountain region. In the east, the development of agri-business has caused parts of Florida, the Megalopolitan strip and Newfoundland to favour large-scale farming, even though farm-sizes are comparatively small (Fig. 5.4).

A more detailed case study of farm-size variations within one individual state has been conducted for Manitoba by Todd (1979). In developing various regression models, relating farm-size variations to such 'spatial' factors as land quality, proximity to markets, intensity of land-use and social conditions, Todd demonstrated the tendency for large farms to be cattle orientated, sited on poorer soils, non-urban biased, run by managers and influenced by the location of medium-size farms. In contrast, medium-size farms operated more alongside small farms, with a majority not seeking to realise economies of scale. Distance to urban markets was a fairly important locational factor and mixed/cereal farming was dominant. Finally, the distribution of small farms was heavily urban-orientated and many were part-time with second occupations. These farms were not in competition with the large farms and their distribution was com-plicated by cultural factors. Manitoba contains a group of Mennonite farmers (Todd, 1979; De Lisle, 1982), of Germano-Dutch origin, who have maintained their small-scale and traditional way of life. Mixed farming with dairying is coupled with alternative urban employment in Winnipeg and vicinity (Todd and Brierley, 1977).

In England and Wales there is a broad relationship between farm-size and enterprise type, with smaller holdings having a greater share of intensive enter-prises like poultry, pigs, dairying and horticulture than larger holdings, which lend themselves more to mechanisation and hence extensive arable activities. The main exception to this trend is livestock rearing which is often practised on large farms that are physically restricted to pastoral land-uses. Therefore, farm-size variations reflect land-use differences (Fig. 5.5), with an east–west division once again prominent. Although the range of farm-sizes is smaller than the USA, areas of larger farms are restricted to eastern counties, reaching a peak in Wiltshire, Oxfordshire and Northamptonshire. Exceptions to this include Powys and Northumberland, both associated with extensive beef and sheep enterprises in upland areas. This provides a broad initial insight into the arable east and pastoral west dichotomy which exists in British agriculture.

Farm enlargement is caused mainly by the process of amalgamation (Britton and Hill, 1975), which has been shown to vary spatially according to certain factors (Kampp, 1979; Clark, 1979). In a study of farm amalgamations in Scotland between 1968 and 1973, Clark (1979) demonstrated how the scale of amalgamations was greatest among larger farms, irrespective of whether they were tenanted or owner-occupied. Three reasons for this were advocated:

(i) Larger farms have more money, or can borrow more easily because of greater assets, and can outbid smaller farms for additional land.

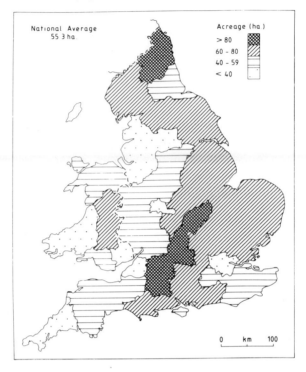

National Average
55 3 ha

Acreage (ha)

> 80
60 - 80
40 - 59
< 40

0   km   100

Fig. 5.5   Average farm-size variations in England and Wales, 1980

(ii) Larger farms need to expand more than smaller farms in order to maintain their relative income.

(iii) Larger farms are more likely to be inherited, whereas prospects for smaller farms are not promising.

Upon mapping the incidence of farm amalgamations (Fig. 5.6), Clark found that there was a spatial concentration in the north-east and Aberdeenshire in particular, in strict contrast to very low rates in the Western Isles, parts of the Inner Hebrides and the western coastal areas of Invernessshire, Ross and Cromarty and Sutherland. The means and the motive for farm enlargement were present in the north-east first, because there was a much higher proportion of vacated holdings in the size range most favoured for amalgamation—4 to 100 ha. (over 70 per cent of holdings in Aberdeenshire fell within this range); and secondly, because more heirs were found on farms in the north-east than on farms of comparable size elsewhere.

The low rates of farm amalgamation in the Western Isles were related to the system of crofting. However, Clark found that this was not due to crofting tenure, which one may expect, but to the small size of farms. In general terms, the pattern and rate of farm amalgamation in Scotland had little to do with land tenure.

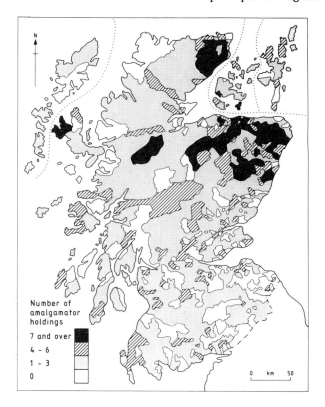

Fig. 5.6   Farm amalgamations in Scotland, 1968–73 (Clark, 1979 p. 101)

With increasing farm-size, through for example the amalgamation of holdings, the problem of farm fragmentation could be reduced. However, the limited amount of work on the topic suggests that increasing farm-size is accompanied by a corresponding rise in fragmentation. The growth in fragmented farms in recent generations is a direct response to modern agricultural technology and advancement. In order to expand his size of business, a farmer is often forced to purchase or rent isolated parcels of land at considerable distances from the main farmstead. Any economies of scale which might be obtained from such an expansion have to be matched against the diseconomies of distance of isolated parcels. As King and Burton (1982) note, fragmentaiton can be a major obstacle to mechanisation and rationalisation and lead to an inefficient spatial organisation of farming.

The relationship between fragmentation and farm-size has been demonstrated by Smith (1975) and Carlyle (1983) in North America, Hill and Smith (1977) in Australia and Edwards (1978) in Somerset, England. Carlyle also found a correlation between fragmentation and land tenure, with consolidated holdings showing a greater tendency to owner-occupancy. As farmers strive to increase the size of their holding, it becomes more difficult to purchase all the land they operate and fragmented parcels are often tenanted.

A study of horticultural holdings in the Vale of Evesham (Ilbery, 1984c) revealed similar important relationships. The extent and characteristics of farm fragmentation were examined by means of Simmons' (1964) index of fragmentation. Fifty-nine per cent of the 205 holdings investigated were fragmented, with 38 per cent of these having three or more isolated parcels. Fragmented farms were mainly concentrated in parishes to the east of Evesham, especially Bretforton, Hampton, Harvington and North Badsey (Fig. 5.7). Significant positive relationships were found between fragmentation and various structural characteristics, including farm-size, horticultural area, changing farm-size and horticultural area, land tenure and tradition. However, all isolated parcels were within 15 km of the main farmstead and, rather than acting as a barrier to efficient horticultural production, many growers stated a preference for having land in different areas. Reasons given for this varied from local variations in soils and climate (hence length of growing season) to water availability (for irrigation), all of which were perceived as spreading the risk of early season frost hazards.

The study concluded that operational processes, in the form of the creation of smallholdings by Worcestershire County Council and the large amount of land available for renting, were responsible for the initially fragmented nature of horticulture in the Vale of Evesham. This was maintained by a unique system of land tenure known as Evesham Custom and reinforced by modern agricultural technology and advancement. Research now needs to incorporate the effects of

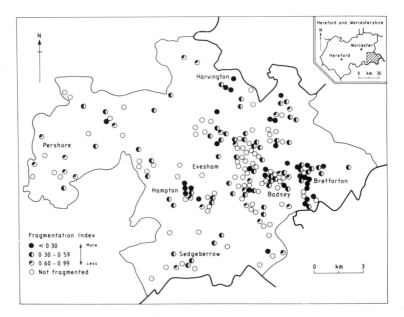

Fig. 5.7   Farm fragmentation in the Vale of Evesham

farm fragmentation on actual farming systems, which can only be achieved by examining the motives and ambitions of farmers as they strive to expand their businesses.

As well as the relationship between farm-size variations and land-use patterns, there is also a positive correlation between efficiency and farm-size (Britton and Hill, 1975). Economies are more easily obtained as the scale of business increases, as producers can use machinery more effectively and get discounts from the bulk buying of inputs. The ratio of inputs to outputs is better on large farms, thus encouraging greater efficiency. Such farms tend to be occupied by the progressive, well-educated farmers who are more ready to accept change and innovate. In this context, the rapid development of agribusiness is not surprising as economies of scale achieved through vertical integration are formidable.

However, studies are beginning to show that the rate of increase in farm-size is slowing down and that diseconomies will set in above a certain optimum size, which varies according to enterprise type. This is a view held by both agricultural economists and geographers alike (Hill and Ingersent, 1977; Todd, 1979; Gregor, 1979; Haines, 1982; Norton-Taylor, 1982) and is well summarised in a statement from Hill and Ingersent (1977 p. 42): 'Most of the empirical evidence on economies of size in farming points to the conclusion that the main reduction in unit costs occurs in moving from small to medium-sized farms: there appears to be little further gain with expansion to very large farm sizes.'

Britton (1977) has graphically demonstrated how the rate of structural change in farm-size is slowing down (Fig. 5.8). Taking the proportion of land in

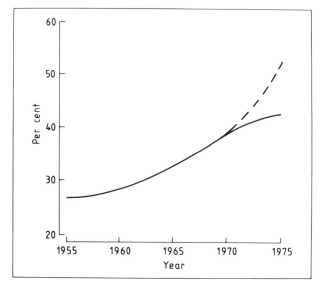

Fig. 5.8   Structural change in farm-size in England and Wales (Britton, 1977 p. 198)

holdings of 120 ha. or more for each year between 1955 and 1975, the actual rate of increase (continuous line) is seen to be less than a projection which would have been made in 1970 on the basis of the trend between 1955 and 1970 (dashed line). As Britton remarks, this could mean that the size structure is reaching stability, with important implications for the future productive efficiency and spatial organisation of British agriculture. Norton-Taylor (1982) suggests that economies of size run out at 100 ha. for dairy enterprises and just over 160 ha. for cropping, and Haines (1982) points to the fact that farms of between 40 and 100 ha., depending on enterprise combinations, are most efficient. In his study of agriculture in Manitoba, Todd (1979) explains how the trend to continued farm enlargement has been tempered by limits imposed through the lack of managerial expertise. Large farming organisations are difficult to co-ordinate, with problems over capital and labour supply and increased risk which accompanies business expansion. Personal individuality plays less part on large farms and the flexibility to respond to changes in economic and environmental conditions is reduced. Behavioural overtones are again apparent, as the majority of farmers prefer to keep control in their own hands. This has an important bearing on farm-size variations and in turn agricultural land-use patterns.

In a study of the Pacific south-west of USA, an area in an advanced state of large-scale farming, Gregor (1979) found that large farms were not a serious threat to the smaller operators. A multivariate analysis of large-scale farming in the area showed that its distribution was urban oreintated, unlike Todd (1979) in Manitoba, and bore little resemblance to the physical environment. Large farms were found in the cooler oases of Nevada, South Arizona and south-east California as well as in the more favourable Central Valley (Fig. 5.9). Gregor concluded that the inefficiencies of larger farms in areas such as the San Joaquin Valley were a greater impediment to viable agriculture than the diseconomies of small farms. This contrasts with a more recent study by the same author (Gregor, 1982) when analysing the conflict between technological change (increasing scale of farming operations) and cultural ideals (equality of opportunity and the right to till the soil in family-sized units) in USA agriculture. Gregor, whilst not emphasising the benefits of large-scale farming, stated that the continued vigour of the family farm was not advisable, for two reasons: first, because it was disadvantaged in all production functions; and secondly, because it was no longer protected by the ideas of labour intensification and production efficiency. He perceived the Western Corn Belt, which contains both large and family farms, to be the most likely area where this clash of ideals would be first resolved.

Despite such propositions, the small farm survives, with its characteristic intensive enterprises and important locational effects on agricultural practices (Hill and Ingersent, 1977; Clark, 1979; Todd, 1979). Various reasons can be forwarded which contribute to its continued vigour:

(i) A majority of small farms finance capital inputs from their own profits and the risks of expansion are often too great.

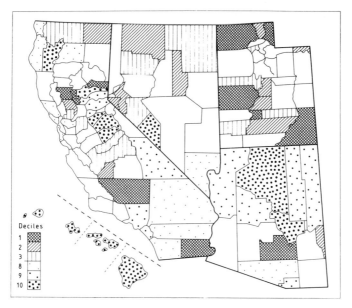

Fig. 5.9   Large-scale farming in the Pacific South-West, USA (Gregor, 1979 p. 83)

(ii) Various government support measures, such as the Small Farmer Scheme in the United Kingdom and guaranteed pricing in the EEC, help maintain many small marginal farms, which would otherwise be forced out of production.

(iii) The general occupational and geographical immobility of such farmers, who stress the importance of independence and 'way of life' aspects of farming, is a dominant force. Often a lack of skills or alternative employment opportunities prevents movement, especially in more isolated regions such as mid-Wales and the crofting areas of western Scotland.

(iv) Agricultural reform and resettlement have often tended to create many small farms from former latifundia and large estates. This is particularly prevalent on the European mainland, in countries like France, West Germany and Italy (Mayhew, 1971; Clout, 1975; Ilbery, 1981b), but is also evident in areas like the Vale of Evesham, where larger farms were split into smallholdings after the First World War, to allow people into agriculture. These have survived to the present day and are mainly associated with horticultural activities.

(v) Many small farms have obtained external economies of scale by pooling their resources together and forming private co-operative organisations (Chapter 7). In the case of the Vale of Evesham, Littleton and Badsey Growers Limited, formed in 1908, has over 1,000 such members and is an important source of farm inputs.

(vi) Cultural factors have been instrumental in maintaining and sometimes encouraging the growth of small farms. Divided inheritance (gavelkind) in the romance language countries of Europe led to continual subdivision and fragmentation of farms. On a reduced scale, it has already been demonstrated how the Mennonite farmers of Manitoba maintain their traditional pattern of small-scale mixed/dairy farming because of cultural factors (Todd, 1979; De Lisle, 1982).

(vii) The growth of part-time and hobby farming, where farmers have second occupations (Layton, 1981a), has ensured the survival of the small farm in certain areas. Such farmers tend to be spatially concentrated in the rural-urban fringe (Chapter 8) as urban proximity is important for employment purposes.

5.3 Enterprise and regional specialisation

Although increases in farm-size have been important in post-war developments in Western agriculture, economies of scale have often been pursued through increased concentration and specialisation of production. Agriculture has become concentrated in the hands of fewer and larger producers. For example, the average area of cereals in the United Kingdom has increased from 22 ha. in 1967 to 40 ha. in 1981. At the same time, the number of cereal holdings has fallen by 27 per cent, with the greatest decline occurring in those holdings growing less than 8 ha. of cereals. Similar trends are apparent in other enterprises, such as sugar-beet, potatoes, dairying, pigs and poultry.

The causes of concentration and larger farm enterprises relate to the significant economies of scale which modern agricultural technology yields. As Bowler (1975a) suggests, specialisation permits a concentration of resources on advanced buildings, machinery and management specific to individual enterprises. Indeed, with improved technology a farmer often has to face the dilemma of increasing the scale of an individual enterprise or giving it up altogether; this is especially the case with the factory-like enterprises of pigs and poultry. As Hill and Ingersent note (1977 p. 46): 'forces making for the enlargement of enterprises also tend to result in a less diversified and more specialised pattern of output on individual farms'. Government policies and advice are contributory to this trend through support systems and guaranteed prices, which have increased the profitability of some products against others and reduced the uncertainty of return and the need for mixed farming. Information from advisory services tends to concentrate on ways of improving the efficiency of each enterprise separately, whereas the interrelationships between enterprises, in a more diversified farm system, are somewhat ignored.

Inevitably there are disadvantages of increased specialisation, which in part can be related to the losses of economies of joint production. Crop and crop/livestock rotations, where one crop replaces in the soil what another has taken out, or where the waste from one enterprise (manure from beef) provides an important input for another (hops), have been reduced. Losses from specialisation include:

(i) Soil deterioration, leading to an increased intensity of fertiliser use.

(ii) Animal manure, previously put on crops, has to be disposed of by costly sewerage processes.

(iii) An increase in the population of specialised pests and diseases, which demands extra application of pesticides and chemicals.

In addition, Bowler (1981a and b) has drawn attention to various ecological, economic and social problems associated with increased regional specialisation. These include a region's reduced ability to respond to changes in production costs and prices, leaving it more susceptible to the market and government decisions, the large increase in fertiliser application which accompanies the trend to monoculture, and physical and social impacts on rural landscapes which large farms bring, in the form of new farm buildings, removal of hedgerows and disruption or rural social patterns.

From a geographical point of view, concentration and specialisation of production have had a marked locational effect on patterns of agricultural land-use. In both the USA and UK, the majority of farming types have become more regionally concentrated. This has been confirmed for England and Wales by Bowler (1981b), where farming types with a high degree of concentration have become more regionally selective, usually in regions traditionally associated with them, whilst farming types appearing on more farms (eg. barley and beef) have become regionally more dispersed. In a general sense, farming types experiencing economic growth are most likely to become more dispersed, whereas types which are stable or declining in numbers will become concentrated in fewer areas. Examples from the USA and Great Britain, at different scales, will be used to examine these trends and the effects of specialisation on agricultural location.

A reduction in transport costs, relative to other production costs, could lead to increased regional specialisation; alternatively modern agricultural technology could reduce the comparative advantage of concentrating farming types in areas that are physically most suitable. In an attempt to solve this apparent contradiction, Winsberg (1980) studied concentration and specialisation in USA agriculture by analysing farm gate sales for 19 commodities between 1939 and 1978. Using the location quotient to study concentration, results showed that the majority of commodities, with the exception of soya beans, had increased their farm sales concentrations. Significantly, an increase in farm sales occurred within those states in which the location quotients were high. Similarly, the index of dissimilarity demonstrated that the distribution of farm sales for most commodities had become increasingly isolated (regionally specialised).

The major change towards regional specialisation occurred between 1939 and 1949, when there was a high demand for home-produced food. Since then more food than required has been produced and farm sales have become increasingly divorced from the distribution of the nation's population; this suggests continued regional specialisation. It also indicates that local comparative advantage outweighs the effects of technical innovations in determining patterns of land-use. However, not all evidence is conclusive as to the extent of regional specialisation in USA agriculture. Various authors have tested the von Thünen model on this macro scale and whilst Muller (1973) and Jones (1976) suggested a zoning of agriculture in the USA, from intensive production in the east to extensive in the west, Kellerman (1977) could find no such pattern.

A similar trend towards increased regional specialisation, associated with a decline in the importance of transport costs, was demonstrated at a reduced scale of analysis in a historical study of agriculture in western New York state between 1840 and 1860 (Leaman and Conkling, 1975). Three hundred and twenty-five townships, in an 18-county area, were selected for study and 21 variables common to both 1840 and 1860 were extracted from the agricultural census for each township, along with information on distance, regionalisation and environmental conditions. Transport facilities improved substantially in the twenty year period, with the railway penetrating most parts of western New York by 1860 and the Genesee Valley canal being extended considerably. In 1840 there was some evidence of specialisation in the east but not in the west, where transport costs and difficulties were more important locational determinants than land quality. By 1860 there was a higher degree of agricultural specialisation in western New York, as farm types had sought particular locations and specific qualities of land. Therefore, local comparative advantage, in association with reduced transport costs and improved accessibility, had become an important determinant of the spatial structure of agriculture, although the major technological advances of the twentieth century were still to be experienced.

The trend towards greater specialisation of production in Britain has been characterised by certain features (Britton, 1977):

(i) The smaller the farm the more rapid the rate of decline in the number of enterprises.

(ii) The decline in farm enterprises largely consists of the elimination of poultry and pig enterprises, which have become increasingly specialised.

(iii) Pig-breeding is no longer a characteristically small-business enterprise, whereas poultry is still more likely to be found in a small farm business.

(iv) The reduction in the number of enterprises per farm has occurred in all farm-types.

None of these changes has been spectacular and on the whole it could be said that 'the type-of-farming structure has been fairly stable, but with mixed farming continuing to give way to more specialised types' (Britton, 1977 p. 203). This was echoed by Bowler (1981b p. 15) who noted that the post-war pattern of farming was being 'modified rather than reinforced'. A process of regional specialisation is occurring, with variations in intensity between different farming types and individual enterprises. The factors at work in this process are complex, but the differential movement in and out of production of certain products is a key element.

In England and Wales, certain farming types, especially beef, cereals, poultry and pigs, increased in absolute numbers between 1965 and 1975. They also increased in proportional terms, along with specialist dairying, general horticulture and livestock rearing and fattening: cattle and sheep (beef/sheep), (Bowler, 1981b). Spatially, a majority of farming types had become more regionally concentrated, especially general horticulture and beef/sheep farms (Table 5.1). However, five farming types (specialist dairying, cereals, vegetables, poultry and mixed) had become locationally more dispersed.

Similarly in Scotland, the trend towards larger units and increased specialisation has not been spatially uniform (Bowler, 1975a and 1981a). Using the coefficient of localisation, for 1961 and 1971 data, Bowler (1975a) was able to show that the rate of change towards dispersion was greatest for barley and beef cow enterprises, with wheat showing the same tendencies. The pre-eminence of the north-east for the beef enterprise had been reduced. Also, the rate of change towards concentration was most marked for pig and poultry enterprises, although dairying, sheep and field crops experienced such a movement. Areas which were traditionally important for these farming types had been reconsolidated, as with poultry in the Firth of Forth, dairying in the south-west and breeding ewes in the hill lands. The only exception to the general trend was pigs, which had increased in numbers but become more concentrated in distribution, due mainly to the growth of large intensive units in the north-east.

Table 5.1

Type of farming change in England and Wales, 1965–75
(percentage of total holdings in each year above 275 SMDs)

Type of farming	1965	1975	Locationally more concentrated (C) or dispersed (D), 1965–75: English and Welsh counties
Mainly dairy	20.0	11.4	C
Beef/sheep	9.6	11.3	C
General cropping	12.1	10.4	C
General horticulture	6.8	8.6	C
Beef	2.2	7.9	C
Pigs/poultry	3.2	5.3	C
Sheep	4.0	2.7	C
Fruit	1.6	1.3	C
Specialist dairy	18.9	24.4	D
Cereals	5.0	6.9	D
Mixed	12.5	6.7	D
Poultry	2.9	2.1	D
Vegetables	1.2	1.0	D
Total holdings	156,207	119,816	

Source: Bowler (1981b p. 7).

A continuation of the same trends in Scotland was apparent for the 1968 to 1975 period (Bowler, 1981a), with five farming types becoming locationally more dispersed and four more concentrated in those regions in which they were already dominant (Table 5.2). Explanation of the pattern was related to two factors in particular: first, the economic viability of individual enterprises, with enterprises experiencing long-term growth demonstrating spatial dispersion (barley and beef) and those with stable or declining numbers becoming more spatially concentrated (dairying, sheep and potatoes); and secondly, 'enterprise concentration', where individual enterprises get bigger and farms specialise on fewer enterprises in their search for economies of scale. This is particularly true of the semi-industrial pig and poultry enterprises, which are becoming regionally concentrated in the north-east and east central regions respectively.

At reduced scales of analysis, evidence of the trend to enterprise and regional specialisation is also available. Using parish data, types of farming and individual enterprises have been shown to become more localised in Leicestershire between 1963 and 1977 (Bowler, 1981b), with the exceptions of beef and cereals (Fig. 5.10). Beef became more dispersed, especially in the north and western areas, and its distribution in 1977 bore little resemblance to the earlier pattern of 1963. On the other hand, cereals continued to be grown in similar areas and the

Table 5.2
Regional farm-type specialisation in Scotland, 1975

Type of farm (% within each region)	Region					Scotland		Locationally more con- centrated (C) or dispersed (D)
	High- land	North- East	East central	South- East	South- West	1968	1975	
Hill sheep	10.9	0.2	3.6	4.7	3.7	5.2	4.2	D
Upland	21.6	10.1	12.0	10.2	27.0	15.8	24.7	D
Rearing with arable	5.9	22.3	8.5	12.4	4.4	12.3	14.1	D
Rearing with intensive livestock	0.3	2.6	0.9	0.9	0.6	2.1	1.5	C
Arable, rearing and feeding	1.6	4.9	4.4	3.8	0.6	4.9	3.6	D
Cropping	2.8	6.9	31.6	19.3	1.8	13.9	11.7	C
Dairy	5.7	4.3	6.6	7.3	34.7	20.0	16.2	C
Intensive	0.8	2.1	8.3	6.4	4.5	4.7	4.7	D
Part-time	42.9	17.2	8.5	8.9	9.8	21.2	19.3	C

Source: Bowler (1981a p. 45).

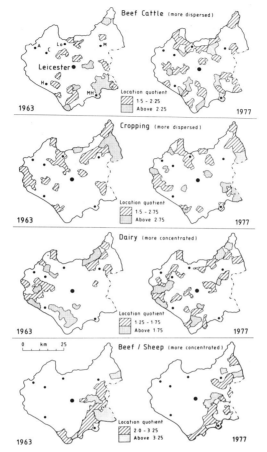

Fig. 5.10   Regional specialisation by type of farming in Leicestershire
(Bowler, 1981b p. 10)

trend towards dispersal was the direct result of the emergence of a new area in
the south-east, traditionally associated with beef and sheep.

Certain farming types, notably livestock rearing and fattening: cattle and
sheep (beef/sheep), dairying and horticulture, had become more concentrated
in those parts of Leicestershire where they were previously important (Fig. 5.10).
Mixed farming and pig and poultry enterprises had also become more spatially
concentrated, but not in their traditional areas. For example, the pattern of pig
and poultry farming altered remarkably between 1963 and 1977 and any
explanation for this change must take account of the industrial and capital-
intensive nature of an enterprise which offers few locational advantages. Therefore, the spatially random pattern is a reflection of entrepreneurial skills and
preferences of individuals within the farming community.

A comparatively rare study of enterprise change at the farm scale was that carried out by Edwards (1980) in central Somerset between 1963 and 1976. Complexity and change were forwarded as keynotes to enterprise structure and whilst a trend towards greater specialisation was recognised, this was not uniform as 31 per cent of the farms had experienced no change between the two dates and a further 16 per cent had actually increased their number of enterprises. A more detailed insight into the changes is afforded in Table 5.3. Dairying had declined in importance in this core dairy area, but was more specialised, with larger herds, on those farms where it had remained. Other noticeable trends included a decline in pig and poultry production and a marked increase in beef production. The latter was seen as either a subsidiary enterprise to rear on and fatten surplus calves from the dairy herd or a primary enterprise replacing dairying since 1963. Reasons cited for the change from dairy to beef included the perceived cost of changing to bulk-tank milk, the age of the farmer and the cost and scarcity of skilled labour. The conclusion drawn from this work was that farmers do respond dynamically in order to remain profitable, 'continuously changing the emphasis of their production systems in response to temporal changes in the factors of production' (Edwards, 1980 p. 51).

These case-studies have demonstrated that the trend to specialisation is a complex one, with much depending on the attitudes of farmers and their perceptions of changing economic circumstances. Despite this, the role of 'behavioural' influences has sadly been neglected, although they did provide the focal point of Bowler's (1975b) study of enterprise specialisation in Montgomeryshire and Ilbery's (1984d) analysis of hop specialisation in Hereford and Worcestershire. As Bowler remarked, the spatial impact of specialisation contains two elements.

Table 5.3
Changing enterprise structure in central Somerset, 1963–76

Enterprise	Total frequency of occurrence		Percentage of sample		Percentage frequency of occurrence as:					
					Only enterprise		First enterprise		Subsidiary enterprise	
	1963	1976	1963	1976	1963	1976	1963	1976	1963	1976
Cereals	39	33	32.0	31.4	–	–	1.7	3.8	30.3	27.6
Potatoes	12	6	9.8	5.7	–	–	–	–	9.8	5.7
Dairy	112	85	91.8	81.0	9.0	20.0	80.3	52.4	2.5	8.6
Beef	22	53	18.0	50.5	–	2.9	1.7	10.5	16.3	37.1
Sheep	35	30	28.7	28.6	–	–	0.8	–	27.9	28.6
Pigs	67	29	54.9	27.6	0.8	1.9	4.9	4.8	49.2	20.9
Poultry	70	17	57.4	16.2	0.8	–	–	3.7	56.6	12.5

Source: Edwards (1980 p. 50).

First, there are changes which are expected from rational economic behaviour, such as the withdrawal from, or entry to, production of farms at the extensive margins of production, and increased output by existing producers at the intensive margins. Greater localisation of production can be explained in terms of agglomeration and scale economies at the intensive margins and dispersion can be attributed to limitations of production or diseconomies of scale at the extensive margins. Secondly, there are changes which do not conform to the trends and are attributable to variations in farmer decision-making behaviour. This aspect has received little attention from geographers and led Bowler to develop a methodological framework for examining its importance, which was extended by Ilbery to include the goals and values of farmers.

A survey of 120 farms in the upland area of Montgomeryshire provided Bowler with his data base. All enterprises were converted to SMDs and expressed as a percentage of total SMDs. Three enterprises were selected for study—dairying, sheep and beef—and farmers deviating in economic behaviour from the norm for the area were identified using trend surface analysis. The trend surfaces modelled the major economic trends in the degree of enterprise specialisation and the residuals were used to identify deviations in economic behaviour; positive residuals indicated more specialisation than the norm for the area and negative residuals less specialisation. An attempt was made to explain the pattern of residuals in terms of 13 physical, economic and social constraints on decision-making. Only six significant relationships emerged (Table 5.4), emphasising the complexity of the processes at work and the lack of direct measures of farmers' goals and values amongst the 13 factors.

Dairying was characterised by high farm business intensities, suggesting that it is an enterprise which is 'more prone to influence by variations in the goals and values held by farmers' (Bowler, 1975b p. 108). The beef enterprise was related to the environmental index (based on soil, slope and climatic character-istics), where adverse physical conditions precluded dairying, and associated with low stocking densities and weakly developed farm business intensities. It is interesting to note that social constraints provided no indication of why these farmers specialised in beef rather than sheep production. As Bowler points out, the best explanation is provided for the sheep enterprise, which was associated with large farms and the high proportion of rough grazing on such farms. This highlighted the importance of physical constraints on decision-making. The remaining important relationship concerned the association of small farms with part-time farming. It is evident that part-time farmers in the area prefer to practice a mixed farming system, in the form of dairy and beef enterprises but not sheep, and so reduce the risks of specialisation.

Although information on the goals and values of farmers was not available in Bowler's analysis, it had been collected in a survey of hop farmers by Ilbery (1983c). Consequently, Bowler's methodology was employed in a study of hop farming in the West Midlands (Ilbery, 1984d), and an attempt was made to explain the pattern of residuals in terms of 13 farm-and-farmer characteristics

Table 5.4

Enterprise specialisation in Montgomeryshire
(Chi-square values for relationship between residuals
and farm and farmer characteristics)

	Nature of enterprise specialisation		
	Dairying	Beef	Sheep
Physical constraints			
1. Proportion of farm in rough grazing	3.97(2)	2.40(2)	6.00(2)*
2. Environmental index	7.22(4)	15.60(4)*	2.59(4)
Economic constraints			
3. Size of farm (hectares)	7.27(6)	6.82(6)	13.47(6)*
4. Size of business (SMDs)	5.60(6)	6.32(6)	10.88(6)
5. Farm business intensity (SMD/100 ha.)	20.76(6)*	31.56(6)*	16.84(6)*
6. Stocking density (LU 100 ha.)	7.89(6)	29.25(6)*	5.58(6)
7. Employment of farm labour	3.91(2)	1.12(2)	3.35(2)
Social constraints			
8. Age of farmer	2.62(6)	0.19(6)	3.20(6)
9. Years in management of farm	3.13(6)	5.07(6)	7.27(6)
10. Part-time farmer	3.14(2)	0.36(2)	9.12(2)*
11. Tenant	2.11(2)	1.80(2)	3.67(2)
12. Innovator	2.74(4)	6.56(4)	5.07(4)
13. Educational attainment	1.76(2)	1.21(2)	2.73(2)
	(degrees of freedom in brackets)		

*   Significant at 0.05 level
SMD standard man days
LU   livestock units

Source: Bowler (1975b p. 107).

and 20 goals and values. Very few significant relationships were revealed by X^2 tests (Table 5.5), even when the 56 farms with a 'normal' level of hop specialisation had been excluded. This emphasizes the complexity of processes at work and the difficulty of generalising about farmers' decision behaviour.

Five factors were statistically significant in explaining variations in the degree of hop specialisation, only one of which was related to direct measures of goals and values; this would appear to be contrary to Bowler's expectations. Three of the four significant farm characteristics were predictable but add weight to the viability of the adopted methodology. These were the number of enterprises, hop acreage and the ranking of the hop enterprise in the farm system. It follows

Table 5.5

Relationship between residuals from regression surface of hop specialisation and farm-and-farmer characteristics and goals and values

	Significant relationship
A. Farm-and-farmer characteristics	
1. Distance from core of hop production	X
2. Farm-size	X
3. Age of hop farmer	√*
4. Education	X
5. Full or part-time	X
6. Agricultural training	X
7. Status	X
8. Experience	X
9. Hop acreage	√†
10. Changing hop acreage	X
11. Father grew hops	X
12. Number of enterprises	√*
13. Rank of hop enterprise	√†
B. Goals and Values	
1. Meeting a challenge	X
2. Being creative	X
3. Belonging to the farming community	X
4. Pride of ownership	X
5. Doing the work you like	X
6. Independence	X
7. Making maximum income	X
8. Working close to family and home	X
9. Self-respect for doing a worthwhile job	X
10. Being able to arrange hours of work	X
11. Continuing the family tradition	√*
12. Expanding the business	X
13. Leading healthy, outdoor life	X
14. Safeguarding income for the future	X
15. Gaining recognition as a farmer	X
16. Earning respect of workers	X
17. Making a satisfactory income	X
18. Exercising special abilities	X
19. Purposeful activity	X
20. Control in a variety of situations	X

*   Significant at 0.05 level
†   Significant at 0.01 level

Source: Ilbery (1984d p. 332).

that the most specialised hop farms in the area will tend to be those with fewer enterprises, larger hop acreages and a hop crop which ranks quite highly within the adopted farm system. However, the fourth significant characteristic was the farmer's age and results show that there is a tendency for the older farmers to be the most specialised hop growers. Of the 37 hop farms with high positive residuals, 57 per cent were run by farmers over the age of 55; in contrast, 79 per cent of the 34 farmers with high negative residuals were less than 55.

Although initially surprising, this relationship can partly be explained by the traditional and declining nature of hop farming in Great Britain. As discussed elsewhere (Ilbery, 1983b), two factors are particularly important in the pattern of hop farming: opportunity cost and social inertia. The former signifies that hops fit well into the adopted agricultural system and cannot be replaced by other intensive crops, which would be either less profitable or unsuited to the prevailing physical conditions. The latter suggests that because of tradition, farmers are reluctant to abandon a crop which has been in the family for years, even if it is a comparatively inefficient enterprise. Consequently, it is the older farmers who remain loyal and devote much of their energy to hop farming, whilst the younger farmers have no such qualms and concentrate on more profitable and less labour-intensive enterprises.

This situation is borne out by the one goal and value that is related to the degree of specialisation. Continuing the family tradition was considered to be an important farming value by those farmers who were more specialised in hops that the 'norm' for the area. Indeed, 65 per cent of the 'overspecialised' hop farmers felt that continuing the family tradition was an important or very important value, compared to a figure of 35 per cent for the 'underspecialised' hop farmers. Interestingly, there was no relationship between specialisation and either farm-size or such goals and values as expanding the business, making maximum income and exercising special abilities.

As with the physically-restricted environment of Montgomery, the study of hops is not truly representative of specialisation trends because it is an enterprise which has experienced post-war decline. The methodology developed needs 'further application to other areas' (Bowler, 1975b p. 109), especially those which permit a wide range of enterprise types and are characterised by patterns of specialisation in such expanding enterprises as cereals and beef.

6

GOVERNMENT POLICY AND AGRICULTURAL MARKETING

6.1 The case for government intervention

'The market is undoubtedly one of the most potent factors in agricultural production' (Morgan and Munton, 1971 p. 70), and if uncontrolled will lead to an
imbalance between the supply and demand for agricultural produce. With the
exception of such long-term changes in taste as the expansion of frozen and
convenience food, the demand for agricultural products has remained relatively
stable and their prices inelastic (Tarrant, 1974). However, the supply of farm
produce is highly variable, reflecting the degree of uncertainty facing farmers.
Uncertainty comes from two major sources (Blandford and Currie, 1975):
first, the characteristic production lags imply that farmers operating in free
markets make production decisions on the basis of imperfect knowledge of
relevant future prices; and secondly, the production of many commodities is
subject to the influence of unpredictable forces, such as the weather and disease.

Therefore, the individual farmer has to consider the market potential for each
enterprise and assess their likely return. Without some form of intervention he
will respond to an advantageous market by producing more. In so doing, supply
is likely to exceed demand, with the resultant overproduction causing prices and
farm incomes to fall. Clearly, with a large number of independent producers
operating under uncertainty the individual farmer has no control over prices and
his own returns. Additionally, he normally has to deal through the traditional
wholesaler–retailer channels, where expensive middlemen can dictate the price
he receives.

Faced with such marketing problems, farmers have different options open to
them. First, they can call for direct government intervention, of various forms,
as discussed in section 6.2. Secondly, they can either group together and form
their own co-operative marketing system or negotiate contracts with food
processors (Chapter 7). Thirdly, they can circumvent the wholesale–retail
channels by embarking upon some form of direct marketing to the public.
Although this latter option is still comparatively rare, producers can increase
profits by selling produce via farm shops, roadside stalls or pick-your-own (PYO)
schemes. America has witnessed this trend for some time (Linstrom, 1978), but
the main expansion of PYO schemes in Britain occurred in the mid 1970s. A
very uneven spatial distribution developed (Fig. 6.1), although there was a
concentration of PYO farms near the major centres of population in south-east
England (Sussex, Kent and Essex) and the West Midlands (Vale of Evesham),
areas traditionally associated with the production of top fruit, soft fruit and

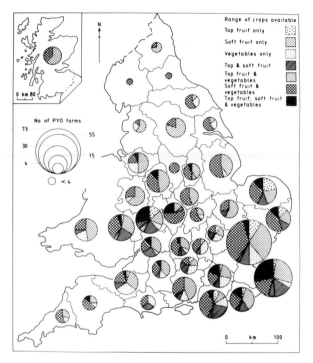

Fig. 6.1   The distribution of PYO farms in England and Wales (Bowler, 1982 p. 26)

vegetables (Bowler, 1981c and 1982). The combination of favourable conditions for horticulture and proximity to urban markets was seen as the crucial factor affecting the location of PYO schemes, which tended to favour small and medium-sized farms, primarily of owner-occupier status.

Over time, agricultural marketing would appear to go through a process of development, which Tarrant (1974) classified into three stages:

(i) Self-sufficiency, where the producer is his own market, as there are as many outlets for produce as there are producers.

(ii) Local markets and exchange facilities, where the number of agricultural outlets declines rapidly and are easily outnumbered by the number of farmers. This gives rise to middlemen who act as distributors to consumers.

(iii) Intervention of large food processing companies and institutional buyers who, with their large scale economies, begin to dominate the market. This is reflected in the growth of food preparation by processors and the demise of home-prepared food. For example, three-quarters of the food produced in Britain and West Germany is processed in some form (Haines, 1982). Such industrialisation of agriculture favours the larger farmers, which leads to a widening of the gap in incomes between different groups of farmers that government intervention is attempting to ameliorate.

Therefore, in the short run, agricultural policy is necessary to even out the worst effects of supply and demand fluctuations on consumers and to provide food at reasonable prices. In the long term, the need for such policy relates to three major considerations (Haines, 1982):

(i) The relatively low incomes of the farm sector *vis-à-vis* other industries and social groups.
(ii) The strategic argument for maintaining a substantial domestic agriculture in order to reduce the dependence on imported food, even though the latter may be cheaper.
(iii) The economic contribution of agriculture to the balance of trade and gross national product. For example, in New Zealand and Jersey agriculture is vital to export income.

Farmers represent one of the most cohesive occupational groups and agricultural policy is greatly influenced by various economic, political and social factors. Economically, the memory of food shortages in Europe during the two World Wars encouraged the EEC to adopt a policy of self-sufficiency in many agricultural products, and agriculture often supports a substantial processing industry, which generates employment and contributes to the gross national product. Politically, concern for agriculture is important because the farm vote can be very significant; also international agreements often include agricultural products, as with the Commonwealth sugar agreement of 1973 which allowed the importation of 1.8 million tonnes of cane sugar into Britain, even though it was much more expensive to refine than local beet sugar. Socially, the desire to prevent rural depopulation and maintain rural services and social stability has meant that many family farms are heavily subsidised (Haines, 1982). Indeed, without government support the incomes of many farmers would be unacceptably low, due to a combination of their location and small size, poor physical conditions and a main enterprise subject to wide price fluctuations.

In most countries farmers benefit financially from government intervention in agriculture, even though such activity is often resented by the farming community (Morgan and Munton, 1971). This is because the idea of independence and the family farm, so important to many farmers, is perceived to be threatened by government action. The wide range of types of government intervention will now be outlined before the locational effects of selected measures on the structure of agriculture are examined. Farmers' responses to these measures will be discussed where relevant.

6.2 Types of government intervention

Various forms of government involvement in agriculture have been experienced in different parts of the world and their spatial ramifications felt at regional, national and international scales. Two categories of measures can be discerned: first, those concerned with controlling and supporting the present system of agriculture; and secondly, those which attempt to improve the efficiency of farming through structural reforms. The two are interrelated but do not necessarily have complementary objectives.

1. Price control

Policies under this category usually protect farmers, by guaranteeing prices for their products, and not consumers. Such measures were extensively used in Great Britain and the USA between the wars, in an attempt to increase output and raise farmers' incomes. The system establishes a support or guaranteed price for a commodity, usually fixed according to the price reached in a mutually agreed base year and at a rate that is judged necessary to maintain farmers' incomes. If the market price falls below this support price, two options are open to the government agency. First, it can subsidise farmers in the form of a deficiency payment (difference between the support price and the market price). This expense is met out of income taxes, with high earners subsidising low food prices. Such a system simultaneously satisfies both the producers, who receive their guaranteed prices, and the consumers, who are shielded against the real cost of food (Haines, 1982), and was implemented in Britain until 1977 when the Common Agricultural Policy (CAP) of the EEC came into full effect. Secondly, the government can 'buy' directly in the market place at the support price, in order to stabilise the market and keep prices high. This intervention buying has the effect of keeping producer prices high, but also raises the cost of food to the consumer who has to pay these artificially high prices. The excess food generated by this system has to be stored and subsequently disposed of, either at cheap prices on the world market or physically destroyed. This form of price support, which distorts the basic principles of supply and demand, is an integral part of the CAP, where the powerful farming lobby has helped to create high guaranteed prices. The creation of massive surpluses, in the shape of butter and beef mountains and milk and wine lakes, is a major disadvantage of the EEC system and it is interesting to note that the deficiency payment idea has been incorporated into the Community's sheepmeat and beef support schemes (Haines, 1982).

The first signs of price control came in the USA with the McNary–Hangen Bill of 1927, which fixed fair prices for agricultural products (Tarrant, 1974). Products which could not be sold at these prices were purchased by the government and sold abroad, in order to avoid depressing the home price. Although the idea met with much opposition and was adversely affected by the depression, the principles were reborn in the Agricultural Marketing Act of 1933. Initially, fair prices were fixed according to a 1910–14 base level, but changing technology and increased mechanisation led in 1948 to the base price being fixed in relation to prices obtained over the preceding ten years. To add flexibility, support prices were later fixed according to production levels and could thus rise and fall accordingly.

Such support is now mandatory for many products and can be applied to others if the market and production levels justify it. The CAP's system of intervention buying through FEOGA (European Guidance and Guarantee Fund) is the modern-day personification of price support and its inherent problems. The latter can be summarised as follows:

(i) Price support requires tariff walls to prevent imported production lowering prices.

(ii) Surplus production has to be disposed of, preferably abroad as in recent large EEC butter sales to Russia.

(iii) With high support prices, the cost to the government can be considerable. In the EEC, the Guarantee section of FEOGA accounts for over 70 per cent of its total funds, leaving very little for the restructuring functions of the Guidance section.

(iv) With increases in world inflation, world prices for products can rise well above support prices. This would necessitate a change in policy, from import controls to export levies, which would help to reduce the differential between home and export prices.

2. Production control

As one of the major consequences of price support is surplus food, the emphasis of government policy changed in such countries as the USA, Canada and Great Britain in the late 1950s towards limiting production. This can take one of two forms (Haines, 1982): first, through the restriction of imports by imposing quotas, tariffs or a variable import levy and so allowing domestic prices to rise to predetermined levels; and secondly, by the imposition of area or quantity quotas.

The latter and more common of the two options again first appeared in the USA, in the 1930s. With farmers planting more to compensate for falling prices, attempts were made to restrict certain commodities, like cotton, tobacco and peanuts, to established production areas. For example, since 1933 the US Department of Agriculture has monitored tobacco acreages and production in all states producing the crop (Raitz, 1971) and in 1936 tobacco acreage allotments were introduced, which the Agricultural Stabilisation and Conservation Service was responsible for enforcing. The same arrangements were made for cotton (Fisher, 1970). Initially, participation in the programmes was voluntary and it was not until the early 1950s that the allotments were enforced. Similarly in the United Kingdom, attempts were made to limit the production of sugar beet (Watts, 1971) and potatoes (Ingersent, 1979) by the introduction of acreage quotas.

However, this form of production control met with little success, primarily because controlling area does not necessarily control the amount of production. With increased inputs, farmers tended to improve their productivity and yields on the allotted areas. Alternatively, they simply shifted their land-use from controlled to uncontrolled crops. This problem of increased intensity could in turn be overcome by allocating each farmer a basic quantity quota and not an area quota, as with hop quotas in England, where the quota was attached to the farm and sold with it (Ilbery, 1984b). Once again, rapid inflation can limit the effectiveness of such measures, although in the case of hops the Hops Marketing Board Limited has an inflation clause in its quota scheme.

In 1958, the USA introduced the National Soil Bank, which had two partly complementary objectives (Tarrant, 1974): first, to reduce the production of surplus farm commodities which the government was finding difficult to dispose of (the Acreage Reserve Programme); and secondly, to promote the conservation of the nation's land and soil resources (Conservation Reserve Programme). The former had more widespread effects as farmers were paid a sum of money in lieu of every acre they withdrew from production. As Morgan and Munton (1971) noted, 11.6 million ha. of land were put into the Bank, but only 4.9 million less were harvested as the majority of land ascribed to the Bank was of low productivity and had not been regularly cropped. In turn, non-participants increased their area or intensity of production in the hope that reduced national output would increase prices. Clearly, the poor rates of compensation made the abandonment of better quality land less financially rewarding. Thus the Bank had a marked spatial impact, with the rate of uptake much higher in the poorer areas of New Mexico than in the productive Corn Belt. For such a scheme to be successful, huge areas of land would have to be withdrawn, necessitating the government to enter the land market.

Ironically, production controls were withdrawn in the USA by the 1970s because of food shortages (Pacione, 1984) and following the Agriculture and Consumer Protection Act of 1973, target prices were substituted for support prices. This situation was quickly reversed by the 1980s when declining consumption, due to world recession and inflation, and bumper harvests turned food shortages into large surpluses. Existing policy was again inappropriate and Pacione (1984) discusses the introduction in 1983 of a 'crop-swap' plan, which was designed to boost prices and reduce production. Under the scheme, farmers agreeing not to plant some of their land would in return receive from the government storage crops up to 80–90 per cent of their normal output.

Such fluctuating fortunes have been characteristic of Europe too and policy in the EEC has shown recent signs of changing from the rigid system of price support to some form of production control. In order to reduce the European milk lake, farmers were paid to transfer cows from milk to beef production. This had a minimal impact and led in March 1984 to a major policy change in the CAP, when Ministers agreed to cut guaranteed prices for the first time in twenty years. Most dramatic was the cut in milk price guarantees to a total of 99.5 million tonnes of Community output (present output is 109 million tonnes, with a consumption of 88 million tonnes). New milk production quotas and prices were set for member states in an attempt to cut the large surplus of milk produced at artificially high prices (Table 6.1). Whilst Ireland, Greece and Luxemburg obtained favourable agreements, most members have had their

Table 6.1

EEC milk production quotas and prices, 1984*

	1	2		1	2
West Germany	−6.7	−0.6	Luxemburg	+3.5	+ 2.8
France	−2.0	+5.0	Britain	−6.5	− 0.6
Italy	nil	+6.4	Ireland	+4.6	+ 2.7
Netherlands	−6.2	−0.5	Denmark	−5.7	+ 1.5
Belgium	−3.0	+2.7	Greece	+7.2	+17.6

* % change in 10 member states of (1) milk production quotas for 1984 and (2) prices expressed in national currencies

Source: The *Guardian* (2 Apr. 1984 p. 5).

quotas reduced and this has caused considerable unrest among the farming communities of countries adversely affected.

3. Marketing Boards

In an attempt to overcome the problems associated with a large number of independent farm operators in the United Kingdom during the economic depression of the 1930s, Marketing Boards were established to organise the marketing of different agricultural products. The Boards would buy from the farmer and sell to the consumer and so cut out expensive middlemen. Their basic objectives were to gain economies of scale through corporate marketing and remove the disparity of bargaining power of small producers, compared to large producers and distributors. The concept of the marketing board was laid down in the Agricultural Marketing Acts of 1931 and 1933, which provided the necessary legislation for the setting up of 'monopolistic selling agencies to act on behalf of producers' (Bowler, 1979 p. 42). Marketing boards were given powers to regulate all sales of the particular commodity, as well as to negotiate prices with distributors and specify terms of trade. All producers of the commodity had to register with it and be subject to the rules and regulations it made (Haines, 1982).

Marketing boards were established for hops (1932), milk (1933), pigs (1933), bacon (1933), potatoes (1934) and eggs (1957), products in which the country was mainly self-sufficient. (The Egg Marketing Board was abolished in 1971 — see Rayner (1977).) In addition, Commissions were set up for those commodities whose producers were unable to organise themselves: these included wheat (1932), livestock (1932) and sugar beet (1936) (Bowler, 1979). Boards were soon established all over the world, with Canada for example having approximately 100 (Haines, 1982), and they became vital to countries dependent on the export of agricultural produce, such as New Zealand.

In Britain, the Boards were reconstructed in the 1950s, under the 1949

Agricultural Marketing Act, but it soon became clear that their function had changed to being an 'administrative agency of the price support system for relevant products' (Bowler, 1979 p. 46). Therefore, the protection of producers was the major objective of the Boards, although they intended to improve the efficiency of the whole marketing channel and ensure that consumer interests were not damaged. In effect, the Boards failed to improve marketing or production efficiency sufficiently and only limited success was achieved in raising farm incomes and expanding the home producers' share of the market.

Such criticism can be levelled at the Hops Marketing Board (HMB). Formed in 1932, the emphasis of the Board was on pricing rather than marketing arrangements and on protecting home production from foreign competition. The imposition of heavy duties and strict quotas on imported hops strengthened the effectiveness of the HMB, but as a consequence it became solely oriented to the demands of the home brewer and made little attempt to explore the export potential of British hops or to examine world hop trends (Ilbery, 1984a). Therefore, when the home market began to decline in the 1960s, due to improved technologies in brewing, changing tastes of consumers and new 'high alpha acid' varieties of hops, the HMB was obliged to introduce a quota redemption scheme in 1968 to remove unwanted areas of hops.

The defects of the producer-controlled statutory of the HMB were further exposed with Britain's entry into the EEC, when at the time of a world surplus of hops import restrictions on hops were removed. Further, the EEC considered the HMB to be a monopoly with statutory rights, not a producer group, and this ran counter to the Treaty of Rome (Griffin, 1982). A consequence of this was that British growers were not eligible for EEC aid or capital grants that were available to members of producer groups. The HMB was finally dismantled in 1982 and replaced by a producer group known as the HMB Limited, of which membership was voluntary. Whilst most growers have rejoined this new group and strongly support the HMB, the Board has not only fossilised the pattern of hop growing in Kent and the West Midlands but contributed to the decline of the hop industry in the 1960s and 1970s. The geographical effects of one marketing board will be examined in section 6.3.

4. Grant aid and income supplement for farming families

This form of government involvement in agriculture is not directly related to marketing, but has often been employed in many countries to help remedy some of the problems of the agricultural industry. Capital investment, by means of grants and subsidies, can help agriculture in various ways:

(i) By reducing the costs of production or farm inputs and so helping to raise farm incomes without a corresponding increase in the produce price paid by consumers.

(ii) By stimulating or retarding food production during periods of shortages and gluts.

(iii) By helping to increase the productivity of the land and the efficiency of farms, especially in such marginal areas as hill land.

(iv) By attempting to ameliorate social conditions in marginal and upland farming areas.

In the United Kingdom, the cost of production grants and subsidies has increased over time, reflecting the importance of capital investment in maintaining productivity and profitability. However, this cost represents less than ten per cent of total government support to agriculture. As Bowler (1979) remarks, production grants have been favoured because they allow price support and price stimulus to be given in a more selective manner than through guaranteed prices. More specifically, Bowler demonstrated how aid can be directed to certain growth points of agricultural practice (silo subsidy, field bean subsidy), to raising husbandry standards (feriliser subsidy, ploughing grants), and to contributing to agricultural credit by providing income before the sale of the end product (calf subsidy, hill sheep subsidy).

A wide range of grants and subsidies have been adopted in the United Kingdom since the war. In the 1940s, these were available for field drainage and water supply, fertilisers, buildings, roads, and farm wages in defined hill farming areas. Attention turned towards stimulating production in the 1950s and grants and subsidies were given on livestock rearing, beef calves, fertilisers and ploughing. For example, the 1957 Farm Improvement Grant attempted to raise the efficiency of production by stimulating capital investment in fixed equipment and land improvement; grants covering one-third of total 'standard' cost were available. The proliferation of grants continued in the 1960s and the major problem at that time was finding measures which were sound in their own right. Bowler (1979) refers to the many 'non-relevant' grants after 1968 and to the fact that by 1970 there were 23 separate measures in existence. The situation was simplified in 1970 with the Farm Capital Grant Scheme, which for the first time placed a ceiling on the amount of money payable to any single farm unit. After entry into the EEC, the UK system began to be dismantled so that by 1977 agricultural policy fell in line with the CAP.

A problem related to subsidy price changes is the time lag between their introduction and the response by farmers. Once again, uncertainty will affect the type and speed of response, which in turn will relate to various farm-and-farmer characteristics. The consequence of this is spatial variations in the input of grants and subsidies, as demonstrated in New Zealand by Fielding (1965), in France by Delamarre (1976) and in England and Wales by Bowler (1976a and b). Therefore, unless spatially restricted to certain defined areas, the adoption of grant aid in most Western countries is not greatly affected by location because of good communication networks and information flows. Instead, it relates to particular structural characteristics of the farm and to the attitudes and perceptions of farmers; this point will be further developed in section 6.3.

Although resented by most farmer organisations, who would prefer to see farm prices maintained, government direct-income supports are a way of helping farmers whose incomes do not reach a minimum level, without raising consumer prices artificially high (Haines, 1982). Indeed, MacEwen and Sinclair (1982) have advocated a package of such supports to help solve the problems facing farmers in the upland areas of the United Kingdom. An important issue in this context is part-time farming, which has been the sole topic of discussion in editions of *GeoJournal* (1982) and *Sociologia Ruralis* (1983). Part-time farming is now very common in many parts of Europe and can be exploited to help solve the farm income problem, as well as overcome the worst aspects of rural depopulation. Special shifts and free transport to factories are offered to attract part-time farmers into industry. This dual existence is important for many small-scale farmers and Haines (1982) has noted that 90 per cent of Japan's five million 'farmers' are employed part-time in industry. However, the process can lead to social fallow (Kunnecke, 1974), where agricultural land is taken out of production, and it is not clear whether part-time farming has a positive or negative effect on rural development (Persson, 1983), especially as it conflicts with attempts to structurally change farm holdings.

5. Structural reform

It has been increasingly recognised in the Western world that a policy of protection is not going to solve the problem of low farm incomes. The major determinant of farm income is farm structure (Bowler, 1983; Pacione, 1984) and both efficiency and income can only be improved by restructuring the farms themselves. Therefore, structural reform is seen as the only long-term solution to poor incomes and Haines (1982) notes that it represents an attempt to ensure that farmers eventually receive an adequate income without government intervention.

A large number of schemes, under the umbrella of structural reform, have been introduced in Europe and countries like Canada and Australia. These can be conveniently categorised into three groups: land consolidation, farm enlargement and land reform. Land consolidation is the solution to farm fragmentation and involves the rearrangement of scattered parcels of·land. Countries with consolidation legislation can be divided into three groups (King and Burton, 1983):

(i) North-west Europe group, including Finland, Sweden, Norway, France, Denmark, Switzerland, West Germany and the United Kingdom.

(ii) Southern Europe or Mediterranean group, including Spain, Portugal, Italy, Greece and Cyprus.

(iii) Developing countries group, of which India, Taiwan and Kenya are most progressive.

Most countries have a consolidation authority, which determines the value of land and patterns of ownership and isolates areas of greatest need. Schemes can be compulsory, as in West Germany, but voluntary and accelerated schemes are usually emphasised in an attempt to get farmers to actively participate in the process. The effect of voluntary schemes is inevitably slow and often enhanced by government intervention. Consequently, accelerated consolidation is usually preferred and occurs once a proportion of landowners (normally 70 per cent) in a designated area agrees to a consolidation plan. Broader integrated schemes of rural reform have also been introduced, as outlined by Mayhew (1970) for West Germany, where consolidation is but one of many measures designed to improve the development of the rural economy. A major problem with the re-allocation of fragmented land is that it does not necessarily lead to an increase in farm-size or a reduction in the number of holdings. It was for this reason that consolidation in Canada was related to a policy of farm enlargement, under the Agriculture and Rehabilitation and Development Act of 1961 (Bunce, 1973).

Farm enlargement is necessary in order to reduce the number of farms which share the income of the agricultural sector. This will help the remaining farmers to fight the price–cost squeeze in agriculture by obtaining economies of scale and taking fuller advantage of modern technology. A reduction in the number of farms is achieved by encouraging out-migration and in this respect three types of scheme have been introduced by different governments (Bowler, 1983): first, retirement pensions or compensation for farmers who voluntarily retire from agriculture and make their land available to enlarge neighbouring farms; secondly, farm amalgamation grants, where aid is given to help with the costs of amalgamation of those farmers remaining in agriculture; and thirdly, retraining schemes for farmers and especially sons of farmers. Whilst the provision of alternative job opportunities helps prevent further fragmentation upon inheritance, it also quickens the pace of rural depopulation and leads to a decline in rural infrastructure. Consequently, social problems often override the economic case for structural reform and the continuing support of farm incomes is a reasonable price to pay for rural social stability (Haines, 1982).

In the United Kingdom, where the problem of small farm-sizes is not so grave, the MAFF administers farm enlargement schemes and there is no real interference in the sale and purchase of land. However, in Sweden a network of County Agricultural Boards was established in 1957 (Whitby, 1968) and these have the authority to intervene in the land market and buy and sell land, in an attempt to produce a more rational pattern of land allocation. The transfer of land is similarly subject to public control in Japan, Denmark and West Germany, and in France regional *Sociétés d'Amenagement et d'Etablissement Rural* (SAFERs) buy and sell farmland. Bunce (1973) has described the operation of similar schemes in Canada.

Farm enlargement schemes have had only limited success and the response from farmers has been poor. This reflects the voluntary nature of the schemes and the non-effectiveness of the financial incentives to leave agriculture. Farmers attracted to such schemes are those who would have retired from farming anyway. Another reason for little success is that many small farmers are part-time and not dependent on farming for their total income. One cannot be surprised at this because it is this group which has been encouraged to take part-time industrial work, to help raise their incomes, but at the same time remain in farming.

The objective of land reform is often contradictory to that of farm enlargement in so far as it is a radical attempt by certain governments to reorganise rural economies, for various social, economic and political reasons (Pacione, 1984). This usually takes the form of a redistribution of property in favour of landless peasants, tenants and small farms (King, 1977) and occurs throughout the world. Examples vary from that in Australia, where the Marginal Land Committee was established to control farm abandonment and amalgamation in the drought-affected margins of the wheat growing areas (Williams, 1976), to the Mezzogiorno of southern Italy, where the large latifundia were possessed and redistributed among the peasantry (King, 1973). Although such measures are useful in areas characterised by poverty, unemployment and exploitation, they have little overall effect on the structure of rural areas and are often not cost-effective because the peasants lack the necessary training and skill to cope with land-ownership and farm management.

As a summary to this section, a definitive solution to the problem of low relative incomes for the majority of small agricultural units is unlikely. This relates to the conflict between economic and social reasoning. Research and improved technology have helped to increase agricultural productivity and consequently the minimum size of farm for efficient production is always increasing (Haines, 1982). This implies a continual reduction in the number of farms, in order to maintain incomes, which may be socially unacceptable as it leads to increased rural depopulation and a decline in the well-being of rural communities.

Over time, agricultural policies have tended to change, from the idea of protection to that of resource adjustment (Bowler, 1979). The farm problem is increasingly being interpreted as a function of the development process, where the demand for food increases less fast than the demand for non-agricultural goods and services. To resolve the ensuing imbalance between supply and demand, fewer farms and farm workers are required, as demonstrated by measures designed to encourage out-migration. However, the trend from protection to adjustment is not without its problems. First, the agricultural labour force is not particularly mobile, either geographically or occupationally (Gasson, 1969), because of family and cultural ties, the loss of status and the fear of an urban way of life. Secondly, a reduction in the number of holdings does not necessarily lead to an increase in income on those remaining. Thirdly, large farms are not necessarily superior economically. It has been shown how an increase in farm size is often accompanied by increased fragmentation (Smith, 1975; Edwards, 1978). Such a process also leads to a decline in the conservation of the environment, as hedgerows and natural habitats are destroyed, and an increase in agribusiness, as processors and financial institutions purchase land and begin to control agriculture, further eroding the social stability of rural communities.

6.3 Geographical consequences of government intervention

The importance of government policy as a factor affecting the spatial structure of agriculture was first recognised fifty years ago by Whittlesey (1935), but surprisingly it has received only limited attention in the academic literature. Despite this, Bowler (1979) was able to classify studies of the relationship between policy measures and land-use into one of two broad categories:

An analysis of areas with similar physical characteristics but different agricultural policies. These areas can be found either side of an administrative boundary. At an international scale, Reitsma (1971) attributed the differences in arable land-use either side of the Canadian/United States border to the wheat acreage allotment programme in the USA. Whilst wheat was the dominant crop in both countries to the west of the Great Lakes, barley was the second ranked crop in the USA whereas oats was in Canada. This is because land in the USA was diverted into barley production, which in turn reduced barley imports from Canada. At a reduced scale, Rose (1955) showed how the intensive fruit area in Stanthorpe, Queensland halted abruptly at the border with New South Wales. The lack of production in the latter was attributed to two factors: first, the lack of state aid for rail transport, refrigeration and extension services; and secondly, to a different land settlement policy for Italian immigrants.

An analysis of the inferred effects of particular policy measures on production patterns. This is a difficult task given the fact that government policy is only one of many influences affecting the spatial distribution of agriculture. Bowler categorised the spatial effects of policy measures into three groups:

(i) Measures which are uniformly available within a country but which have a variable impact on agricultural patterns. Examples would include the USA Soil Bank and the Milk Marketing Board and Calf Subsidy and Ploughing Grant in England and Wales. The variable impact relates to differences in physical, farm-and-farmer characteristics and will be further discussed below.

(ii) Measures which are restricted to defined areas of a country and thus by definition have a spatially selective influence. Bowler (1976a) has described the effects of the Hill Cow and Hill Sheep Subsidies in defined upland areas of England and Wales. Similarly, Cabouret (1976) has shown how the three altitudinal zones in Swiss agriculture have separate policy measures and different rates of support for farm improvements. At the international scale, the introduction of different policies for priority agricultural areas in the EEC is a good example of spatially selective measures.

(iii) Measures which create inertia rather than change in production patterns. The already-mentioned cotton and tobacco allotments in the USA, which fossilised production in specific core areas, are good examples. In the United Kingdom, a similar situation has arisen with sugar beet and hops. The area of sugar beet is limited by the government and the British Sugar

Corporation has a monopoly as buyer of beet for processing (Watts, 1974). Therefore, the decision to invest in existing rather than new factories has meant the fossilisation of the prevailing pattern and no new areas of production. With the formation of the HMB in 1932, quotas were given to farms growing hops at that time. Although theoretically possible for farms in other areas to obtain quotas, the pattern of hop farming has become concentrated in the traditional growing areas of Kent and Hereford and Worcestershire.

In preference to providing a superficial analysis of the geographical consequences of all types of policy measure in agriculture, three case studies will be developed, each representing one of the last three major forms of intervention outlined in section 6.2.

1. Marketing Boards: the Milk Marketing Board

According to Tarrant (1974), the concept of a marketing board is epitomised in the British Milk Marketing Board (MMB), which conducts a range of functions, from quality control to advice on farm management, but whose primary objective is the protection of producers. The MMB was formed in 1933, at a time when the dairy industry was characterised by a very large number of small producers (75 per cent of which were less than 40 ha.), and of all the Boards it has received considerable coverage in the economic and geographical fields (Chisholm, 1957; Barnes, 1958; Simpson, 1959; Strauss and Churcher, 1967; Tarrant, 1974 and Rayner, 1977). It has a duty to purchase all milk from dairy farmers and to sell it to wholesale dairymen; it must accept all milk offered and cannot exercise any form of quantity control. The Board actually collects the milk from the producers, who receive approximately the same price for the same quality of milk. In turn, as much milk as possible is sold to the highest priced market—the liquid market (Haines, 1982). The revenue is pooled and producers are paid a pool price per litre. Additionally, the MMB has a statutory responsibility to ensure supplies of milk for the liquid market; to this end it encourages winter production by paying a premium for winter milk.

Therefore, the basic objectives of the MMB are threefold:

(i) To establish a marketing organisation which ensures that no producers have special advantages over others.

(ii) To reduce the cost of transporting milk from the farms to the dairies and from the dairies to centres of demand.

(iii) To balance the differences between the supply and demand for milk and milk products between different seasons and regions. This is particularly important as there is little geographical coincidence between the main production areas and areas of demand (Strauss and Churcher, 1967).

In relation to these objectives, the MMB established eleven regions in England and Wales (Fig. 6.2). Within each region, two features were important. First, producers paid a standard collection charge to the Board, irrespective of their

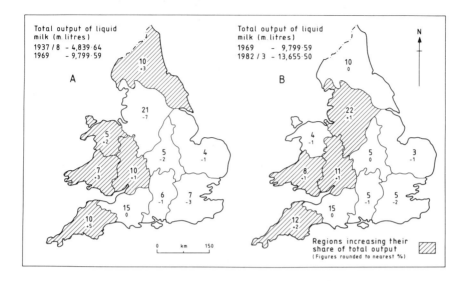

Fig. 6.2   Milk Marketing Board regions: percentage of total output of liquid milk in 1969 and 1982/3 and percentage change 1937/8–69 and 1969–82/3 (Morgan and Munton, 1971 p. 96 and MMB Dairy Facts and Figures, 1983)

location in relation to the nearest dairy. Differences in collection charges between regions were minimised and in 1970, for example, the maximum difference in regional charge amounted to 1.7 per cent of the producer milk price (Morgan and Munton, 1971). Secondly, producers received a fixed pool price for their milk, which was based on the financial returns from all milk sold in that region. The higher the proportion going to the liquid milk market the higher the pool price. Consequently, those regions with the highest demand for milk, such as the south-east and north-west, received the highest pool price. However, in an effort to stabilise prices throughout the country, a system of regional compensation was introduced so that inter-regional pool prices never varied by more than a very small amount (around 1 per cent of the total price).

This equalisation of prices and transport costs has had a considerable impact upon the distribution of dairy farming in England and Wales (Fig. 6.2). In particular, distance from the market no longer acts as a prime locating factor and the production of milk has become more dispersed. With a greater reliance on the sale of milk for manufacture, production has become more viable in the 'isolated' western areas, especially as physical conditions favour pastoral activities. This westward movement is clearly shown in Figs. 6.2(*a*) and (*b*). Between 1937/8 and 1969, output of liquid milk more than doubled and the whole of Wales, the northern and west Midland regions and in particular the south-western region (which doubled its percentage share of national output) made noticeable gains over the thirty-year period. In contrast, the traditional dairying area of the north-western region recorded a large 7 per cent fall in its percentage share of total production. The pace of change slowed down for the 1969 to 1982/3 period, but the general trend of growth in the west and decline in the east continued. For example, the four regions to the east of the Humber–Solent line (southern, south-east, eastern and east Midlands) accounted for just 18 per cent of total liquid milk production in 1982/3 compared to 29 per cent in 1937/8. Over the whole study period, (1937/8 to 1982/3), the 7 and 4 per cent gains in the far western and south Wales regions were counter-balanced by losses of 6 and 5 per cent in the north-western and south-eastern regions.

Whilst favourable physical conditions are partly responsible for the expansion of dairying in western areas, other factors have contributed to the decline in the east. The increased production of milk in the 1960s and 1970s tended to lower prices at the time of a marked price–cost squeeze in agriculture, forcing many smaller-scale operators into more profitable enterprises (Tarrant, 1974). This was most noticeable in southern and eastern areas, where other forms of production were possible and where proximity to the major milk market of London was no longer a strong locating factor. Therefore, the policies of the MMB have tended to reverse the pattern of intensive dairy farming as envisaged by von Thünen, encouraging production in outlying areas which are more physically restricted to pastoral activities. However, production costs are higher in such peripheral areas and the MMB may in the long-term 'have increased the consumer price of milk' (Morgan and Munton, 1971 p. 96). Indeed, the MMB has been criticised by Whetstone (1970 and 1975), who advocated a return to a free market in milk, and by Bowler (1979), who feels that only limited success has been achieved in expanding the home producers' share of the market and raising farm incomes. Despite these observations, Rayner (1977) used partial welfare economics and quantitative analysis to show that the policy of the MMB had not worked against the 'public interest', although its regional pricing system appeared to work to the disadvantage of producers in the south-east.

2. Grant aid in England and Wales

The importance of grants and subsidies in the United Kingdom, as a means of maintaining production and profits, has increased over time, but the spatial dimension of such support had not really been examined until the work of Bowler (1976a and b; 1979), upon which this section is inevitably based. His research concentrated upon two main themes: first, the spatial responses to particular production grants; and secondly, the factors affecting the adoption and distribution of grant-aided investment. With regards to the former, the spatial effects of four production grants up to 1974 were examined, two of which were uniformly available within England and Wales (the Calf Subsidy and Ploughing Grant) and two that were spatially restricted to defined hill and

upland areas (Hill Cow and Hill Sheep Subsidies). Bowler made three broad observations of value to the geographer:
  (i) No grant changed fundamentally the overall pattern of production of the item to which it related.
 (ii) The influence of production grants varied according to the agricultural geography of the area concerned.
(iii) It was difficult to make valid generalisations, except that the analysis high-lighted the limitations of government action rather than any positive influences.

The Calf and Hill Cow Subsidies can be taken as examples of uniformly available and spatially restricted subsidies respectively. Paid directly to breeders and/or rearers of beef animals, the Calf Subsidy was introduced to 'encourage the retention of beef type calves of specified standards and breeds for rearing rather than slaughter' (Bowler, 1979 p. 67). The number of beef calves in England and Wales increased by 232 per cent between 1949 and 1975, but there is no evidence that this was due to the Calf Subsidy. However, the input of capital to agriculture through this subsidy rose from £7 million in 1955 to £59 million in 1975 and although it had no explicit spatial objectives, Fig. 6.3 shows that spatially it was biased towards traditional beef breeding and rearing areas in

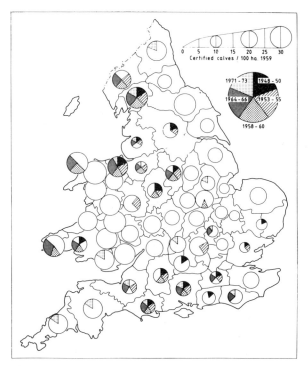

Fig. 6.3   Spatial variations in production responses in calf-rearing, 1948–75 (Bowler, 1979 p. 71)

the uplands. The Calf Subsidy proved to be of more benefit to cattle-with-sheep and mixed farms, on which beef rearing was a main enterprise, than to other farm types.

Whilst the north-west and south-central regions witnessed the most noticeable increases in calf production throughout the study period, expansion varied spatially at different times. For example, between 1958 and 1960 it was greatest in upland areas, particularly north Wales, whereas between 1971 and 1973 south-west England experienced the largest gains. Such variations cannot be related directly to the Calf Subsidy, although an association with different farming systems seems likely. Bowler noted how the improving profitability of beef as compared with milk production was an important feature in the long-term movement from dairying to livestock rearing, as reflected in the increased inputs of the Calf Subsidy to the dairy regions of north-west and south-central England.

Despite government statements to the contrary, the long-term role of the Calf Subsidy was interpreted by Bowler as an income supplement rather than a stimulus to production. This is not the case with the Hill Cow Subsidy which had a considerable production effect in hill and upland areas. It had two main objectives (Bowler, 1979): first, to encourage the development of beef-breeding herds in hill areas; and secondly, to provide direct financial assistance to hill and upland farms on socio-economic grounds. Originally introduced in 1943 to cover all mature beef cattle kept on hill land, the subsidy was paid annually from 1953 on hill cows as a direct payment to beef breeders. The two measures had different responses and the 1943 scheme failed to lead to a substantial increase in the number of beef cattle kept on hill land; the only significant rise occurred on lower hill land in the Welsh Borderland and Devon (Fig. 6.4(*b*)). However, the 1953 subsidy was higher in value and stimulated a more noticeable increase in beef breeding cows in upland areas. Expansion was spatially variable (Fig. 6.4(*c*)) and greatest in the northern uplands of England. Once again this can in part be explained by the conversion of herds on marginal dairy farms to beef breeding. Within each county, the area of land eligible for the subsidy is not known and so the spatial pattern of the Hill Cow Subsidy is difficult to identify accurately. However, Fig. 6.4(*a*), which shows the proportion of beef cows receiving the subsidy in counties with eligible land, gives a guide. This depicts the Welsh uplands as receiving the largest inputs of support, which have been necessary to 'prevent a fall in relative income levels of hill and upland farms' (Bowler, 1979 p. 81).

The second major aspect of Bowler's work (1976a) was concerned with the factors influencing the spatial incidence of grant-aided investment. Three schemes were analysed—the Farm Improvement Grant (1965-70), the Hill Farming and Livestock Rearing Grant (1946-63) and the Small Farm Grant (1959-70)—and the spatial pattern of each was viewed as the outcome of the adoption process, which in turn was likely to be influenced by such 'resistances' as the amount of capital needed to adopt the innovation, the rate at which

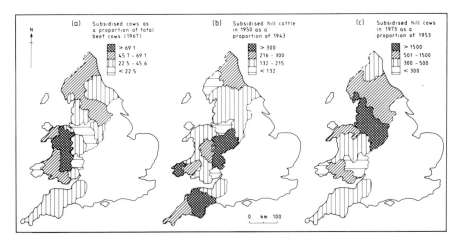

Fig. 6.4   Input of the Hill Cow Subsidy: (*a*) spatial variations in input;
(*b*) increase in input of Hill Cattle Subsidy, 1943–50; (*c*) increase in input of
Hill Cow Subsidy, 1953–73 (Bowler, 1979 p. 80)

investment is recovered, the degree of risk and uncertainty involved and the
socio-economic characteristics of the farmers.

Although evidence of a Hagerstrand-type diffusion was not shown, the spatial
distribution of resistance factors was thought to account for the varying
responses of farmers to the schemes. Bowler was able to make four general
conclusions:

(i) There was considerable spatial variation in the incidence of grant-aided
investment, even though the grants had no spatial objectives.

(ii) For all grants, a distinction could be made between the innovativeness of
areas in adopting a measure and the subsequent resistances in the adoption
process. The relative importance of influencing factors varied according
to the type of measure.

(iii) Although a considerable degree of spatial randomness existed in the input
of grant aid, farm-size emerged as the major influence on levels of adoption
and the amount of investment undertaken. Type of farming and land
occupancy were also important influences.

(iv) The distribution of grant aid has tended to increase rather than reduce inter-
regional differences in farm incomes. This is because aid has been allocated
to those regions, parishes and farms where the returns from investment are
most favourable, whereas 'resistances' have limited the uptake of grant aid
in counties, parishes and farms in most need of capital investment.

These points can be further developed in relation to the Farm Improvement
Grant (FIG) and Small Farm Grant (SFG). The former attempted to raise the
efficiency of production by stimulating capital investment in fixed equipment
and land improvement, whilst the objective of the latter was to enable

economically marginal small farms (8 to 40 ha. and 250 to 450 SMDs) to become properly equipped, stocked and managed. Neither grant received promotion on an individual farm basis, but formal information was available. Consequently, the initiative for assistance came from the farmer himself, implying that the adoption of the grants was related to certain farm-and-farmer characteristics.

The adoption of grant aid was measured as the proportion of potential adopters who had an approved scheme. At the county level, the pattern of adoption was initially very uneven, reflecting the interaction between the characteristics of both the grant aid and the potential adopters. Innovative counties for the FIG were Devon, and Westmorland/Cumberland/Northumberland, and for the SFG Devon, Durham, Lincoln and Denbigh/Flint. In an attempt to account for these variations, the importance of a number of socio-economic 'resistances' was examined. Five indices were derived in this context by Bowler:

(i) Size of farm index, on the basis that larger farms are more innovative.
(ii) Dairy farm index, on the basis that innovativeness is related to the type of farming and that dairy farms are particularly capital intensive.
(iii) Profitability index, on the basis that the availability of capital affects levels of innovation.
(iv) Social environment index, on the basis that levels of innovation are related to the degree of urban influence.
(v) Investment context index, on the basis that innovativeness is positively associated with the proportion of owner-occupied holdings in an area.

Spearman's rank correlation coefficients were used to relate these indices to both levels of adoption and the average cost per scheme for each county (Table 6.2). In terms of adoption, the FIG was initially associated with the distribution of dairy farming and owner occupation, unlike the SFG which was not related to any of the resistances. Re-testing the five indices for 1965, only the influence of farm-size was significant for the FIG and the association with the dairy farm index was lost. Therefore, counties with a high proportion of large farms experienced less resistance to the adoption process, despite the long-term fall in the average size of farm adopting grant aid. Consequently, the East Riding of Yorkshire, Suffolk, Essex and Hertford exhibited high final levels of adoption (Fig. 6.5(a)), with the Welsh hill counties and Lancashire recording the lowest. Adoption of the SFG was obviously more relevant to the problem of the small farm in hill areas, than elsewhere.

Turning attention to the value of aid received by the adopters, the cost per approved scheme for the FIG in 1965 was highest in southern and eastern counties (Fig. 6.5(a)), and the distribution was associated with farm-size, as well as with the profitability and dairy farm indices (Table 6.2). Significantly, counties with higher adoption levels also experienced higher investment levels per scheme. For the SFG, the input per scheme was associated with the dairy farm index, indicating that small dairy farms received the highest inputs of grant aid. Also, the input per scheme was again related to the level of adoption and

Table 6.2

Correlation coefficients between (a) the level of adoption and
(b) the average cost per scheme, and the independent variables

	Farm improvement grants			Small-farm grants		
	Adoption		Cost	Adoption		Cost
	1957	1965	1965	1959	1965	1965
1. Size of farm index	+0.1112	+0.7372*	+0.8321*	+0.2750	not applicable	+0.4148*
2. Dairy farm index	+0.3241*	−0.2334	−0.3982*	−0.2891	+0.2514	−0.1771
3. Profitability index	−0.0432	+0.2290	+0.4408*	+0.0121	−0.4030*	−0.2407
4. Social environment index	+0.0466	+0.0454	+0.0638	−0.0217	−0.2733	−0.0149
5. Investment context index	+0.3711*	+0.0821	+0.1014		−0.0573	
6. Initial level of adoption or cost per scheme	—	+0.5695*	+0.5702*	—	+0.6669*	+0.5967*

Source: Bowler (1976a p. 146).

* Significant at the 0.05 level.

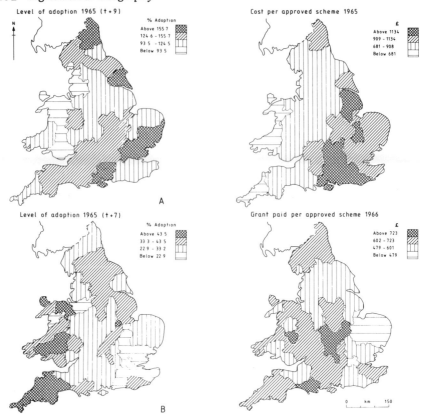

Fig. 6.5   Input of grant aid: (*a*) Farm Improvement Grant; (*b*) Small Farm
Grant (Bowler, 1976a p. 148)

counties with higher adoption levels experienced higher investment levels per
scheme (Fig. 6.5(*b*)).

Bowler's work has been commented upon at length because of the relative
paucity of literature on the subject and also because it demonstrates clearly the
spatial significance of the allocation of grant aid in England and Wales. Further,
it has shown how the socio-economic characteristics of farmers influence their
willingness to adopt an innovation. These include their status, age and education,
as well as their values, attitudes and perceptions. Clearly, more work on these
aspects is required before the distribution of grant aid can be fully explained.

3. Structural reform in French agriculture

There has long existed a drastic need for structural change in French farming.
In 1891 the cultivated area of France consisted of 151 million parcels of land,
averaging just 0.36 ha. in size (Baker, 1961), and even in the late 1960s 47 per
cent of the 1.69 million farms were less than 10 ha. (Clout, 1972). Such extreme

partitioning of land encourages a large labour force and impedes mechanisation and the introduction of technological and biological advances in agriculture.

Although planning legislation for agriculture first began with laws in 1918 and 1919, the basis of modern consolidation in France was the adoption of the *remembrement* policy in 1941, when 14 million ha. of land were in need of immediate reorganisation (King and Burton, 1983). Under the scheme, a special commission invested the possibilities of consolidation in any commune where 75 per cent of the local landowners demanded change. The actual task of re-grouping was undertaken by the *Service du Remembrement*, whose main aim was the improvement of land cultivation by the introduction of a new division of land into larger parcels, more suitable for machinery and more easily accessible (Ilbery, 1981b). However, problems were soon evident and complete consolidation became very difficult. The first problem related to local variations in soil productivity and the farmers' desire to work land from each 'zone' of soil. Secondly, with many farm houses being located in the villages it was necessary to allocate land in various zones of distance away from them. Thirdly, the procedure involved, from the evaluation of land potential to the removal of hedges and the building of roads, meant that reform was slow once it had been initiated in a commune.

As a result of these problems, *remembrement* took 28 years to consolidate 43 per cent of the land in need of treatment (Pacione, 1984) and had only achieved one half of its target by the mid-1970s (Hirsch and Maunder, 1978). However, the scheme had some noticeable geographical effects. At a local scale, Baker (1961) studied four communes in Beauce and found that *remembrement* had led to a decline of 75–80 per cent in the number of farms in each one. Similarly, Thompson (1961) described the process of change in Vézelise, where *remembrement* was completed by 1960, and showed how the number of fields had been reduced from 2,643 in 1811 to 358 in 1960 (Fig. 6.6). At the regional scale, most progress was made in areas already supporting the larger, more modernised farms, where there was a high level of tenancy and a large number of younger farmers. Consequently, the openfield zone of northern France benefited (Fig. 6.7(*a*)), with 19 *départements* in the Paris Basin each having over 100,000 ha. of restructured land (Clout, 1968 and 1972). In contrast, poorer areas like Brittany, Aquitaine and the Massif Central experienced much less success, due to physical disadvantages, smaller farm units, higher levels of owner-occupancy, older farmers, traditional farming systems and strong peasant antipathy.

Therefore, areas in most need of structural reform got left behind and *remembrement* had the effect of increasing rather than reducing regional disparities in agriculture. As a result, the government intervened and 29 regional SAFERs were created in 1960, with the simple objective of buying land on the open market and using it to enlarge farms which were too small for efficient production. They could also acquire abandoned land, improve it and use it for the same purpose (Perry, 1969) or to create new viable units. At the same time they had the rather contradictory task of safeguarding the family character of

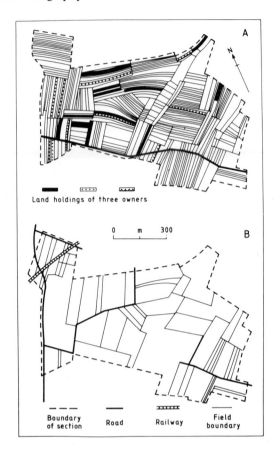

Fig. 6.6   Pre and post land consolidation field boundaries in Vézelise
(Lorraine) (Thompson, 1961 p. 241)

French farming (Clout, 1972). Although the SAFERs' powers were strengthened
in 1962, when they were given the right of pre-emption to acquire land in
certain cases, compulsory purchase has not been used because of its perceived
detrimental effect on their public image. As with *remembrement*, a limited
budget restricted the scope of the scheme and the volume of land handled was
comparatively small, even though it increased annually throughout the 1960s.

Three main factors determined the regional impact of the SAFERs: the
amount of land coming up for sale, the complexity of tenancy arrangements and
the price of land (Clout, 1968). As a result, the effect of the SAFERs has been
most marked in southern areas, where land tenure is simple, land is comparatively
cheap and rural outmigration is highest (Figure 6.7(*b*)). In one respect this
complements the work of *remembrement*, yet in another it works against it.
This is because in order to achieve their policy of making the family farm more

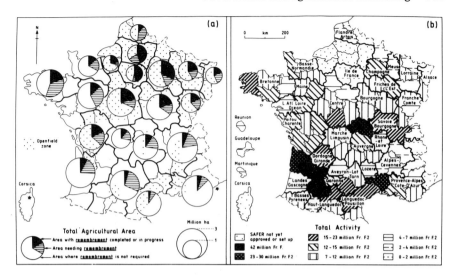

Fig. 6.7   Structural reform in French agriculture: (*a*) *Remembrement* operations (Clout, 1972 p. 40); (*b*) SAFER activity in 1970: value of acquisitions, assignments and improvement work (OECD, 1972 p. 114)

viable, the SAFERs often increase the size of smaller units at the expense of larger farms.

Further incentives for farm enlargement came in 1962 with the introduction of *Fonds d'Action Social l'Amenagement des Structures Agraries* (FASASA). Under this scheme, various funds were established, including one designed to help re-train farm operators who were prepared to leave non-viable holdings. Similarly, installation grants were available to those farmers prepared to move from overcrowded 'departure' zones in the north to designated 'reception' zones in central and southern France, where there was a shortage of young farmers. Possibly the most widely adopted measure from FASASA was the retirement pension scheme (IVDs). If, at the age of 65, farmers voluntarily retired and vacated their land they would receive an annuity to supplement the state old-age pension. The vacated land could be used for the installation of farmers under 45 years of age on the same unit, for farm enlargement, or for transfer to the SAFER: the retiring farmer could retain a small subsistence plot (Naylor, 1982).

The basic retirement grant (IVD *complément de retraite*) had a limited up-take and declined after 1966 (Fig. 6.8), mainly because land passed to relatives had to be by gift or sale. As a consequence, numerous amendments were made to the scheme. First, an early retirement premium (IVD *non complemént de retraite*) was available from 1968 for farmers between 60 and 65 years of age, in such problem areas as Brittany and the Massif Central, and the within-family transfer of land was allowed by leasing. In the same year, farm enlargement was

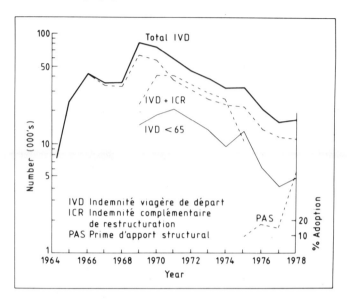

Fig. 6.8   Number of retirement grants in France, 1964–78 (Naylor, 1982 p. 28)

encouraged through a restructuring grant (*Indemnité complémentaire de re-structuration*), which was given to retiring farmers creating an amalgamated unit larger than one and a half times the minimum settlement area. Finally, in 1974 the early retirement premium became available throughout France and the additional restructuring grant was replaced by a supplementary payment (*prime d'apport structural*), independent of the IVD scheme, given to farmers of any age transferring their land to the SAFER, for farm enlargement or the installation of suitably qualified young farmers (Naylor, 1982).

The adoption of these various schemes is shown in Fig. 6.8 and the maximum number of IVDs was granted in 1969. Since then they have declined in attrac-tion, due primarily to the increase in land values. The IVDs have been more popular among tenant farmers, but less effective in areas with a high proportion of part-time farming. One-third of the country's agricultural land has been transferred through the scheme, which has been most successful in central and south-western areas, where the small-farm problem is particularly acute. Local custom, farmers' age, the impact of advisers and opportunities for selling land to industry, housing and tourist interests are all factors affecting the spatial pattern of IVD adoption (Bowler, 1979). As with *remembrement* and the SAFERs, FASASA has been restricted by a lack of funds and criticised for merely financing farmer retirement that would have taken place anyway. This is especially the case as many of the transfers of land have simply involved young family members taking over land previously managed by elderly farmers (Clout, 1972).

Overall, structural reform in French agriculture has been operating far too slowly and radical changes are required before an efficient system of farming will be achieved. The situation has been aggravated in the 1970s and 1980s by the CAP of the EEC, which encourages the maintenance of small farms (through its system of price support) and thus contradicts French measures. Price support to farmers is in proportion to output and larger producers and richer regions benefit considerably more than smaller farmers who are often located in poorer regions and restricted by adverse environmental conditions. Therefore, EEC policy has led to a widening of the income gap between farmers in different regions (Cuddy, 1980) and, as in France, has not been designed to resolve wider rural problems. In this context, the EEC introduced a 'less favoured areas' scheme, effectively a package of social measures designed to maintain the rural population. Many parts of France are eligible, under this scheme, for a compensatory allowance to cover increasing costs of production (Fig. 5.3). Clearly, social objectives overrule the argument for fewer and bigger farms, which French structural reform measures seek to achieve.

7

CO-OPERATIVES, CONTRACTS, AND AGRIBUSINESS

With changes in demand, markets and techniques of production, agriculture has become increasingly dynamic and farmers have been forced to reappraise their practices. However, the individual farmer is in a weak bargaining position when isolated and has often found it difficult to make the necessary adaptations. The failure to adapt to new circumstances relates to a lack of specialist knowledge and information about the nature of change and pressures in the outside world, and to an instinctive attitude to resist change rather than to adopt new ideas (Pickard, 1970). These difficultires can, in part, be overcome by co-operation, a private enterprise solution, often with government assistance, to the problems of agricultural marketing and low farm incomes. Alternatively, farmers can seek contracts with the many food processing companies which now dominate the market place. Either way, specialist information and skills are provided and, in the case of co-operatives, resistance to change should be mitigated by the fact that they are owned by the farmers.

The existence of a sophisticated food industry has created new and varied opportunities for farmers, whose farm systems have sometimes been radically changed as a result (Haines, 1982). Horizontal and vertical integration is now a characteristic feature of much of Western agriculture and complex links between farmers, co-operatives and processors have developed. In turn, the decision-making milieu of the individual farm has become more complicated, with important decisions, especially in relation to marketing, increasingly being taken by either groups of people or processing companies.

7.1 Agricultural co-operation

In general terms, co-operation involves individual farmers acting in combination for mutual benefit (Bowler, 1972). More specifically, co-operative groups are hard to define, although Dodds (1965) stated that a group was 'a number of farmers who join together to market their produce and accept the view that their production should be orientated to meeting the requirements of the market and are prepared to accept reasonable restrictions on individual action to fulfill this objective'. This definition is effectively restricted to marketing co-operatives and excludes groups formed to supply requisites and share machinery and buildings.

Co-operatives are normally voluntary organisations, financed and controlled by farmer shareholders, which attempt to provide services to members at cost (Haines, 1982). Their basic philosophy is not to maximise profits, as in private companies, and Bateman *et al.* (1979) emphasised the importance of three non-maximising objectives:

(i) The self-help argument, whereby co-operatives encourage a spirit of independence amongst disadvantaged groups.

(ii) Satisficing behaviour, whereby prices, dividends, capital accumulation and managerial salary are acceptable rather than optimal.

(iii) To act as a pacemaker and prevent oligopolistic industry from exploiting primary producers.

The major objective of a co-operative is to allow farmers to reach backwards towards their suppliers and forwards towards their markets (Tarrant, 1974), and so provide protection against the rise of specialist organisations and agribusiness. Indeed, co-operatives can be distinguished from companies, partnerships and societies by many features (Bowler, 1972), including ownership by members, open membership, equality of members, and the payment of any trading surplus in proportion to patronage of the co-operative.

Co-operatives have been looked upon as mechanisms which assist farmers in the process of adaptation (Pickard, 1970). They provide an 'effective communicating link between the market and the farm, one along which real signals and not just noise will pass; the group must be mentally alert to these signals and structured so as to be able to take action on the messages received' (p. 110). More radically, Baron (1978) saw the role of co-operatives in agricultural marketing as relieving social tensions while structural changes are being made. Such organisations should be looked upon as a holding device while farm sizes adjust to an economic size and changes in market processes are assimilated. According to Baron, co-operatives are not a complete solution to structural difficulties in farming, but rather a supplement to other structural policies in times of rapid change.

Theoretically, the benefits of co-operation are manifest (LeVay, 1983), although in reality there is often suspicion and mistrust. Multiples and retailing supermarkets have increasingly demanded high standards of grading and packaging from their suppliers, which in turn has placed new pressures on growers to improve the quality of their produce. Co-operatives can offer these services and help members to turn out a more uniform product and find the best channels and methods of disposal. Economies of scale are achieved, in such items as storage and transport, and the farmers benefit through lower costs and higher product prices, especially the smaller ones who, through co-operation, are more able to compete with larger businesses. In turn, greater specialisation of production on individual farms is permitted. Whilst helping to preserve the economic independence of producers, co-operatives can regulate competition in the agricultural community for the benefit of all farmers, secure a greater share of the marketing margin and provide a countervailing power against business concerns (Gasson, 1977). Access to specialist knowledge and expertise, the removal of the uncertainty of marketing, the stabilisation of fluctuating prices and the joint purchase of high capital expenditure items like harvesters, viners and silos are other often quoted advantages of co-operative organisations.

In a survey of 20, essentially marketing, agricultural and horticultural co-operatives, the Central Council for Agricultural and Horticultural Co-operation (CCAHC, 1979a) classified the benefits of agricultural co-operation into two categories: first, those relating to members within specific co-operatives; and secondly, those with broader effects on third parties (Table 7.1). Of the twelve benefits, greater security, a higher overall return and new market outlets were dominant, although the saving of time and anxiety and better facilities to prepare for the market (transport, grading, storage and packaging) were significant. Also important from the point of view of the farm system and the spatial structure of agriculture were improved methods of production and changes in the pattern of production. Membership of a co-operative can lead to a review of the adopted methods of production, in order to make the product more marketable, or to the production and marketing of new and profitable crops. In one noted case, producers were forced to develop a new break crop, due to circumstances outside their control, and the formation of a co-operative was an essential means to this end.

Table 7.1

Benefits of agricultural co-operation

	Times mentioned (max. of 20)
A. Benefits to members	
1. Reduced cost of inputs/services	8
2. Improved methods of production	11
3. Change in pattern of production	9
4. Better facilities for preparation for market	12
5. New market outlets	16
6. Higher overall return	17
7. Greater security (personal and commercial)	18
8. Saving of time and anxiety	12
B. Other benefits	
1. To non-members	11
2. To other co-operatives	11
3. To consumers	8
4. To national economy	4

Source: Derived from CCAHC (1979a pp. 4 and 5).

The main benefits to third parties were those to non-members and other co-operatives. In the first group, benefits included the ability of a co-operative in an area to keep down prices, add stability and force marketing competitors to lower profit margins. Co-operatives were also seen as aiding the formation of other, often interdependent, co-operative groups which could be used for mutual advantage. Consumers benefited as well from co-operative activities, through reduced prices for better quality produce, the availability of a product over a longer period of time and the satisfaction of changing tastes. Finally, one-fifth of the co-operatives thought they had helped the national economy through the development of exports and provision of employment opportunities.

Against this long list of real and apparent advantages of agricultural co-operation must be set a number of actual and perceived disadvantages, which vary spatially and cause the success of co-operatives to differ between areas and countries. The loss of flexibility in the choice of marketing channels for the farmer is a commonly quoted problem, along with the need and desire to attend markets in order to 'keep in touch'. Farmers have often developed a satisfactory system of farming, which involves close links with dealers to whom they remain loyal, and they dislike the idea of discipline being imposed upon them from outside (LeVay, 1976). Loss of independence is a major perceived problem amongst a group of people which usually prefers to make its own bargains, even if lower prices result. Indeed, many farmers believe that they can obtain better prices on the open market. Barker (1981) also commented upon the relatively low standards of management in co-operatives, but this is primarily because farmers are reluctant to pay sufficient salaries to attract the most able men.

Co-operatives can be grouped into one of three basic types, although many perform a combination of functions (Bowler, 1972):

(i) *Supply co-operatives* (single or multipurpose). These reduce input costs on the farm by providing members with agricultural supplies, mainly in the form of feedstuffs and fertilisers.

(ii) *Marketing co-operatives*. On the basis of a uniform flow in quality and volume of output, these attempt to increase product prices received by members by negotiating more favourable prices than is possible by individual farmers.

(iii) *Production co-operatives*. These aim to reduce unit costs in actual farming processes by organising the partial or full joint use of land, machinery and buildings.

This simple classification fails to take full account of the changing nature of farmer co-operatives over time. For example, in the USA co-operatives have grown in size from local to regional organisations which then merged and integrated their operations, with decision-making becoming more centralised and management more bureaucratic. Second-tier co-operation, between different farmers' co-operatives, has increased in popularity and three types of second-tie enterprise can be distinguished (CCAHC, 1979b):

(i) *An Association*. This is a loose-knit group whose main function is the sharing of market or buying information, but which does not generally have any central policy making or trading functions.

(ii) *A Federation*. This is an incorporated society or company with some central management acting on behalf of its member co-operatives, but where each co-operative makes its own final decisions, within the overall policy.

(iii) *A Federal.* Co-operative members have delegated full responsibility to the second-tier management for the execution of an agreed policy.

These differing approaches often represent successive stages of development along the path of involvement in second-tier enterprise.

The type and degree of co-operation has varied considerably over space, according to local and national traditions and because co-operation lends itself to some crops better than others, especially those of a horticultural nature. Co-operatives have been far more successful in the USA, on the European continent and in some developing countries than they have in the United Kingdom. This led Hewlett (1967) to conclude that interest in co-operative movements has been in inverse proportion to the level of contemporary agricultural prosperity, with the peak in USA activity, for example, being reached during the depression after the First World War. Tarrant (1974) notes that another reason for the growth of co-operatives in the USA, relative to the United Kingdom, is their success in areas of bulk production of single crops.

The low incidence of formal co-operation in the United Kingdom, in comparison to other EEC members in the mid 1970s, is shown in Table 7.2, which

Table 7.2

Proportion of produce sold through co-operatives in
EEC members in 1975 (%)*

	Milk	Beef	Pigmeat	Fruit	Vegetables	Cereals
Germany	78	19	20	26	36	52
France	46	15	50	40	30	70
Italy	35	5	5	46	5	15
Netherlands	90	20	30	82	85	60
Belgium	65	small	15	35	50	15
Luxemburg	90	22		30–55	–	65–70
Eire	88	28	32	16	18	30
Denmark	87	60	90	55–60	50	40
UK	–	9	5	15†	9	20

* based on estimates by Commission departments.
† for tree fruits alone the figure would be nearer 50%.

Source: Sargent (1978 p. 22).

indicates that the proportion of fruits and vegetables marketed co-operatively was greater in all other countries except Italy (Sargent, 1978). In Sweden, government assistance enabled co-operative structures to be established at national, regional and local levels in the 1930s (Tarrant, 1974) and in Finland and Denmark agricultural education and product quality control are provided (Morgan and Munton, 1971). In searching for an explanation of the different levels of co-operation, the CCAHC (1978, p. 5) stated that it

cannot be doubted that the strength of continental co-operatives owed much to the fact that, in their early days, they were all institutions of unlimited liability, which members neglected at their peril ... whereas ... in the United Kingdom co-operatives have always had limited liability, whereby members could and did neglect them without incurring penalty.

From another viewpoint, Malcolm (1983) argued that the small continental farmers had no real alternative but to unite in marketing through co-operatives.

Despite a long history and renewed emphasis in recent times, agricultural co-operation in the United Kingdom has achieved only moderate gains (Baron, 1976). Reasons for this have been advanced by numerous authors (see Tarrant, 1974; Sargent, 1978) and include the following:

  (i) The lack of government support for co-operatives until 1967.
 (ii) The existence of government support prices and statutory, monopoly marketing boards for certain commodities, which were able to control prices.
(iii) The lack of any significant export trade in agricultural produce, which has been an important incentive to collective action in such exporting countries as New Zealand and Denmark.
 (iv) The general prosperity of British post-war farming, according with Hewlett's (1967) statement.
  (v) The heterogeneous nature and spatial diversity of British agriculture, unlike areas with the bulk production of single crops, as in the USA.
 (vi) The independent, conservative and mistrusting nature of British farmers, who have been slow to recognise the need to devote more time to the marketing of their produce.

However, signs of increasing co-operation were apparent during the 1970s, representing a response to a fall in real product prices, increasing input costs and the general deficiency in farmer-bargaining power (Bowler, 1972). Economies of scale through co-operation could be viewed as a possible alternative to economies gained through farm amalgamation. In more detail, Murray (1983) listed five factors which were instrumental in the growing interest shown in agricultural co-operation. The increasing experience of co-operatives in operating as successful commercial businesses offering their members competitively priced and efficient services was the first factor. This was followed by the cost–price squeeze on the net incomes of producers, resulting from the continued high level of cost inflation, the downward pressure on farm prices as a result of a chronic structural surplus of several commodities within the EEC, and the continuing threat of EEC produce imports into the UK domestic market. The third factor was the rising importance of food processing and distributional/retail companies within the agribusiness sector. The demands of these buyers for large volume and consistent supplies of high-quality produce will further encourage trends towards the collective organisation of produce marketing. Fourthly, the increasing importance and number of large farm businesses within the agricultural economy, whose managers and owners will be more disposed to the transfer of requisite buying and produce marketing decisions to specialist co-operative organisations, is a major stimulus to co-operative developments. Finally, growth in co-operative activities can be related to the increase in government and EEC financial support for improved produce marketing through farmer-controlled organisations.

In relation to this last point, the Agricultural and Horticultural Co-operation Scheme was introduced to foster the development of marketing and production groups, especially amongst smaller farmers; the fairly well-developed sector of supply co-operatives was excluded from the scheme (Bowler, 1972). Farmers became eligible for grant aid, which was to be administered by the CCAHC, formed in 1967 (known as 'Food from Britain' from 1983), and applied to new and existing organisations. The terms of reference of the Council were very positive—to organise, promote, encourage, develop and co-ordinate co-operation in agriculture and horticulture—and it was to be just as concerned with small farmers, with less prosperous farmers and with farmers operating in the more difficult areas, as it was with farmers in the more favoured areas. Emphasis was placed on aiding the establishment of single enterprise production groups and the development of new marketing groups was restricted, reflecting the previous development of this sector and CCAHC policy of avoiding conflict with existing organisations (Bowler, 1972).

One sector which has shown a recent surge in co-operative activity is horticultural marketing. Dominated by small-scale family units dealing with a highly perishable product, growers have often been keen to co-operate. The stimulii for this were essentially four-fold (Sargent and Roxburgh, 1976; Sargent, 1978): first, the greater potential in horticulture to 'add value' in the marketing process, through grading, sorting, packaging and transport; secondly, the considerable publicity given to the vulnerability of horticulture from overseas competition, especially with entry into the EEC in 1973; thirdly, the desire to gain security from collective action and to shed the worry and time involved in marketing; and fourthly, the positive government support since 1967. Horticulture received a major proportion of grant aid proposals approved by the CCAHC in the early 1970s; indeed, 61 per cent of grants went to horticulture between 1971 and 1975 (70 per cent of total value). Although declining by the late 1970s, 45 per cent of grants (26 per cent of total value) were assigned to horticultural co-operatives in 1976/7 (Sargent, 1978).

Inspired by the work of the CCAHC, agricultural co-operation has been most successful in areas of large, mainly arable farms and hence the eastern counties of England and Scotland. These areas were highlighted by Bowler (1972), in a study which interpreted the adoption of grant aid in co-operatives as the diffusion of an innovation (Figure 7.1(a)). Secondary centres were shown to have evolved in Northern Ireland and isolated counties throughout Britain. Whilst the CCAHC was also concerned with small farms and poor farming areas, smaller units found it difficult to set aside a certain amount of their land or capital for use in production or marketing groups and there was much resistance amongst smaller farmers to placing all of the farm in a group.

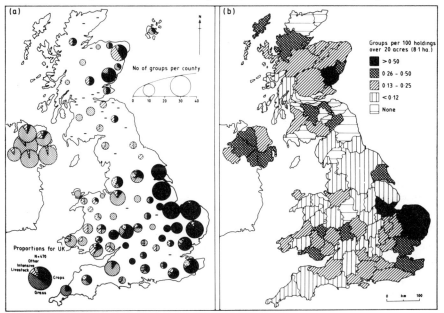

Fig. 7.1   Distribution of co-operative grant aid in the United Kingdom:
(*a*) diffusion of grant-aided co-operative groups by county (October, 1970);
(*b*) types of grant-aided co-operative groups by county (Bowler, 1972 p. 172)

Significantly, Bowler found that the type of crop involved in group formation in the east varied with location. For example, new pea production groups characterised developments in Norfolk, Suffolk and the East Riding of Yorkshire in the early 1970s, whereas in Lindsey (Lincolnshire) existing pea production groups were dominant. Pea marketing groups have also been important, as demonstrated by the link between Essex Peas Ltd. and Frozen Quality Ltd. The former was established in 1968, by five members with very extensive farms, and washes, cools and transports peas to Frozen Quality Ltd., a co-operative which markets them and finds customers, dealing directly with wholesalers and super-markets and by-passing the large frozen food companies. Interestingly, Frozen Quality Ltd. was formed with the help of Essex Peas Ltd., which owns one-third of the former's shares (Heiseler, 1977). Despite this arrangement, it is more common for co-operative pea groups to deal with the main processors and often they have been formed under the influence of companies like Birds Eye and

Findus and are especially concerned with the ownership and use of mobile pea viners (Rosales and Vargas, 1979).

Besides pea groups, new potato production groups were important in Norfolk and Suffolk, just as pre-existing fruit marketing groups were locally significant in Kent and Sussex and new vegetable production groups in Angus and Worcestershire. In contrast, the secondary centres of innovation were associated more with grass production groups (Figure 7.1(*b*)), although the number of farmers involved in each group has been lower than in crop co-operatives (Bowler, 1972). Silage groups were encouraged by the CCAHC and became relatively important in Northern Ireland and in the dairying areas of Cheshire, Somerset, Carmarthen (Dyfed) and Lanarkshire. Livestock co-operatives were weakly developed and of local importance only in Aberdeenshire (new cattle production), Cardiganshire (existing lamb marketing) and Lancashire and Kent (pigs and poultry).

The formation of second-tier co-operatives is not well advanced and out of more than 600 agricultural and horticultural co-operatives in the United Kingdom, 164 are involved in one or more second-tier commercial enterprises (CCAHC, 1979b). Most of the second-tier bodies established belong to the 'Association' and 'Federation' categories and have been formed for the purpose of marketing agricultural and horticultural products. The main exceptions are those set up in Scotland and Wales for the purpose of supplying requisites.

As well as being influenced by the type of crop grown and farm-size, spatial variations in the success of co-operative activities reflect the attitudes of farmers themselves and their resistance to change. Answers to such questions as 'What do potential co-operators want?', 'What sort of farmers are potential co-operators?', and 'What effects do co-operatives have on farmers and society?', need to be found (Bateman, 1976) and this has encouraged studies of attitudes and decision-behaviour in different farming areas. Many such studies are required before general conclusions concerning the spatial characteristics of agricultural co-operation can be drawn.

In a study of two marketing co-operatives (vegetables and potatoes) in Bedfordshire and Yorkshire respectively, Gasson (1977) classified the reasons, given by the farmers themselves, for joining a co-operative into five groups:

(i) *Commercial strength*, relating to the ability to secure for producers a greater share of the marketing margin and exercise countervailing power, as well as being able to influence producer prices.

(ii) *Convenient service*, relating to economies of scale and the supply of boxes. This category also includes the saving in time, trouble and worry.

(iii) *Best alternative*, relating to dissatisfaction with existing marketing outlets and the possibility of a fairer deal for the producer.

(iv) *Co-operative principles*, relating to the ethics of co-operation and the belief that farmers ought to work together and help one another.

(v) *Persuasion*, relating to the influence to join a co-operative by another person or by such organisations as the National Farmers Union or the EEC.

Convenient service and best alternative emerged as the favourite reasons for joining the two co-operatives studied, suggesting that farmers join co-operatives for many reasons other than economic advantage. In an attempt to test the general applicability of the findings, Gasson compared her results with those obtained in studies carried out in Northumberland (Foxall and McConnell-Wood, 1976), Dyfed (LeVay, 1975), and Iowa (Beal, 1954). Table 7.3 lists the results for the five different areas and whilst commercial motives were most important in the Dyfed and Iowa samples, reasons associated with convenient service and best alternative were of the same order of importance as in Gasson's study. For members of the Northumberland requisites co-operative, convenient service was dominant and commercial strength and best alternative were unimportant. Results seem to vary according to the type of crop or co-operative concerned, which has important geographical connotations, and overall farmers appear to join co-operatives for other reasons besides commercial advantage. Similar findings were reported by Aitchison and Knowles (1979), in a survey of four co-operatives in Lancashire and Yorkshire, and in a study of farmer participation in co-operatives in Brecon and Radnor, LeVay and Lewis (1977) highlighted the importance of convenience above high prices and the principles of co-operation.

It is not clear from these quoted examples whether the reasons for joining a co-operative varied according to particular farm and farmer characteristics, such as farm-size, age and education. In line with the behavioural approach to geographical studies, answers to such questions are important in helping to understand the spatial structure of co-operative activity. A survey of horticultural marketing in the Vale of Eveshem (Ilbery, 1985b), an area where many small-scale growers would have formerly been forced out of production without the existence of co-operative organisations, was able to relate growers' attitudes to a range of socio-economic influences.

Three grower co-operatives are important in the Vale:

Littleton and Badsey Growers Limited (LBG). This traditional co-operative was established in 1908, with its headquarters in the core horticultural area to the east of Evesham. Membership is over 1,000, although many are non-active and retired growers, and there is a tendency to deal with the smaller growers. Turnover is approximately £2 million per year. Active membership is very localised, with over 50 per cent concentrated in the parishes of Evesham, Offenham, Badsey and Bretforton (Fig. 7.2(*a*)).

Grower Marketing Services Limited (GMS). This was established in 1919 and has over 500 members in 26 counties of England and Wales. It is a much bigger concern than LBG, with a turnover of £10 million, and became the largest co-operative marketing organisation in horticultural produce in the United Kingdom in 1973. With headquarters outside the Vale, at Cheltenham, it tends to attract the larger growers in the Vale, although its takeover of Pershore Growers in 1977 has enabled it to become concentrated in the parish of that name (Fig. 7.2(*b*)).

Table 7.3

Reasons for joining co-operatives

Per cent of reasons given

Type of reason	Vegetable Marketing: East England	Potato Marketing: Yorkshire	Supply of Requisites: Northumberland	Livestock Marketing: Dyfed	All types: Iowa
Commercial strength	14	8	9	41	40
Convenient service	32	24	56	26	15
Best alternative	27	29	1	20	23
Co-op principles	14	18	22	4	15
Persuasion	13	21	12	9	7
All reasons	100	100	100	100	100
Number in sample	86	20	139	74	259

Source: Gasson (1977 p. 32).

Midland Shires Farmers Limited (MSF). The branch of MSF based in the centre of Evesham (Smithfield) deals only in horticultural produce and disposes of produce through a daily auction market. Growers do not have to be members to sell their produce in this way, but non-members miss out on bonuses at the end of the financial year. Membership is again very localised, perhaps because MSF provides a collection service. Another attraction of the co-operative is the very large sundries section and MSF is the main supplier of farm machinery, parts and wholesale seed, fertiliser and pesticide in the area.

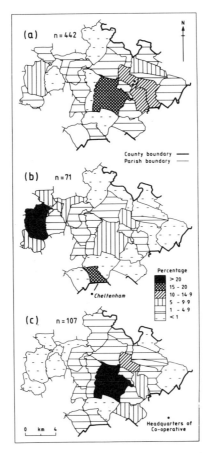

Fig. 7.2   Active membership of co-operative groups in the Vale of Evesham:
(*a*) LBG; (*b*) GMS; (*c*) MSF

Also in the Vale are two smaller and more specialised co-operatives: Evesham Glasshouse Produce (EGP) and Evesham Vale Growers (EVG). The former was established with help from the CCAHC and its small number of members (less than ten) deal in salad crops. EGP does not grade or pack produce, which is done on members' farms, but markets it centrally. EVG is the Italian growers' co-operative which was formed in the late 1970s and which specialises in spring onions.

Sixty-nine per cent of the 299 holdings with horticultural production, in 27 parishes, were surveyed in 1982. The sample of 205 holdings was characterised by very small farm-sizes (84 per cent less than 25 ha.) and horticultural areas (50 per cent less than 6 ha.). However, 90 per cent were full-time growers, with most practising diversified systems of fruit and/or vegetable production. There was evidence of considerable tradition and experience amongst the growers as 69 per cent had fathers who were growers and 75 per cent had been in charge of their present holding for more than ten years.

Only 13 per cent of the sample did not belong to a local co-operative organisation and of the 179 members, 42 per cent belonged to one, 44 per cent to two and 14 per cent to three or more. The 76 growers belonging to just one co-operative favoured LBG (41), followed by MSF (22) and GMS (8). Most of the members (93 per cent) had joined over fifteen years ago, emphasising the tradition and family-based nature of membership. Indeed, general apathy towards co-operation prevailed in the area, with less than half of the membership actually marketing their produce through the co-operatives. Their main value appeared to be in the supply of sundries and co-operatives could only rank third in terms of the disposal of produce off the farm, after local wholesale markets and dealers within the Vale and distant wholesale markets (mainly Birmingham). The surprising fact was that 111 of the 179 members failed to market any of their produce through the co-operatives, with just 24 marketing all of it through them. Why then do the growers continue to belong to these co-operatives? Reasons given by the members, in rank order, were the bonus, sundries, convenience and continuation of father's membership; two additional reasons of minor importance were higher returns and the basic principles of co-operation, which had obtained similarly low ranks in Gasson's (1977) studies.

When asked to place eight possible advantages of co-operatives into rank order, 131 growers stated that there were no real advantages! The composite rank order for the remaining 74 growers is given in Table 7.4. Once again, convenience is a very strong influence, as indicated in the first three ranked factors, whereas better prices, for sundries and products, access to knowledge and the idea of countervailing power fared rather badly. In developing an index of co-operative satisfaction, only 34 per cent of members obtained a score of over 50 per cent of the possible maximum. Consequently, it was envisaged that the perceived disadvantages of co-operation would be worth eliciting (Table 7.4). It is clear from this that the 136 growers concerned were not critical of the co-operatives just for the sake of it, but rather were satisfied with their existing system of production and marketing, and preferred to deal on the open market and trust their own ability to sell at the best time. Loss of independence and lower prices were the lowest-ranked disadvantages.

An attempt was made to relate the growers' attitudes towards agricultural

Table 7.4

Advantages and disadvantages of co-operatives in the Vale of Evesham

	Points
A. Advantages (Rank order; N = 74 growers)	
1. Saves looking around for marketing outlets	148
2. Collects, grades, packs and markets produce	73
3. Reduces uncertainty	66
4. Buy supplies at discount	46
5. Only way to compete with large growers	24
6. United force against middlemen	21
7. Better prices for products	21
8. Access to specialist knowledge and expertise	18
B. Disadvantages (Rank order; N = 136 growers)	
1. Prefer to deal on the open market	233
2. Confidence in own ability to sell at the best time	210
3. Satisfied with existing system	178
4. Lower prices	130
5. Loss of independence	58

Source: Author's survey.

co-operation to a set of farm and farmer characteristics, ranging from farm-size, horticultural area, number of enterprises and the percentage of holding owned, to the age, education and experience of the growers. Very few significant relationships emerged and attitudes were found not to vary according to farm-size and horticultural area, possibly because only a small proportion of the sample had more than 25 ha. of land or horticultural crops. However, ·the importance of convenience as a reason for joining a co-operative varied according to whether or not. growers were expanding their horticultural area, with the latter group emphasising its importance. Similarly, it was this group which felt that co-operatives were more for the progressive farmers. With regards to age, the younger growers ranked access to specialist knowledge and expertise more highly as an advantage of co-operation than the older growers, who also felt that lower prices represented one of the major disadvantages of co-operative groups. Finally, it was the more experienced growers who felt that the continuation of their fathers' membership was an important reason for joining a co-operative, just as they were most satisfied with the services offered by their own co-operative.

This brief resumé of findings helps to demonstrate why the level of agri-cultural co-operation varies spatially within the United Kingdom. Essentially, the Vale of Evesham is a long-established area of horticultural production characterised by very small farm units run by growers according to the ties and traditions developed by their fathers; social inertia, rather than a response to contemporary agricultural trends and problems, is a major reason for the continuation of co-operative membership. Horticulture in the area is in decline, partly because it cannot compete with larger, field-scale developments in vegetable production in eastern England, an area which has also benefited from the existence of a much greater food processing capacity than in the Vale (Ilbery, 1985b). Rather than attempt to adjust to changing technology and trends, many growers abandon their way of life altogether and the most important co-operative in the area, LBG, has been criticised for bad management and a failure to 'change its ways' and help members develop new ideas. Consequently, it is not surprising that apathy towards co-operation prevails and unless the marketing of horticultural produce in the Vale improves to meet modern requirements, the area devoted to horticulture will continue to fall. More smaller growers will be forced out of production, mainly because they resent change and fail to make proper use of their own co-operatives. Eventually, the Vale could be characterised by a much smaller number of large growers and a polarisation of agricultural society which government policies have sought to prevent.

7.2 Contract farming

The growth in the frozen food sector since the 1950s has encouraged many companies to offer farmers written contracts to produce a given volume of produce, of a specified quality, for which they undertake to pay an agreed price (Haines, 1982). Rarely, if ever, initiated by the farmers themselves, contracting is an attempt by the processing industries to increase their level of integration between the production and marketing of farm produce. This type of control is considered necessary in order to ensure the highest possible quality for freezing, dehydration and canning. To achieve this, the speed and timing of harvesting and factory processing are very important considerations. From the farmers' point of view, they are in a better negotiating position over contracts if they belong to a co-operative group which can deal on their behalf with the processing companies and act as a kind of countervailing force.

In common with co-operatives, contract farming has various real and assumed advantages, but it also presents certain social and economic problems which affect the spatial nature of its pattern of adoption. Advantages include:
  (i) A reduction in risk, which is shared with the contracting company.
 (ii) Higher prices than those obtained on the open market.
(iii) Greater certainty surrounding both the outlet for products and price received.
(iv) Access to specialised knowledge and expertise.
 (v) Reduction in the capital requirements of farmers.
However, contract farming is often viewed with suspicion by the agricultural industry, except where it is used to limit production generally or to factory processing capacity, as with sugar-beet in the United Kingdom (Watts, 1974).

The following disadvantages of the system have been advocated:

(i) The farmer loses his independent status.

(ii) The freedom to seek higher prices on the open market, and hence the flexibility of marketing, is lost.

(iii) Contracting favours larger farmers who can more easily cope with the requirements of processing companies.

(iv) Bargaining power is heavily tilted in favour of the processing companies and contract terms can vary between farmers according to their relative bargaining strength (Allen, 1972).

(v) The farmer is no longer the major decision-taker and can become little more than a caretaker as the processor dictates the date of harvest and the variety of peas, type of fertiliser and amount of weed control to be used.

(vi) The basic mistrust of industrialists, who fail to understand farming requirements.

(vii) If the contractor misjudges the needs of consumers and commercial potentiality, failures can be speedy and large. Therefore the contracting farmer has more to gain and more to lose (Allen, 1972).

In America, contracting has been successful in matching farm production to the needs of consumers more quickly and economically than would otherwise have been possible (Allen, 1972). The strong farmers' co-operative movement has helped to ensure fair contractual terms, especially as regional co-operatives are large-scale agribusinesses in their own right. Allen noted that by the early 1960s there were over 325 co-operative bargaining associations involved in contract negotiations. Contracting has been particularly important in fruit, vegetables and poultry production. Jesse and Johnson (1970) showed how in 1964 canners of fruit and vegetables offered contracts, among which 90 per cent contained a guaranteed price provision, 80 per cent provided information on crop technology and 69 per cent covered the provision of harvesting containers. Bucksar (1968) demonstrated how the development of the American egg industry has been characterised by three distinct stages — the farm flock, the chicken range and the egg factory — and how location is a major determinant of the success or failure of an egg factory. The latter needs to be located within a corn surplus area, which coincides with major markets, high population density and a well-developed transport network. The first requirement is particularly important as feed accounts for approximately two-thirds of overhead costs. These trends in broiler and egg production have enabled the purchasing companies to dictate contract terms and many provide the chicks, feed, vaccines, fuel, litter, advice and general supervision; the farmer is little more than a caretaker of an industry which is using a portion of his land (Tarrant, 1974).

In the United Kingdom, the independent and conservative nature of farmers has helped to restrict the development of contract farming, the need for which will be reduced as co-operative marketing groups are formed and enlarged (Allen, 1972). Whilst published figures on contract marketing are unavailable, the Baker Report (1972) estimated that 40 per cent of the total output of UK farms in 1971 was disposed of under either written contracts or some other formal, direct-selling arrangements. Contracting favours certain types of crops, including sugar beet and many kinds of fruit and vegetables, especially peas, broad beans, blackcurrants and raspberries. The spatial pattern of contract farming reflects the agricultural geography of these particular crops and thus is primarily concentrated in the eastern counties of England. This is typified by the freezing and canning of peas (Dalton, 1971; Hart, 1978).

Peas for freezing were first grown in Norfolk in the 1940s, with surplus capacity in Birdseye's fish-packing factories at Lowestoft and Great Yarmouth being the main locating factor. However, demand soon exceeded supply and Birdseye initiated a similar scheme in Lincolnshire, based on Grimsby. Other companies soon followed and the area of peas trebled during the 1960s, reaching 19,541 ha. by 1969. The greatest concentration, with 50 per cent of the national area in 1965, occurred in the Lindsey district and was caused by close proximity to the fish-freezing centre of Grimsby and the 'large, highly capitalised arable-biased units capable of adaption to stringent contract terms laid down by the companies' (Dalton, 1971 p. 133). Once again, capacity was reached in the late 1960s, causing the companies to develop new areas, notably north Humberside based on Hull, where the area of peas for processing increased from 276 ha. in 1965 to 3,953 in 1975 (Aitchison and Knowles, 1979).

The main pea-growing areas of Lincolnshire in 1969 are shown in Fig. 7.3(*a*). Whilst the distribution partly reflects soil type, Dalton (1971) attributed it more to the policies of the processing companies and the location of processing plants. The supply areas of the five main processing companies are outlined in Fig. 7.3(*b*), with Birdseye and Findus controlling three-quarters of the total area. Birdseye draws most of its peas from a radius of less than 25 miles from Grimsby, reflecting their early interest in the area, but also the importance of transport costs and the need to reduce travelling time to less than 90 minutes in order to preserve the quality of the final product. In contrast, the supply area of Findus is to the south of Birdseye's, even though its freezer plant is near Grimsby, at Cleethorpes. Therefore, peas have to be transported over 50 miles and this is made possible by the establishment of chilling plants in association with static and mobile viners. A problem with using former fishing ports for the freezing of peas is that they do not provide ideal locations because due to the sea, only one half of their potential catchment area is available. It is noticeable that new freezing factories established in the 1970s were sited further inland, at places like Grantham and Spalding (Dalton, 1971).

In terms of company policy, the processing companies in Lincolnshire only offered contracts to large farmers. Some contracts were for over 100 acres (40 ha.) of peas and, working on a four-year rotation, farms had to be in excess of 400 acres (160 ha.). Therefore, only certain farms within a defined catchment area were eligible and once a contract was agreed, the processors could dictate the drilling programme, the variety and types of inputs and the date of harvest. Many farmers resented this type of interference and refused to seek contracts;

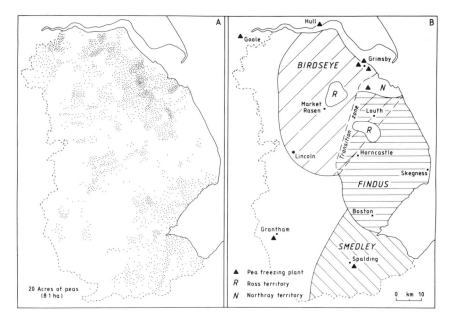

Fig. 7.3   The pea-growing areas of Lincolnshire in 1969: (*a*) peas for freezing, canning and dehydration; (*b*) supply areas of the main companies and location of pea-freezing plants (Dalton, 1971 pp. 135 and 136)

this further modified the pattern of contract farming within the supply areas. Additionally, the processors preferred to deal with co-operative groups, whose members were often in close spatial proximity, and this led to clusters of farmers with contracts. Farmers tended to join these groups in order to pool such resources as mobile viners, labour and drilling equipment. Also, by joining a co-operative, smaller farms could possibly grow peas, as long as vining capacity was greater than the group's own contracted area.

Adopting modern geographical methodologies to contract pea farming in Norfolk, Hart (1978) suggested that the spatial pattern of growers with contracts was determined by two factors: first, the farmers' attitudes as to whether they will seek a contract; and secondly, the decision-making procedures of the processing companies. Of the two, the 'policies of the processing companies can be regarded as the single most important factor determining the location of production' (p. 213).

Hart's survey of 195 farmers, each within 23 miles of one of five processing plants at Lowestoft and Great Yarmouth, revealed that 57 had contracts for vining peas, 33 had tried but were unsuccessful and 105 had no wish to seek contracts. Given the fact that no farmer could be prevented from growing peas on account of the distance criterion, other reasons were sought for the breakdown of the 195 farmers. The 33 unsuccessful applicants were rejected for one or more of four possible reasons: first, because they did not satisfy the minimum size requirement of 32 ha. (8 ha. per year on a four-year rotation); secondly, because an inspection of their farms by the companies had revealed unsatisfactory husbandry, field sizes or farm roads; thirdly, because they had applied to only one company, which happened to be the wrong one in terms of distance; and fourthly, because they were not members of co-operative groups, which the companies insisted upon.

Regarding the majority of growers not seeking a contract, Hart cited five main reasons for their non-adoption. In rank order these were:
  (i) Incompatability with the prevailing production system.
 (ii) Interference and encroachment upon independent decision-making.
(iii) Scale of operations (farm-size) not large enough.
 (iv) Satisfaction with the results of the system in operation.
  (v) Negative experience in regard to contract marketing and dislike of processing companies.
To these can be added unsuitable physical conditions, the need to belong to co-operative vining syndicates and give fieldsmen access to farms, the inability to seek better prices on the open market and the loss of social contacts at the market place.

The distribution of the 57 farmers with contracts (Fig. 7.4) shows a tendency to decline with distance from the processing plants, although there is still a strong random element. In dismissing the effects of physical factors in the final pattern, Hart (1978) developed three principles—random, market proximity and cluster—to help explain the distribution and foster links between empirical studies and theoretical concepts. Decision-making processes under contracting were considered to be more complex than on the open market because farmers had to take into account a much wider range of factors and the policies of processors varied. Consequently, spatial patterns of contract farming will be more complex than patterns of production in free market conditions.

Hart's simple descriptive model of contract farming is essentially a two-stage model, with the second stage concerned with the three locational principles (Fig. 7.5). Stage one identifies those factors which define the spatial margins of the production areas. If these are based on classical theory, with its assumptions of an isotropic surface, uniform transport facilities and cost–distance relationships, a circular market area will be established around the processing plant (Fig. 7.5(a)). In reality, this will be distorted by physical factors, competition and local markets. Classical theory is too blunt to determine patterns of production within these spatial limits and consideration of decision-making aspects is necessary as only certain farmers will seek contracts. The policies of the processing companies become the dominant factor in the final pattern (stage 2), which relates to three principles (Fig. 7.5(b)):
  (i) *Random principle.* Contracts impose conditions upon farmers, and restrict their own ability to make decisions. A random pattern can result from either a first-come-first-served policy or the company's policy of favouring large farms (assuming a random distribution of different sized farms).

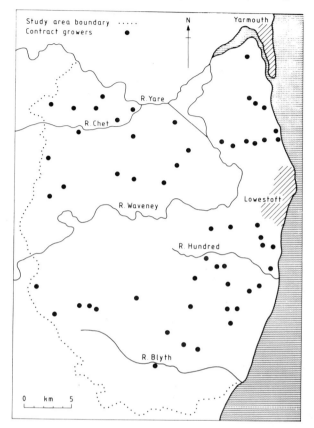

Fig. 7.4   Farmers with contracts to grow vining peas in Norfolk (Hart, 1978 p. 210)

(ii) *Market proximity principle*. This is likely to grow in importance as the size of study area increases. This principle can apply in three situations:
    (*a*) where the processing company is partly responsible for the cost of transport;
    (*b*) where crops are grown near the factory in order to maintain close contact between growers and field staff;
    (*c*) where crops are perishable, as with vining peas.
(iii) *Cluster principle*. This might be applicable in certain situations. The first is where the company offers contracts to farmers' groups rather than on an individual basis. Group dealings and the sharing of resources could help to ensure that members are located close to each other; this would also aid the work of field staff. The second situation is where physical conditions are particularly favourable, and the third is in the early stages of the general diffusion process where innovators first take up contracts and this spreads to neighbours.

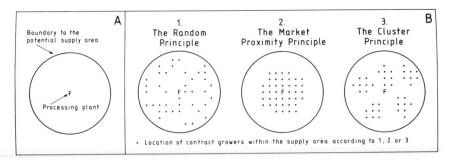

Fig. 7.5   Simple descriptive model of contract farming (Hart, 1978 p. 214)

Although applicable to the five processing companies examined by Hart, these theoretical principles await vigorous empirical testing. The representatives of the selected companies of contract farming in general is unknown and the relevance of the model cannot be assessed without application to other types of contracted crop and to different areas and countries of the Western world. However, the work is important in attempting to develop conceptual ideas about contract farming and for demonstrating that both behavioural and structuralist approaches need to be employed when attempting to explain the spatial characteristics of this type of agricultural integration.

Whilst contract farming is often viewed with distrust by farmers, 'the economic criticisms which can be raised against contracting are minor' (Allen, 1972 p. 98). Indeed, Haines (1982) argued that farmers will increasingly need to overcome their traditional suspicion of vertical integration and work more closely with marketing and processing companies to establish joint ventures, even if it means a loss of some independence. He could find no evidence to show that farmers become mere caretakers or that companies wished to become their own suppliers, especially as they could make higher returns on alternative investments. Allen (1972 p. 98) went further by stating that 'widespread contracting, or failing that complete vertical integration, is necessary if the full opportunities of modern technology are to be realised'. However, the less progressive farmer may not have such objectives (Bateman, 1976) and Allen himself was concerned about the social dangers of biasing contract farming towards larger farmers. To overcome this problem, he advocated a system whereby public finance should be made available to agricultural co-operatives that agreed to take on the welfare function of helping smaller farmers to benefit from the opportunities provided by contract farming.

7.3 The rise of agribusiness

In the post-war period, the agricultural economy has undergone a process of profound change, commonly referred to as the second agricultural revolution.

This has been characterised by 'the progressive extension of technological, organisational and economic rationality into the arena of farm operations, linking them even more closely to the other sectors of the economy both materially and in ethos' (Wallace, 1985 p. 6). In the Western world, this has been associated with the growth of large, predominantly transnational corporations which have become involved in one or more stages of the agri-food production system. As Newby and Utting (1981) remarked, agricultural entrepreneurship has increasingly followed the precepts of rationalisation apparent in other industries, and farms have become bigger, more capital-intensive and more specialised in production. This they interpreted as a move from agriculture to agribusiness. Indeed, farm capitalisation has emerged as a critical variable determining the profitability of contemporary agricultural production (Gregor, 1982), with the larger farms most able to benefit from agribusiness developments.

Agribusiness has been defined as agriculture organised around scientific, rational and industrial business principles and agribusinessmen as farmers who share this approach to crop and animal husbandry (Newby, 1979). At the heart of the concept is the relationship between the agricultural production industry and two related sets of industries: upstream, the agricultural supply industries (e.g. machinery, chemicals); and downstream, the food-processing industries (Bowers, 1985). In reality, agribusiness is the incorporation of agriculture into sectors which deal with both the provision of farm inputs and the marketing and processing of agricultural produce. This is reflected in the high level of concentration in both supply and food-processing industries. In the United Kingdom, for example, in half of the agricultural processing industries, the five largest firms constitute over 80 per cent of total sales (Bowers, 1985). Similarly, agro-engineering, agro-chemical, feedstuff and seed supply industries are dominated by such multi-national corporations as Massey Ferguson, ICI, Shell, Rank-Hovis-MacDougall and Spillers-French (Dalgetty), all of which are characterised by forward integration into food production. Unilever is probably the most spectacular example of a vertically integrated, multinational agribusiness corporation which controls both inputs into agricultural production and marketing and processing outlets, as well as restaurants which sell the food to customers; it comprises 812 companies in 75 countries and manufactures over 1,000 products (Newby and Utting, 1981).

The growth of agribusiness is a response to such developments in the food production system as convenience frozen foods, supermarkets and media advertising. In turn, the demand for convenience foods has been caused by such factors as an increasingly urbanised and affluent population and higher female participation rates in the labour force (Wallace, 1984). Three companies controlled 90 per cent of the frozen food market in Britain prior to the recession of the mid 1970s: Unilever (Birdseye), Nestlé (Findus) and Imperial Tobacco (Ross). Birdseye accounted for 60 per cent of the British market, whilst the other two controlled 70 per cent of the market in Western Europe (Newby and Utting, 1981).

It is clear from this preamble that farmers have become more dependent upon non-farm inputs and drawn further into the complex of industrial companies concerned with food marketing, processing and distribution. Adjustments to such change have progressively polarised the farming community into 'a minority of highly capitalised, large-scale enterprises (which account for an increasing proportion of total agricultural production) and the vulnerable majority of inadequately capitalised farms whose ability to provide their proprietors with a livelihood is increasingly undermined' (Wallace, 1985 p. 14). This raises social and cultural issues (Gregor, 1982), some of which are the direct result of government policies. Although committed to maintaining the family farm, policy has benefited the larger and more agribusiness concerned holdings disproportionately, as demonstrated by the CAP of the EEC. Newby and Utting (1981 p. 2) are more condemning when they state that 'the technological trans-formation of agriculture is not a product of the hidden hand of the market, but of quite deliberate policy decisions, consciously pursued and publicly encouraged up until the present day'. Technological change and the trend to fewer, larger and more capital-intensive farms have been aided directly, through grants and subsidies for farm capitalisation and amalgamation, and indirectly, through manipulation of price supports and guarantees.

Although the rise of agribusiness is fairly well-documented, spatial differences in its growth have received little attention from agricultural geographers, who have been more concerned with empirical studies of recent agricultural trends (Bowler, 1984). With the exception of Gregor's (1982) study on the role of capital in agricultural change, little theoretical work has been developed. In an attempt to overcome this deficiency, Wallace (1985) has suggested four areas of the agri-food system which warrant future geographical examination:
(i) The global food production system.
(ii) The industrialisation of agriculture and the relationship between economic and production (biological) systems.
(iii) The theoretical interpretation of contemporary agricultural evolution and the political economy of agricultural food production, including an examin-ation of the relations between farmers and agricultural corporations.
(iv) The social and economic benefits of the emergence of bio-technology and its distribution within the world's major ecological zones.

An important geographical starting point is to seek reasons for spatial contrasts in the growth of agribusiness within the Western world. For example, whilst British and American agriculture is similar technologically, it is insti-tutionally very different and agribusiness is much further developed in the USA (Smith, 1980). Here, large companies, like Tenneco, Taggares and De Kalb Agresearch, control most of the processes in the food chain, from the manu-facture of seeds and the farming of the land, to the storage, marketing, packaging, processing, distribution and retailing of agricultural produce and the ownership of food outlets. Despite factory farming developments in pigs and poultry, vertical integration has not progressed in Britain to the same degree and most food processors and agricultural supply industries are not directly involved in farming the land. Newby and Utting forwarded three reasons for the lower level of agribusiness developments in Britain than in the USA:

(i) Technological developments in food processing and marketing in Britain occurred when a highly commercialised farming class was already in existence; a class which could ensure quality and continuity of supply on a contractual basis.

(ii) There are few economies of scale in farming (unlike processing) which are not attainable at a level well below that of agribusiness involvement and within striking distance of family proprietorships.

(iii) The historic cost of land is much higher in Britain and the rate of return on capital invested in agriculture is below that in other sectors.

Therefore, in Britain the integration of farm operations into the activities of non-farm businesses is not by direct investment. Instead, it is characterised by agribusiness companies seeking out highly market-oriented agribusinessmen farmers with whom to place contracts. However, it has already been shown how contracting favours the larger farms, which are the first to become organised according to non-agricultural criteria. In contrast, the smaller farms become increasingly marginal as they cannot generate sufficient capital to support profitable farm operations. This capital could be provided by manufacturing companies and financial institutions, but knowledge of their activities is limited (Wallace, 1985). Information which does exist (Munton, 1977) shows that financial institutions (insurance companies, public and private pension funds, and property unit trusts) buying land on a rising market in the early 1970s were interested not in small farms but in large, economically viable properties on high quality land. Consequently, activities were once again biased towards the eastern counties of England. Munton's (1977) survey of 14 institutions showed 46 per cent of their land to be concentrated in Norfolk, Lincoln, Humberside and Cambridge (Fig. 7.6). Their interests were essentially financial and they became landlords on a sale and leaseback basis. Although this is not agribusiness, the signs are ominous and if companies become interested in purchasing and working the land, as a basis for achieving full vertical integration, it is the eastern counties which are most likely to attract their attention.

It seems appropriate to finish this chapter by referring to one geographical study of agribusiness developments in a country where it is most advanced— the USA. In a novel but important paper, Smith (1980) used Dunn and Bradstreet directories for the late 1970s to analyse the distribution of America's richest farms and ranches. On the basis of two criteria—an indicated or inferred annual sales of over one million dollars, and a standard industrialisation classification (SIC) code number of 01 for crops and 02 for livestock, with this SIC agricultural number listed first if the business claimed more than one function—770 businesses where agriculture was the primary activity were identified. The distribution of these rich farms and ranches showed areas of economic power for different agricultural types and reflected regions of prime

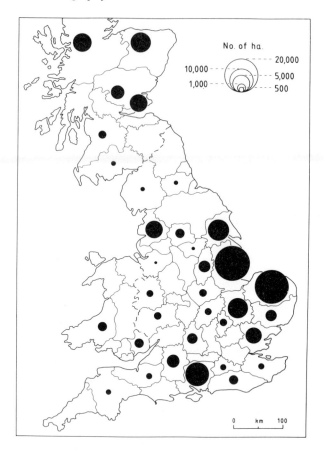

Fig. 7.6   Distribution of agricultural land owned by financial institutions, 1975 (Munton, 1977 p. 33)

agricultural land as well as lands less well regarded (Fig. 7.7). Smith found that 'California valleys and peninsula Florida exhibited the most striking concentrations of wealthy agricultural enterprises in the late 1970s' (p. 529). Other important locations were more diverse and included the Columbia Plain in the Pacific north-west, the low desert in the south-west, the Mississippi alluvial plain and scattered sites in the east. In more detail, approximately one half of the enterprises had headquarters in metropolitan counties, emphasising the importance of proximity to urban areas in large-scale farming, a force previously emphasised by Gregor (1979) in a study of the Pacific south-west. Indeed, many large concerns conducted business from offices in such cities as Washington DC, Miami and Los Angeles. For example, the J. G. Boswell Company, with headquarters in Los Angeles, achieved sales of $100 million in 1977, generated from over 62,750 ha.

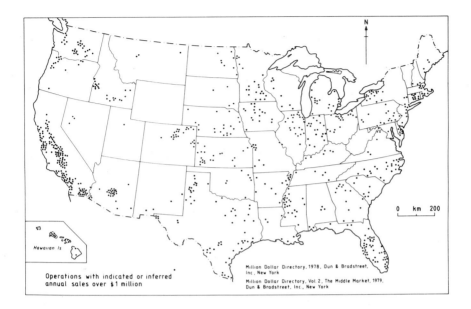

Fig. 7.7   America's richest farms and ranches, late 1970s (Smith, 1980 p. 530)

of land and the following functions: general livestock farming, crop harvesting, manufacturing cotton-seed oil and cattle feeding and ranching.

One of the most important findings of Smith's work, in the context of this section, was that nearly three firms in five were integrated agribusinesses that supplemented production from the land with related activities. In the late 1970s, these were still biased towards the producing end of the agribusiness chain, although diversification into processing, marketing, manufacturing, retailing and restaurants was increasing. Geographically, they were distributed throughout the USA and often had international significance. One quoted example of a vertically integrated superfarm was the P. J. Taggares Company, based in Othello, with a turnover of $50 million and employing 600 people. Among its list of activities are general farming, the manufacture of alfalfa cubes, retail and wholesale fertiliser and pesticides, wholesale fresh vegetables and crop preparation services. Towards the end of the 1970s, the company became one of America's leading processors of frozen french fry potatoes, which provides a good outlet for the interest P. J. Taggares has (with J. R. Simplot) in the country's largest potato farm—SimTag Farms, with 10,121 ha.—in Oregon.

It is clear that modern forms of agriculture are more capital-intensive and that agribusiness is partly responsible for promoting social and economic change in rural areas. This process has been strengthened by government policies which favour the rich and influential large-scale farmers at the expense of the family farm, whose share of retail food prices is likely to continue to decline. From a marketing viewpoint, vertical co-operation with the rest of the food chain is necessary, but this is often at the expense of many of the features which have characterised the agricultural landscape for many years.

AGRICULTURE IN THE RURAL–URBAN FRINGE

8.1 Problems of definition

The rural–urban fringe is a zone of intermingling land-uses, characterised by an irregular transition from farm to non-farm land. Agricultural patterns begin to relate to the demands for rural land by numerous urban-oriented functions. Change is the 'order of the day', related to such processes as urbanisation, industrialisation, land speculation and increasing personal mobility. Demands on the fringe can be both complementary and conflicting, as city and countryside become integral parts of the same social and economic system (Jung, 1971).

It is difficult to delimit the spatial extent of this dynamic zone, as it appears to vary according to the size of the urban centre and the severity of the processes at work. For this reason, various overlapping terms have been used in the literature, ranging from fringe, inner fringe and rural–urban fringe, to urban shadow, exurban zone and urban fringe (Martin, 1975); the OECD (1979) used the phrase peri-urban. An early definition by Wehrwein (1942 p. 218) saw the fringe as 'the area of transition, between recognised urban land-uses and the area devoted to agriculture'. A more detailed view was presented by Pryor (1968 p. 206), 'the zone of transition in land-use, social and demographic characteristics, lying between the continuously built-up urban and suburban area of the city and the rural hinterland and characterised by an almost complete absence of non-farm dwellings, occupations and land-use'. Both definitions contain the distinct notion of transition, or a continuum from urban to agricultural areas characterised by changing relationships between a whole series of 'indicators'. This continuum between urban and rural was schematically portrayed by Bryant *et al.* (1982) and is shown in Fig. 8.1. Four 'zones' are recognisable in the diagram. The first is the *inner fringe*, where there is little doubt about the ultimate conversion of rural land to urban uses; much land is already under construction or has planning permission. Secondly, the *outer fringe* is characterised by rural land-uses. However, the infiltration of such urban-oriented elements as single family dwellings along routeways, trading estates and stock yards is clear. Together, the inner and outer fringes form the rural–urban fringe, which can extend for up to six to ten miles from the edge of the city. Many properties in the rural–urban fringe belong to non-farm people who acquire land in anticipation of future urban expansion. As a consequence, farmers may reduce their investment in agriculture, lowering the intensity of production or leaving the land completely idle. Alternatively, they may decide to increase intensity and exhaust the soil, in an attempt to make high short-term profits before urban development. The thrid zone is the *urban shadow*, where the physical evidence of urban influences is minimal, but where the metropolitan presence is felt through commuting patterns, non-farm residences and the non-farm ownership of land. Metropolitan influences do not stop in the fourth zone, the *rural hinterland*, and are felt through such items as second homes.

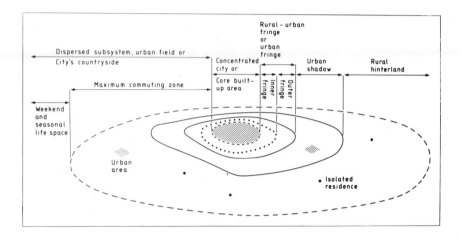

Fig. 8.1   Relationship between rural–urban fringe, urban shadow and rural hinterland (Bryant *et al.*, 1982 p. 25 after Russwurm, 1975)

It is clear that very few areas in the urbanised Western world are unaffected by urban processes, except possibly for the remoter rural regions (Cloke, 1977). However, Bryant *et al.* (1982) point out that Fig. 8.1 is an idealised sequence and that in reality much variation exists. One should think of the rural–urban fringe as a 'discontinuous spatial phenomenon around most cities' (p. 14), where the key to the understanding of the various zones is that they 'are simply different parts of a continuum and that they are the result of a very complex and dynamic set of processes' (p. 14). It is also important to recognise that the preceding discussion has been based on land-use and not land-ownership. The latter undoubtedly affects the former and only by investigating ownership structure and change can the full extent of urban influences in rural areas be assessed. A lack of adequate data on land ownership in the rural-urban fringe has meant that this important control is sadly under-researched (Munton, 1977 and 1983). This is not true of agriculture in the fringe in general, an area of ever-increasing research from numerous viewpoints. Indeed, in line with the broad objectives of this book, recent studies have demonstrated the need to incorporate behavioural considerations into their understanding of rural–urban fringe agriculture. These will be developed in the next section, on fringe processes, and in the presented case-study evidence.

8.2 Rural–urban fringe processes

Agriculture around cities has continued to attract the attention of geographers since the writings on von Thünen (Hall, 1966). However, for a long period this work was mainly descriptive and ignored the processes operating on the urban fringe (Munton, 1974). It was also commonly assumed that agriculture in the rural–urban fringe was explicable in terms of direct urban influences; in reality, non-metropolitan influences on agriculture occur independently of proximity to a city. Therefore, the pattern of land-use in the fringe is complex, probably with no real zoning, and it is impossible to present one model relating land-use to proximity to urban areas. Instead, various concepts have been formulated to help understand the processes at work in this dynamic area.

A combination of urban pressures and non-metropolitan forces acts upon farming in the rural–urban fringe (Fig. 8.2). Three urban-generated processes are particularly important:

  (i) The increased demand for land for urban development.

 (ii) New employment opportunities in urban areas.

(iii) Increased market opportunities for local producers.

These forces either complement or conflict with non-metropolitan processes, which include technological change and managerial innovations, increasing inter-regional competition, government policies, changes in living standards, and increasing capital investment and the decline of land and labour as factors of production (Munton, 1974; Bryant *et al.*, 1982). Complementarity can occur when, for example, technological change and non-farm employment oppor-

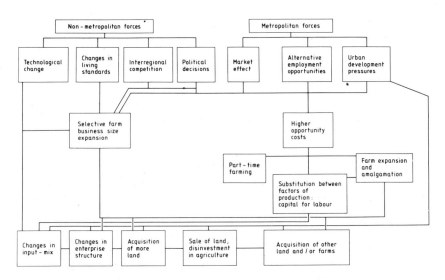

Fig. 8.2   Metropolitan and non-metropolitan forces affecting agriculture in the rural–urban fringe (Bryant *et al.*, 1982 p. 94 after Bryant, 1970)

tunities combine to produce a reduction in the agricultural population, farm-size expansion and increased mechanisation. In contrast, conflict will become evident when urbanisation pressures reach a threshold beyond which agricultural progress is retarded; investment is risky and farm fragmentation could increase (Bryant *et al.*, 1982). These interactions are not constant and will vary according to the type of enterprise practised and the level of regional specialisation in agriculture.

Whilst non-metropolitan forces must not be ignored, this chapter will focus attention on urban-generated processes and in particular the three depicted in Fig. 8.2.

1. The land transfer mechanism

As cities expand, the pressure on rural land-uses becomes very great and agriculture can rarely compete with the higher prices paid for land by such urban uses as residential, commercial and industrial. Under these circumstances, a farmer often has to make two sets of linked decisions (Munton, 1974): first, the timing of the sale of his land and the price he is prepared to accept; and secondly, the kind of farming he should pursue in the meantime. Indeed, the future possibility of rural land coming under the influence of urban development can affect both the current value and use of that land. Assuming a relatively free land market and no government control over land-use, the value of land is increased if an area of future development is known. Where land is likely to become urban in a short period of time, the present value will be very high, whereas land to be developed in the future will have a lower present value (Found, 1971). This is known as the speculative process, evidence of which can be seen in both the purchase of land by speculators and the amount of land lying idle in the rural–urban fringe. A zoning of land values is likely to occur, in a distance–decay relationship from the edge of the city.

Regarding land-use, the speculative process can have both positive and negative effects on intensity. Upon realising that his land will soon be taken over for urban use, a farmer may increase his intensity of production, by abandoning rotation and conservation measures and so depleting his land resources; in other words, he may be 'farming to quit'. Alternatively, he may withdraw his labour and capital and simply await the developer's offer. Optimum profits are forgone in the light of future profits from urban development and intensity of production is correspondingly reduced. The choice of options depends very much upon the farmers' attitudes and perceptions, which will vary according to previous experiences of urban development (Kaiser, 1968). Non-economic motives, such as the maintenance of status and privacy, together with individual rights and desires for a country living (Gertler and Crowley, 1977), can affect the decision of whether or not to sell and the intensity of production.

Inevitably, urban growth is irregular and this creates uncertainty for land-owners in the rural–urban fringe. As Munton (1974) remarked, it is the uncertain nature of the decision-making environment in which an urban-fringe farmer operates that could help to explain the declining intensity of agricultural production. A farmer making large gains from the sale of his land in the fringe is able to purchase land in either the urban shadow or rural hinterland. This could have the effect of raising the price of general farmland. A similar effect could occur with the imposition of government controls on urban sprawl, as for example with land-use zoning laws in the USA (Snyder, 1966) and green belts in the United Kingdom (Boal, 1970; Thomas, 1970). Such controls can lead to an increase in prices beyond the particular zone, which in turn will place extra pressure on the zone itself (Munton, 1974), as speculators and farmers speculate against a change in policy. The price of land in the green belt area becomes inflated and the extra security provided is lost.

2. Increased employment opportunities in urban areas.

Proximity to urban areas and the prospect of higher wages could create a drift of workers from the land and rural depopulation. This decline in agricultural labour is most evident in the rural–urban fringe, as demonstrated by Boddington (1968), who showed that the 'urban' counties of Derbyshire, Hertfordshire and Essex lost 27, 25 and 24 per cent of their agricultural workforce between 1951 and 1961, compared to figures of 8, 9 and 12 per cent for the more 'rural' counties of Lincolnshire, Herefordshire and Westmorland. Farm employers can either increase wages or substitute extra capital inputs for labour inputs in order to maintain their intensity of production. Failing that, they have the option of changing to more extensive types of farming, as for example from dairying to beef production. Assuming that the availability of urban employment increases with proximity to the city, intensity of agricultural production could increase with distance away from the city edge (Sinclair, 1967).

Another adjustment to urban pressure is the growth of part-time farming, which has been the subject of much recent debate (Fuller and Mage, 1976; *GeoJournal*, 1982; *Sociologia Ruralis*, 1983; Gasson, 1983). In Britain, this phenomenon is most prevalent in the highly urbanised south-east region, but it is also important in areas of small farms and marginal farming (Gasson, 1966). The presence of part-time farming increases with proximity to urban areas, until one reaches the inner fringe where competition with speculators is prohibitive. The overall effect of part-time farming is to lower the intensity of agricultural production, although it is important to distinguish between two types of part-time farmers (Munton, 1974; Van Otten, 1980; Layton, 1981a): first, those who seek non-farm employment to supplement their farm incomes; and secondly, hobby farmers who obtain only a nominal income from the farm. The former are more likely to adopt similar farming systems to full-time farmers, whereas the latter tend to originate in urban areas and have little farming background. Hobby farmers tend to be motivated by non-economic considerations, such as status, desirable location and a wish to 'get back' to nature (McKay, 1976), as well as by such factors as tax concessions, a desire to reduce the estate duty and the purchase of land as an investment. However, Layton (1979 and 1981a) has shown that hobby farmers are not a homogeneous group, but can be divided into motivated and non-motivated sub-groups. This will be further developed in section 8.3. One important characteristic of hobby farming is the leasing of land to full-time farmers. Therefore, the rural–urban fringe tends to witness a growth in both part-time and large farms (which are better able to compete with urban pressures), at the expense of the traditional family farm (Munton, 1974).

3. Increased market opportunities

Whilst urban pressures are primarily seen as a major constraint on agriculture, proximity to a large and expanding urban market can present new opportunities to farmers (Blair, 1980). Agriculture may be maintained partly because of the very strong attachment of some farmers to the land. In addition, the leaseback to farmers of land purchased by non-farm interests can release much needed capital for improvements and intensive production. However, with speculation this lease can be uncertain, encouraging the farmer to 'mine' the land in the short-term future.

An increasing urban demand for food can present certain advantages to local producers, especially if they engage in such intensive enterprises as horticulture. This relates in part to von Thünen's principles of locational rent, although inter-regional competition from low-cost producing areas has rather reduced these kinds of effects (Bryant *et al.*, 1982). Despite this, increasing personal wealth and mobility have presented farmers with new opportunities to embark on direct marketing and farm-based recreation schemes. Farmers have been rather slow to develop the income potential of farm-gate sales, retail distribution of milk, eggs and vegetables, and garden centres and nurseries (Munton, 1974), but the 1970s did witness an upsurge in the importance of PYO schemes, even if this was not necessarily urban-oriented (Bowler, 1982). Similarly, signs of such recreational pursuits as horse-riding (horsiculture—Layton, 1981b), caravanning and shooting have been emerging on many farms in the rural–urban fringe (Blair, 1980).

All or none of these three processes may be relevant in given situations and it is for this reason that nobody has formulated a combined model of general application. However, Kellerman (1978) did attempt to incorporate three urban determinants of rent from metropolitan areas—the market, space consumption and economic change—into one rent model. Using the interrelationships between an increase in the demand for food and urban space, both resulting from urban growth, as an example, the model attempted to analyse the interactions among the three factors over time. With the aid of graphical representations, Kellerman demonstrated how in the long run all three urban determinants would have a positive impact on agriculture, by increasing the value of agricultural land in an outer zone and encouraging more efficient locally-oriented production. In contrast, expansion of the city would have a negative impact on rural land in the short run, as competition between urban and rural activities would cause abandonment of agricultural land. Economic change was seen to have a mixed impact: whilst an increasing flow of capital would help to stimulate productivity, the pressure of urban wages on rural labour would cause a necessary reorganisation of farms, which in turn could reduce the farmers' income.

In summarising the various processes at work in the rural–urban fringe, Bryant *et al.* (1982) classified urban effects on agriculture into two groups: direct and indirect. The former has a negative impact in that land is removed from its agricultural production function and is either used for urban development or lies idle awaiting future residential or industrial use. The latter tends to modify existing farming systems and can be either positive or negative for agriculture. Positive effects could stem from a fall in the number of farm operators and employees, encouraging farm amalgamation and an increase in capital inputs; intensification could also be encouaraged by the expanding urban market. Negative effects could result from land speculation, farm fragmentation, increasing property taxes, trespass and vandalism.

Anticipation of urban development is an indirect impact and various viewpoints exist upon its effect on agricultural intensity in the rural–urban fringe. Four possibilities are demonstrated in Fig. 8.3:

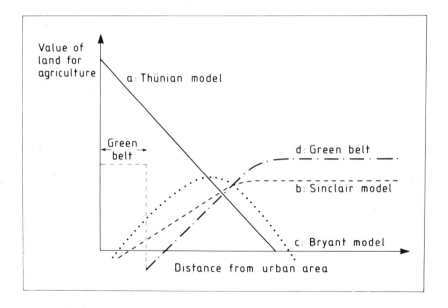

Fig. 8.3   Models of agricultural intensity in the rural–urban fringe (Bryant *et al.*, 1982 p. 103)

(*a*) *Thünian model*, or direct approach. In accordance with the concept of economic rent, which is related to distance and transport costs, intensity of production declines with distance from the city edge. This traditional view has received empirical support from numerous researchers, notably in the 1960s (Golledge, 1960; Higbee, 1961; Muth, 1961; Goldsmith and Cropp, 1964; Schmid, 1968). Although the demand from urban areas encourages intensive dairy farming and market gardening, another reason given for increased intensity in the fringe is the better quality of land near cities, especially if they developed as trade centres for agriculture (Griffen and Chatham, 1958). However, the counter-argument to that reasoning is that land lost to urban development is often of above-average quality (Wibberley, 1968; Coleman, 1978a; Platt, 1981). Also, the direct approach assumes that economic rent from agriculture in the rural–urban fringe is determined independently from rent achieved from urban uses. In reality, rents from agriculture in the fringe depend very much on urban pressures.

(*b*) *Sinclair model*, or reverse approach. Sinclair (1967) argued that rapid urban development, rather than transport costs to the market, would cause farmers to reduce their level of investment in agriculture. Land speculators push prices beyond the reach of ordinary farmers and idle land, together with the growth of part-time and hobby farming, leads to more extensive agriculture in the rural–urban fringe. Consequently, the value of land for agricultural production (and intensity) would increase with distance from the city edge. This is the more modern theory, supported by another group of researchers (Clawson, 1962; Best and Gasson, 1966; Mattingly, 1972; Bryant, 1974 and 1981; Berry, 1979).

(*c*) *Bryant model* (1973). This is the compromise solution between von Thünen and Sinclair. Bryant argued that only certain types of agriculture are negatively effected by urban pressure, depending on the time the farmer needs to get a return on the capital invested; orchards and vineyards would be good examples (Krueger, 1978). This could help determine whether the farmer will abandon the enterprise or farm to quit. A variety of 'value for agriculture' curves are possible, depending on the degree to which particular enterprises are effected by potential urban development, and if proximity to the market is considered as a factor too, agricultural intensity could first increase and then decline with distance from the city edge.

(*d*) *Green belt model.* If strict policy was enforced, the demand for urban land could be deflected beyond the belt (Boal, 1970). This would have an adverse effect on the value of land for agriculture, at considerable distances from the edge of the city.

Each of these four situations assumes homogeneity of response on the part of the farming community. In reality, farmers' responses to the threat of urban development are likely to vary according various socio-economic factors and the strength of potential urban development indicators (Bryant, 1981). A model showing the possible range of variation in farmers' evaluations is given in Fig. 8.4. In situation I there is little possibility of an agricultural future as the farming community is close to or has already experienced non-farm development; consequently, the variation in farmers' evaluations is likely to be small. Similarly in the urban shadow (situation III), there is little variation in farmers' responses, but this time the evaluation of the probability of an agricultural future is high as there is little experience of urban development. However, in the outer fringe (situation II) there is more uncertainty than in the two other zones and, due to differences in optimism and awareness of potential urban development, this

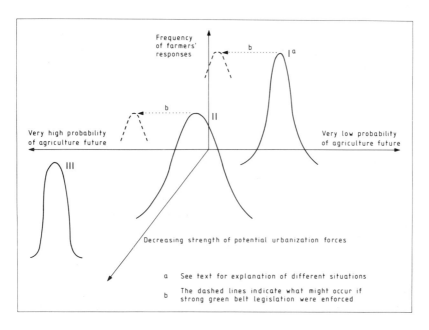

Fig. 8.4   Evaluation of the probability of an agricultural future by farmers (Bryant, 1981 p. 29)

could lead to a wider variation in the evaluation of an agricultural future. The model is valuable in so far as it attempts to incorporate 'behavioural' consider-ations into the understanding of rural–urban fringe agriculture and was partly successful when applied in a case study of Paris (Bryant, 1981).

   This section has attempted to outline the wide range of processes at work in the rural–urban fringe and emphasise the possible effects on agricultural production. It is clear that there is continual change in the social structure of those engaged in farming in the fringe. The decline in traditional farmers and farm labour and the entry of professional men with urban backgrounds into farming means that the family farm is being squeezed out by hobby farms and large farming companies. As Munton (1974) demonstrates, this is unlikely to lead to a clearly-defined metropolitan agriculture. The behaviour of farmers, in face of changing urban pressures, has also been shown to be inconsistent; this is not surprising in a dynamic zone where both economic efficiency and non-agricultural motives for land-ownership are being emphasised (Munton, 1974).

8.3 Case-study evidence

Throughout the 1970s and early 1980s, numerous studies have been published on agriculture in the rural–urban fringe, with many testing the concepts outlined in section 8.2. Most of these studies emphasised the complex interplay of factors at work, which created varied patterns of land-use in different areas; for example, in a study of Hong Kong, Sit (1979) found evidence to support both direct (Thünen) and reverse (Sinclair) approaches to fringe farming. Consequently, the objective of this section is to present six case-studies, from different parts of the Western world, which demonstrate the contrasting importance of many of the processes already described. In addition, the studies have been ordered in such a manner to show the changing emphasis placed upon economic and behavioural considerations on the structure of metropolitan agriculture.

1. The Niagara fruit belt (Krueger, 1959 and 1978)

First delimited in the 1950s, on the basis of the area devoted to fruit and vegetables as a percentage of the total area in occupied farmland, the belt consists of ten townships in close proximity to the southern shore of Lake Ontario. Fruit growing reached its maximum spatial extent in 1951 and orchards and vineyards accounted for over 99 per cent of the total Niagara fruit crop. Between 1951 and 1971 the fruit area declined by 19 per cent and all fruit crops experienced this demise, except grapes which increased by 7 per cent. This trend continued between 1971 and 1976, when tree fruits declined by a further 400 ha. and grapes increased by 800 ha., providing evidence of both increasing and declining intensity.

Using Russwurm's (1970) classification of urban, semi-urban, semi-rural and rural, and township concession blocks as his mapping units, Krueger indicated the increasing degree of urbanisation over the 1934–75 period (Fig. 8.5). The tabulated results in Table 8.1 show this progression, with the number of concession blocks classified as urban increasing from five to 34 per cent, whilst rural declined from 59 to 28 per cent. A major jump in the number of urban concession blocks occurred between 1965 and 1975, a decade when 346 blocks changed by one category, 37 by two and 17 by three (i.e. rural to urban). Significantly, most of the urbanisation occurred in the most intensive fruit-growing areas and on better quality land. The decline in orchards has been most severe on tender fruit soils near the city edge. Some of this loss has been compensated for by increased intensification of orcharding on similar soils further removed from the city; a similar trend for vineyards could be observed.

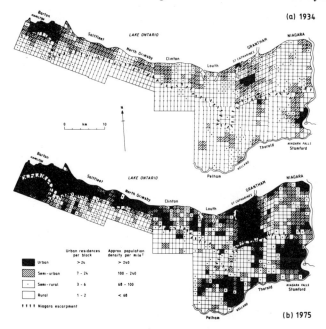

Fig. 8.5 Urbanisation of the Niagara fruit belt: (*a*) 1934; (*b*) 1975 (Krueger, 1978 pp. 186 and 187)

Therefore, intensity of fruit production increased with distance from the edge of the city, lending support to Sinclair's (1967) assumed relationship. However, Krueger pointed out that the stage had been reached when all available tender fruit soils had been fully cultivated, implying that any future urban expansion would result in a greater rate of decline in fruit production than in the past.

Two further factors affect agriculture in this fringe area. The first is that only one major tree fruit-processing plant remains in the fruit belt. This creates a constant state of uncertainty for the farmer, because if the plant was forced to close, through a lack of adequate supply or increased competition from imported fruit, the complete collapse of the tree fruit-growing industry would

Table 8.1

Percentage of township blocks by degree of urbanisation, 1934–75

	1934	1954	1965	1975
Rural	59	46	39	28
Semi-rural	19	16	19	17
Semi-urban	17	30	30	21
Urban	5	8	12	34

Source: Krueger (1978 p. 188).

occur. The second factor is the lack of government commitment to preserve the fruitlands. There is no tariff protection against imported fruit and the provincial government has no strategy for urban growth and no agricultural land preservation policy. These two factors and the indirect effects of urbanisation are felt most strongly in the semi-urban blocks (outer fringe), which are characterised by high land prices, the subdivision of land into uneconomic units, pilfering and the harassment of farmers by 'urbanites'. The result is a lack of long-term investments in agriculture, especially orchards. Hopefully, the slowing down of metropolitan growth in Canada will provide much-needed time to enable planners to direct urbanisation towards less valuable agricultural land.

2. *Dairying in the Illinois fringe* (Berry, 1979)

Eleven counties in north-east Illinois formed the study area for an examination of the relationship between agricultural land-use and urban pressure. In particular, the decline in dairy cows, from 149,885 in 1965 to 87,148 in 1975, formed the focus of attention. One hundred and twenty-four townships, each with more than 100 milk cows and heifers in 1964, were selected for detailed study and classified into three categories to reflect the severity of urban pressure: strong, moderate and weak (Fig. 8.6). The area is a continuation of the Upper Great Lakes dairy region and consists of high quality, flat land, suitable for many types of farming.

For each township two measures were obtained: first, an index of change in

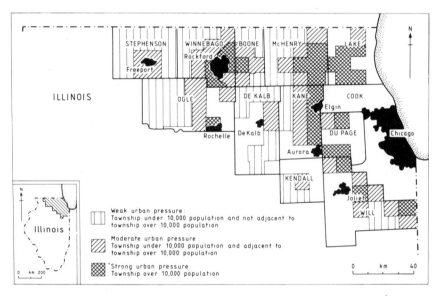

Fig. 8.6   Townships in north-eastern Illinois classified by degree of urban pressure (Berry, 1979 fig. 1 p. 171)

dairying; and secondly, a summary measure of farming in general. The former was obtained by dividing the number of milk cows and heifers in 1974 by the number in 1964, although it was recognised that this took no account of the increased output of milk per cow. The latter was calculated by dividing the acreage of land in farms in 1974 by the acreage in 1964. Ratios were calculated for each township in the three urbanisation groups and a summary median value entered in a final table of results (Table 8.2). Using the Kruskal–Wallis analysis of variance, significant differences were shown to exist between the three levels of urban pressure. For example, in areas of little urban pressure 64 per cent of the number of cows and heifers recorded in 1964 still existed in 1974; this compared with figures of 53 and 34 per cent in areas of moderate and strong urban pressure respectively. Therefore, it was assumed that strong urban pressures were associated with a major decline in dairying. Similar figures were obtained for the general farming measure, but the rate of decline was much less marked, implying that general farming was less sensitive than dairying to urban processes.

Table 8.2

Median change in dairying and land in farms for 124 townships in north-eastern Illinois, 1964–74

	Townships with 1970 pop. > 10,000	Townships with 1970 pop. < 10,000	
		Adjacent to township with pop. > 10,000	Others
Milk cows and heifers	.34	.53	.64
Land in farms	.66	.90	.97
Number of townships	24	37	63

Source: Berry (1979 Table 1 p. 172).

In searching for an explanation of these trends, Berry attributed the greater decline in dairying to certain characteristics associated with both labour and capital inputs. Urban growth presents the farmer with the opportunity of obtaining off-farm income in the city. However, the time-consuming nature of dairying means that it does not lend itself to this possibility very well; in 1974, 43 per cent of dairy farmers in Illinois had off-farm work, compared with figures of 53 per cent for livestock and 54 per cent for cash grain farming. Consequently, some farmers were encouraged to change from dairying to less time-consuming enterprises.

Dairying was also shown to be more sensitive than other farming types because of differences in the mobility of capital and the ability to recover costs. Fixed costs in dairying are primarily immobile and, with the threat of land speculation and urban development, there is an increased risk of not being able to recover one's investment in capital. Therefore, uncertainty relates more to costs than to intensity of production, although a reduction in investment is likely to lead to declining yields.

It was concluded that capital plays a major role in changing the patterns of land-use in the rural–urban fringe. Where urban pressures are moderate (outer fringe), dairy farmers may be outbid for land by cash grain farmers whose capital is more mobile. Where urban pressures are strong, all farming will be outbid by speculation and there will be general disinvestment and an idling of land.

3. The Auckland rural–urban fringe (Moran, 1979)

Characterised by much physical diversity, there is healthy competition between the various types of farming in the fringe area of Auckland. Extensive rearing and fattening of sheep and beef compete with the more intensive dairying for factory and town supply, orcharding, viticulture, market gardening and poultry. The result is a complicated pattern of land-use which fails to follow either von Thünen's or Sinclair's idealised types. Vineyards and orchards are concentrated to the west and north of Auckland, whilst market gardening favours the southern districts. Pastoral farming does display some zonal pattern of distribution, with dairying for town supply dominating the inner fringe, especially to the south of Auckland where it survives alongside residential land (Fig. 8.7). In turn, dairying for factory supply produces a concentric pattern around town supply areas, whilst the rearing and fattening of beef and sheep is most prominent in the urban shadow.

Overall, there is only a weak correlation between the intensity of production and distance from the city, but as Moran indicates, intensity of farming types does not decline with proximity to the city either. Evidence of both the positive and negative effects of urbanisation can be found, producing a complex pattern which is difficult to explain. In searching for explanations, Moran pointed to five factors in particular:

(i) *Historical legacy and competitive agriculture.* This included many considerations, ranging from the natural advantages of basaltic soils and frost-free slopes to the speculative subdivision of land for orcharding, the distribution of Yugoslav and Chinese ethnic groups for market gardening, viticulture and orcharding, and the method of allocating milk supply quotas (see below). These factors enabled many capital and labour-intensive enterprises to maintain their momentum, despite increasing urban pressure.

(ii) *The allocation of town supply quotas for milk.* In order to supply milk for direct consumption in urban areas, farmers are allocated a quota by the producer associations to which they belong. Farmers are contracted to supply a minimum quantity of milk every day, in return for which they receive almost twice the price as farmers supplying for factory production. An important policy of the Milk Board is to 'ensure that in the allocation of quotas, some preference is given to farmers close to the urban area' (p. 173).

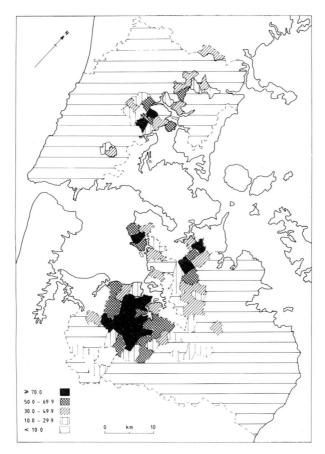

Fig. 8.7 Town supply dairying in Auckland, 1970 (area in holdings classified as town supply dairy farms as a percentage of total area in holdings over 1 ha.) (Moran, 1979 p. 169)

Therefore, it is not surprising that 38 of the 89 quotas allocated in the 1960s were within 6 km. of the built-up area, compared to only five that were more than 21 km. away from the city edge. As well as maintaining land in the inner fringe in agricultural use, the spatial extent of town supply dairy farming (Fig. 8.7) has changed very little since its inception in 1944.

(iii) *The role of individuals and planning.* Existing land-use patterns and the strong farm lobby have influenced the direction of urban growth and maintained particular parcels of land in agricultural production. If current attitudes are to be met, planners have to make definite attempts to protect productive farmland.

(iv) *Differential assessment of farmland.* In order that the increase in the value of land attributable to urban influences is not felt fully by the farmers, in the form of land taxes, legislation has been passed specifically to assess rates on a different basis for land that is being farmed, compared with other land on the urban periphery. These special rates, which are usually less than 70 per cent of the normal rate, permit farmers to continue in the inner fringe, even though the value of their land has been increased by urban potential.

(v) *Proximity to Auckland.* Although distance to the market has lost much of its importance, it has been partly responsible for the growing trend of the market moving to the producer. This is reflected in the number of roadside stalls and PYO schemes, both of which have increased on the periphery of Auckland. Direct marketing of this form enables farmers to overcome otherwise very tight marketing controls. Auckland has many other effects on fringe agriculture and is the provider of capital for innovations, amenities for the rural population, employment for part-time farmers, hobby farmers and many agricultural supply inputs such as labour for harvesting.

All of these influences combine to produce a heterogeneous pattern of agricultural land-use in Auckland's rural–urban fringe. The formal and informal controls of institutional restrictions have produced a much greater diversity of responses than Sinclair's model permits and Moran suggests that furture work on agriculture in the rural–urban fringe should look more at the motivation of land-owners and occupiers than search for patterns of intensity. It is to this point that the remaining case-studies are addressed.

4. The Île de France region (Bryant, 1981)

A neglected aspect in studies of agriculture in the rural–urban fringe has been the extent to which farmers vary in their responses to the threat of urban expansion. Variations can result from many factors, such as the perceptions of threat, the ability to interpret changes in the surrounding environment, personal preferences and resources available to the individual farmer. This formed the focus of attention in Bryant's study of two areas within the rural–urban fringe of Paris. Sixty-three farmers were surveyed; 21 in the northern suburbs of Paris and 42 to the south-west of the city. Each farm was classified into one of three urbanisation categories: very strong (23 farms), relatively strong (20) and low (20).

In order to test his own model of farmers' evaluations of urbanisation forces (Fig. 8.4), Bryant established three working hypotheses (p. 30):

(i) The direction and degree of variation in farmers' evaluations of the likelihood of an agricultural future in the area are related to the strength of potential urbanisation forces.

(ii) The mix of patterns of farm change is related directly to the strength of potential urbanisation forces and to farmers' evaluations of these forces, with fixed investment (capital-intensive enterprises) being substantially reduced in areas where development pressures are strong.

(iii) Part of the variation in farmers' responses is related to farm and farmer characteristics in an as yet unspecified manner.

For each farm, information was elicited on five subject areas: urbanisation, attitudes and feelings, problems expressed, farm-and-farmer characteristics, and components of farm change. The farms were then classified on the basis of each of these areas, using dissimilarity analysis, and the following number of groups emerged:

urbanisation	3
attitudes	3
problems expressed	3
farm change	2
farm/farmer characteristics	2

Interrelationships between the five subject areas were examined by means of X^2. Urbanisation was shown to be strongly related to both 'attitudes' and 'problems expressed' groups, and it was farmers in areas of high urbanisation that had the most negative response profile on attitudes. In contrast, farmers in the intermediate urban zone were more evenly divided, supporting the variability aspect of hypothesis (i). The same pattern emerged with the 'problems expressed' group. Although the relationship between urbanisation and the pattern of 'farm change' was not significant at the 95 per cent level, three-quarters of the farmers in the most urbanised cateogry were in the farm change group characterised by simplification of the systems of production and by acquisition of farms elsewhere. The more intensified systems tended to be located in the moderate and low urbanisation areas. Evidence was found to show that whilst some farmers in the highly urbanised areas had lowered their investment in fixed capital, others had intensified production to benefit from changing market conditions. As a result of this adaptive behaviour, hypothesis (ii) was not strongly supported by the data. Finally, no significant relationships emerged between farm and farmer characteristics and either urbanisation or patterns of farm change, leading to the rejection of hypothesis (iii).

In reviewing the results, Bryant made four general conclusions. First, it would seem that farmers' evaluations are systematically differentiated according to the strength of potential urbanisation forces. The greatest variability in responses was found amongst the farmers in the intermediate urbanisation category, supporting the conceptual framework outlined in Fig. 8.4. Secondly, differences in evaluations were not matched by comparable variations in types of farm change. Whilst many farmers in the more highly urbanised zone had tended to simplify their systems, there was some evidence of increased investment. Thirdly, there was no relationship between the farmers' evaluation of urbanisation forces and farm change. Perceived problems in the rural–urban fringe were more of a nuisance than a disincentive and not sufficient to have a marked impact on farm investment. Finally, farmers' evaluations were not related to farm and farmer characteristics. This last conclusion needs to be treated with some caution for as Bryant remarked, the size of farm sample was rather small and variation in urbanisation forces may have overridden the operation of farm and farmer characteristics in influencing response profiles.

5. Urban influences in Essex (Blair, 1980)

In a survey of 1,129 farm businesses in Essex, the structure of agriculture was interpreted in terms of both opportunities and constraints placed upon farmers. In particular 'it is the farmers' responses to these constraints and opportunities within the urban fringe that need to be examined rather than a catalogue of land-use' (p. 373). Four classes of urban influence were isolated for special attention: first, as markets for agricultural products; secondly, as consumers of agricultural resources, especially land; thirdly, the interaction of farmers with urban dwellers and its reflection in part-time farming, farm-based recreation and farm-gate sales; and fourthly, the effects of planning legislation.

Between 1960 and 1973, 2.3 per cent of the sample farm area was transferred out of agriculture. Although this is a relatively small amount, 77 per cent of the farmers experienced at least one land conversion, mainly in amounts of less than 2 ha. Spatially, land loss was understandably concentrated in the shadow of the major urban centres. Interestingly, one-quarter of the land transfers and 35 per cent of the area converted was accomplished through compulsory purchase orders, mainly for road building but also for housing.

Full-time farm labour declined by 17.3 per cent over the 1960–73 study period, but there was no simple relationship between the types of farming practised and the rates of loss. However, it was the more urbanised districts that lost most labour and this in turn lead to a growth in part-time farming. Twenty per cent of the sample were part-time and these were randomly distributed in Essex (Fig. 8.8). Of this total, 59 per cent had local occupations, 22 per cent commuted to local urban centres and just 10 per cent went to London. Little difference could be discerned between full and part-time farmers in terms of farm type, farm-size and tenure. However, the part-time farmers were far from a homogeneous group and included semi-retired farmers, people working in ancillary agricultural work, and professional and managerial people.

Whilst 70 per cent of the farmers were troubled by one or more urban hazards (trespass, litter, dogs, vandals, pollution), the majority took no action and only a small proportion changed their farming systems. This negative aspect of fringe agriculture appeared to be outweighed by positive effects on farm-gate sales and farm-based recreation. Nearly 30 per cent of the sample engaged in some form of direct marketing, through farm stalls and shops, deliveries to households and PYO schemes. The latter were particularly concentrated in the soft fruit-growing areas of Witham and Tiptree and not the inner fringe of cities. One-tenth of the farmers also undertook farm-based recreation, in the form of campsites, horse-riding, farmhouse holidays, farm trails, shooting and fishing. However, this is possibly a trend of the future as only 25 per cent of those involved gained a worthwhile income from it. Horse-riding and educational visits showed some affinity to urban-fringe locations but the distribution of other activities was determined more by the location of relevant resources.

Blair concludes his study by demonstrating how both land loss and urban

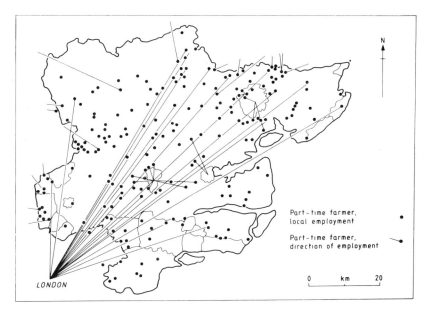

Fig. 8.8   Location of part-time farmers in Essex, with direction of other employment (Blair, 1980 p. 378)

hazards have had a minimal impact upon the structure of fringe farming, whereas the potential benefits of both farm-based recreation and farm-gate sales are considerable, presenting farmers with enhanced rather than reduced opportunities. Although the growth of part-time farming may be interpreted as a negative effect of urban pressures, farming on the urban fringe is more variable than the usual stereotype of declining intensity allows.

6.   *The rural–urban fringe of London, Ontario* (Layton, 1978, 1979 and 1981a)

A comparison of attitudes between commercial and hobby farmers is the focus of attention in a study of 450 farmers in a 20-mile zone around London, Ontario. Commercial farmers are those with a traditional rural and agricultural background, primarily involved in farming for a living. These can be subdivided into two groups: full-time farmers, fully engaged in farming; and part-time farmers, with non-farm employment to supplement their income. Hobby farmers have a more urban background, with urban employment and residence, but purchase farms for personal recreation and residence whilst retaining their jobs in the city. Two sub-groups of hobby farmers can also be identified: motivated, towards farming on a commercial basis, and non-motivated.

The 450 farmers in Layton's study included a small percentage which could be classified as non-resident. With these excluded, there were 187 full-time farmers, 109 part-time and 114 hobby farmers; the latter included 64 non-motivated and 50 motivated. These groupings formed the basis of analysis and five working hypotheses were established (pp. 36 and 37):

(i) The hobby farming group would perceive living in the rural-urban fringe as an advantage, unlike the commercial farmers who perceive it as a disadvantage.

(ii) The commercially-motivated hobby farmer would perceive living in the fringe as a greater locational disadvantage than the commercially non-motivated hobby farmer.

(iii) The commercial farmer would view landscape features that are of value to agriculture as more important than the hobby farmer who places more emphasis on aesthetic features.

(iv) For hobby farmers, the commercially-motivated would place more importance on features of agricultural importance whereas the non-motivated would emphasise aesthetic features.

(v) The location of hobby farms would reflect the attitude of the owner.

Two levels of analysis were undertaken: first, three-way cross-tabulations of full-time, part-time and hobby farmers; and secondly, two-way cross-tabulations comparing the two hobby farming sub-groups. Considering the advantages of owning land in the fringe, most were perceived by the hobby farmers. These included close proximity to the city for commuting, business and shopping, the varied landscape and novelty of growing one's own food, and recreational activities. There was little difference between the two hobby farming groups, although the non-motivated were more interested in growing their own food and in personal recreation. With regards to the disadvantages of a rural–urban fringe location, it was the commercial farmers who were concerned about increased urbanisation, especially the rise in land values which limited farm amalgamations. In contrast, the hobby farmer perceived taxation and land prices as being relatively cheap. Similarly, the commercial farmer was more concerned about the problems of noise and trespass and pressures on the land, just as the motivated hobby farmer saw more disadvantages than the non-motivated.

Notable differences also emerged between the groups of farmers in terms of the perception of desirable features. For example, the hobby farmers, especially the non-motivated ones, felt that features like a stream, a wood and rolling land were important, whereas the commercial farmers viewed features that were more conducive to good agriculture, such as class one land and drainage. These differences were borne out by the fact that the hobby farmers tended to cluster along certain streams and in areas of rugged topography, although the more-motivated ones sought good land. This in turn is a reflection of larger farm-sizes for the motivated hobby farmer compared to the non-motivated and the tendency to rent land by the motivated group. Generally, the hobby farmers tended to be clustered nearer the city than the commercial farmers, but surprisingly it was the more-motivated sub-group of hobby farmers that was found in the inner zone; no explanation was forthcoming for this.

It is clear from Layton's study that farmers of different background characteristics and aspirations vary in their attitudes towards the rural–urban fringe. Hobby farming, located in aesthetic areas and near the city, is creating problems, especially that of inflated land prices. This is preventing the amalgamation of farm units and causing polarisation in the agricultural community, whereby the family farm is being 'squeezed out' by very small and very large farm units.

8.4 Urban encroachment and land loss

Urbanisation is in part a function of continuous population growth which, together with rising income levels, lead to an increasing demand for both land and food. Conflict is immediately apparent as more food is required from less land. This in turn leads to further arguments as to whether agricultural production should continue to be intensified or whether land should be conserved in order to maintain its quality and associated ecosystems. These problems are magnified in the rural–urban fringe, a zone of conflicts and competition between the different uses of land.

Urban expansion is a major consumer of agricultural land, although evidence suggests that this loss has been more than offset by substantial increases in the output of food per hectare. The major question is whether production can continue to compensate for further agricultural losses, without affecting the 'quality' of the environment. Understandably, there is concern about urban encroachment and Hart (1976) believes that this has been motivated by three interrelated anxieties:
  (i) Uncontrolled urban development is wasteful, economically.
 (ii) Urban expansion is depriving nations of some of their prime agriculture land.
(iii) Urban sprawl is an aesthetic abomination, causing irreparable damage to the environment or the 'ecology'.
A related problem is that this conversion process is almost certainly irreversible and land is highly unlikely to return to agriculture. It cannot be denied that agricultural land is being lost to urban development, but a healthy debate has developed as to how much is actually being lost and how serious the problem is.

The extent of agricultural land loss is naturally most pronounced in the more urbanised countries. For this reason, the USA and United Kingdom will be used as case-studies, although the problem is evident elsewhere, as for example in Canada (Pierce, 1981). In the United Kingdom, the 'urban area' doubled between 1900 and the 1950s. The peak in the conversion of agricultural land to urban uses occurred in the 1930s, when 25,000 ha. per year were being transferred in England and Wales. Since 1945 the annual losses have continued to fall, from an average of less than 16,000 ha. in the 1960s to 12,400 ha. in the 1970s (England and Wales); indeed, the average annual rate of conversion for the 1975–80 period was less than 10,000 ha. Figures for Scotland tend to vary between 2,000 and 3,000 ha. per year. In 1971, urban development accounted for 11 per cent of the total land surface of England and Wales (3 per cent in Scotland). Estimates for the year 2000 show that this figure will not rise to more than 15 or 16 per cent (Best, 1968; Edwards, 1969); precise figures quoted by Best (1981) were 14.1 per cent for England and Wales and 10.6 per cent for Great Britain. As the same author demonstrated (Best, 1977 p. 18), the transfer of agricultural land to urban use is 'distributed very unevenly across the surface of England and Wales and there are considerable areas of the country in which the impact of urban growth is still relatively weak'. Even in the most heavily urbanised south-eastern part of England only 18 per cent of the land is urbanised (Hall *et al.*, 1973).

In the USA, a wide range of estimates have been forwarded as to the amount of land lost to urban development, from 141,700 ha. to 2,020,000 ha. per year. A detailed survey conducted by the Conservation Needs Inventory in 1967 produced a more realistic figure of 464,777 ha. per year. Indeed, the built-up area in that year was 24,693,500 ha., or just 2.7 per cent of the total land surface. Assuming similar rates of land transfer, it has been estimated that by the year 2000 little more than 4 per cent of the land area will be urbanised (Hart, 1976).

These figures show that relatively small amounts of agricultural land are being lost to urban development in the United Kingdom and the USA. However, this has not prevented two opposing schools of thought to emerge with regards to the extent of the problem. This is typified by the diverging views of Best (1968, 1977 and 1981) and Coleman (1976, 1978a and b) for the United Kingdom (see Rogers, 1978).

Alarm over the loss of agricultural land is evident in the United Kingdom (Edwards and Wibberley, 1971; Coleman, 1976, 1978a and b) and the USA (Bogue, 1956; Gregor, 1957 and 1963; Krueger, 1959 and 1978; Platt, 1977 and 1981). A central concern is not only that land is being lost but that it is often good quality land (Edwards and Wibberley, 1971). In England, urbanisation is concentrated in the south and east where the better land is also found (Coleman, 1978a). Similarly, Gregor (1963) noted a tendency towards the urbanisation of the better soils in California; this was due to the gentle terrain and the fact that urban centres originated as service centres for the farming community. Platt (1977) estimated that 21 per cent of California's prime agricultural land had been urbanised. In the Niagara fruit belt, Krueger (1978) established that urbanisation was occurring on land where the ratio of 'tender fruit' soils to 'tender' climate was most favourable.

As well as land quality, certain other 'urban' effects have given cause for concern. One is the problem of increased fragmentation of agricultural land in the rural–urban fringe, which helps to accelerate the rate of land transfer. Another is the imposition of a property tax on agricultural land in the fringe, to pay for urban services and facilities. This tax does not apply in the United Kingdom, provided that the land and buildings are used wholly for agricultural purposes, but it has had detrimental effects in the USA, as demonstrated by

Gregor (1957) in California. Many farmers cannot afford these high taxes and so sell their land to developers and speculators, with the result that the intensity of agricultural production is reduced, in line with the Sinclair (1967) model. Other areas of concern include the effects of pollution from the city, increased pilferage and impediments to the spraying of crops, all of which have a negative effect on agricultural output.

This alarm over land loss and urban effects on agriculture is not shared by all economists and geographers. To people like Harris (1956), Hart (1976), Best (1977 and 1981) and Best and Champion (1970), the problem is more of a myth than a reality. Best has argued that, with nearly 80 per cent of the land surface devoted to agriculture, the United Kingdom is not running out of productive land. He makes a number of pertinent points: first, that there is no increase in the rate of land loss; secondly, that grade one quality land only occupies 3 per cent of the land surface and urban areas have not absorbed a disproportionate share of it; thirdly, that since the 1960s the north and western urban regions have outpaced the London region in its rate of urban growth, thus emphasising the potential for urban development in the more peripheral areas where land quality is lower; fourthly, that at current rates of urban growth it would take a further 800 years before all land was urban; fifthly, that only one-third of the land surface of England and Wales is not protected by amenity and land quality restraints on development; and finally, that land budgets up to the year 2000 show that land losses are not likely to affect the ability of agriculture to feed a growing population.

In America, urban encroachment has been interpreted as only a minor induce- ment to land abandonment and Hart (1976) has argued that little has happened since 1956 to modify Harris's (1956 p. 889) concluding remark that 'neither the present nor the potential total land pressures of urban agglomerations are critical'. The only real problems were thought to occur in areas of high urbanisation and limited agricultural land, as in California. Harris felt that the role of cities as centres of culture and economic change was more important than their role as competitors with agriculture for space. More recently, Hart (1976 p. 11) has stated that 'the evidence of urbanised areas indicates that urban encroachment does not represent a serious immediate threat to the nation's supply of land' and 'the nation has far more millions of acres of rural land than will ever be needed for any foreseeable urban growth'.

Indeed, urbanisation has been slowing down in many parts of the Western world since the early 1970s and with it has been a noticeable change in direction of interest, away from the loss of agricultural land to urban development and towards the general conservation of the rural landscape. A conflict of interests, between specialisation of agricultural production for short-term efficiency and diversification for long-term ecological survival, is once again in evidence. In line with the radical approach described in Chapter 1, conservationists argue that land should be used in such a way as to maximise its use over a very long time- period. This would involve the development of soil management principles, the 'wise' use of resources and the maintenance of the natural ecosystem (i.e. a state of balance). What is needed is a balance between food production and environmental conservation. With various incentives given to farmers to increase production, this is unlikely to be achieved and many Sites of Special Scientific Interest (SSSIs) in Britain, for example, are being seriously threatened by the relentless drive to produce more, often unwanted, food. This opens up another exciting area of interest but one which is unfortunately outside the scope of this text.

An attempt has been made in this final chapter to examine the processes affecting agriculture in the rural–urban fringe and to demonstrate the complexity of farming, by means of selected case studies, in this dynamic zone. As well as being one of agriculture's 'problem regions', the rural–urban fringe represents a microcosm of many of the trends and processes studied in agricultural geography. It is a zone where physical, economic, social and political factors all interact, making it difficult to establish generalisations. However, this represents the real flavour of farming and agricultural geography, a part of which has hopefully been portrayed in this short book.

REFERENCES

Adeemy, M. (1968), 'Types of farming in North Wales', *Journal of Agricultural Economics*, 19, 301–15.

Agnew, J. A. (1979), 'Instrumentalism, realism and research on the diffusion of innovation', *Professional Geographer*, 31, 364–70.

Agrawal, R. C. and Heady, E. O. (1968), 'Application of game theory models in agriculture', *Journal of Agricultural Economics*, 19, 207–18.

Aitchison, J. W. (1979), 'The agricultural landscape of Wales', Part 1, 'The structure of agricultural holdings, 1964–74', *Cambria*, 6, 32–53.

—— and Knowles, S. E. (1979), *Intensive crop marketing in Lancashire and Yorkshire*, Department of Geography, University College, Aberystwyth.

Allan, J. (1980), 'Remote sensing in land and land-use studies', *Geography*, 65, 35–43.

Allen, G. R. (1972), 'An appraisal of contract farming', *Journal of Agricultural Economics*, 23, 89–98.

Anderson, K. (1975), 'An agricultural classification of England and Wales', *Tijdschrift voor Economische en Sociale Geografie*, 66, 148–58.

Ashby, A. W. (1926), 'Human motives in farming', *Welsh Journal of Agriculture*, 2, 1–9.

Ashby, W. R. (1964), *An introduction to cybernetics* (Methuen, London).

Ashton, J. and Cracknell, B. (1960–1), 'Agricultural holdings and farm business structure in England and Wales', *Journal of Agricultural Economics*, 14, 472–506.

Bakcr, A. R. H. (1961), 'Le remembrement rural en France', *Geography*, 46, 60–2.

Baker REPORT (1972), *Contract farming report to the Committee of Enquiry*, Cmnd 5099 (HMSO, London).

Bannister D. and Mair, J. (1968), *The evaluation of personal constructs* (Academic Press, London).

Barker, J. W. (1981), *Agricultural Marketing* (Oxford University Press, Oxford).

Barnes, F. A. (1958), 'The evolution of the salient patterns of milk production in England and Wales, *Transactions of the Institute of British Geographers*, 25, 167–95.

Baron, P. J. (1978), 'Why co-operate in agricultural marketing?', *Journal of Agricultural Economics*, 29, 109–16.

Bateman, D. I. (1976), 'A review of the literature of marketing theory and of selected applications', *Journal of Agricultural Economics*, 27, 171–227.

——, Edwards, J. R. and LeVay, C. (1979), 'Agricultural co-operatives and the theory of the firm', *Oxford Agrarian Studies*, 8, 63–81.

Bayliss-Smith, T. P. (1982), *The ecology of agricultural systems* (Cambridge University Press, Cambridge).

Beal, G. M. (1954), *The roots of participation in farmer co-operatives* (College Book Store, Iowa).

Belding, R. (1981), 'A test of the von Thünen locational model of agricultural land use with accountancy data from the European Economic Community', *Transactions of the Institute of British Geographers*, 6, 176–87.

Berry, D. (1979), 'Sensitivity of dairying to urbanisation: a study of North-East Illinois', *The Professional Geographer* of the Association of American Geographers, 31, 170–6.

Best, R. H. (1968), 'Competition for land between rural and urban uses', in *Land use and resources: studies in applied geography*, Institute of British Geographers, Special Publication 1, 89–100.

— — (1977), 'Agricultural land loss: myth or reality?', *The Planner*, 63, 15–16.

— — (1981), *Land use and living space* (Methuen, London).

— — and Gasson, R. M. (1966), 'The changing location of intensive crops', *Studies in Rural Land Use 6*, Wye College, Kent.

— — and Champion, A. (1970), 'Regional conversions of agricultural land to urban land in England and Wales', *Transactions of the Institute of British Geographers*, 49, 15–31.

Bibby, J. and Mackney, D. (1969), *Land-use capability classification: soil survey of Great Britain*, Technical Monograph, Number 1.

Birch, J. (1954), 'Observations on the delimitation of farming-type regions, with special reference to the Isle of Man', *Transactions of the Institute of British Geographers*, 20, 141–58.

Blaikie, P. M. (1971), 'Spatial organization of agriculture in some North Indian villages', *Transactions of the Institute of British Geographers*, 52, 1–40.

— (1978), 'The theory of the spatial diffusion of innovations: a spatial cul-de-sac', *Progress in Human Geography*, 2, 268–95.

Blair, A. M. (1980), 'Urban influences on farming in Essex', *Geoforum*, 11, 371–84.

Blandford, D. and Currie, J. M. (1975), 'Price uncertainty—the case for government intervention', *Journal of Agricultural Economics*, 26, 37–51.

Blunden, J. (1977), 'Rural land use', in *Fundamentals of human geography*, Section II, spatial analysis, D204 (Open University, Milton Keynes).

Boal, F. W. (1970), 'Urban growth and land value patterns: government influence', *Professional Geographer*, 22, 79–82.

Boddington, M. A. (1968), 'Urban pressure', *Farm Business*, 9, 6–12.

— — (1978), *The classification of agricultural land in England and Wales: a critique*, Rural Planning Series, No. 4, Ipsden, Oxfordshire.

Bogue, D. J. (1956), *Metropolitan growth and the conversion of land to non-agricultural uses*, Scripps Foundation Series in Population Distribution (Oxford, Ohio).

Bosanquet C. I. (1968), 'Investment in agriculture', *Journal of Agricultural Economics*, 19, 3–12.

Bourliand, J., Boussard, J. M. and Leblanc, J. (1977), 'Linear programming as a means of studying African peasant behaviour: an experimental study in Senegal; *Mondes en Développement*, 17, 49–74.

Bowden, L. W. (1965), *Diffusion of the decision to irrigate*, Research Paper Series, Department of Geography, University of Chicago.

Bowers, J. (1985), 'The economics of agribusiness,' in Healey, M. J. and Ilbery, B. W. (eds.), *Industrialisation of the countryside* (Geo Books, Norwich).

Bowler, I. R. (1972), 'Co-operation: a note on governmental promotion of change in agriculture', *Area*, 4, 169–73.

Bowler, I. R. (1975a), 'Regional variations in Scottish agricultural trends', *Scottish Geographical Magazine*, 91, 114–22.

—— (1975b), 'Factors affecting the trend to enterprise specialisation in agriculture: a case study in Wales', *Cambria*, 2, 100–111.

—— (1976a), 'Adoption of grant aid in agriculture', *Transactions of the Institute of British Geographers*, 1, 143–58.

—— (1976b), 'Regional agricultural policies: experience in the United Kingdom', *Economic geography*, 52, 267–80.

—— (1976c), 'Recent developments in the agricultural policy of the EEC', *Geography* 61, 28–31.

—— (1979), *Government and agriculture: a spatial perspective* (Longman, London).

—— (1981a), 'Regional specialisation in the agricultural industry', *Journal of Agricultural Economics*, 32, 43–54.

—— (1981b), 'Regional specialisation in Leicestershire's agricultural industry', in Turnock, D. (ed.), *Leicester Geographical Essays*, Leicester.

—— (1981c), 'Self-service down on the farm', *Geography*, 66, 147–50.

—— (1982), 'Direct marketing in agriculture: a British example', *Tijdschrift voor Economische en Sociale Geografie*, 73, 22–31.

—— (1983), Structural change in agriculture, in Pacione, M. (ed.), *Progress in Rural Geography* (Croom Helm, London).

—— (1984), 'Agricultural geography', *Progress in Human Geography*, 8, 256–62.

Briggs, D. (1981), 'Environmental influences on the yield of spring barley in England and Wales', *Geoforum*, 12, 99–106.

Britton, D. K. (1977), 'Some explorations in the analysis of long-term changes in the structure of agriculture', *Journal of Agricultural Economics*, 28, 197–209.

—— and Hill, B. E. (1975), *Size and efficiency in farming* (Saxon House, Farnbourough).

Brown, L. A. (1968), *Diffusion processes and location: a conceptual framework and bibliography* (Regional Science Research Institute, Philadelphia).

– (1975), 'The market and infrastructure context of adoption: a spatial perspective on the diffusion of innovation', *Economic Geography*, 51, 185–216.

—— (1981), *Innovation diffusion: a new perspective* (Methuen, London).

—— and Moore, E. G. (1969), 'Diffusion research in geography: a perspective', in Board, C., Chorley, R. J., Haggett, P. and Stoddart, D. R. (eds.), *Progress in Geography, Volume 1* (Edward Arnold, London).

—— and Lentnek, B. (1973), 'Innovation diffusion in a developing economy: a mesoscale view', *Economic Development and Cultural Change*, 21, 274–92.

Brown, M. A. (1977), 'The role of diffusion agencies in innovation adoption; a behavioural approach', Department of Geography, Ohio State University.

—— (1980), 'Attitudes and social categories: complementary explanations of innovation adoption', *Environment and Planning A*, 12, 175–86.

—— (1981), 'Behavioural approaches to the geographic study of innovation diffusion: problems and prospects', in Cox, K. and Gulledge, R., *Behavioural problems in geography revisited* (Methuen, New York).

—, Maxon, G. E. and Brown, L. A. (1977), 'Diffusion-agency strategy and innovation diffusion: a case study of the Eastern Ohio Resource Development Centre, *Regional Science Perspectives*, 7, 1–26.

Brunn, S. and Raitz, K. (1978), 'Regional patterns of farm magazine publication', *Economic Geography*, 54, 277–90.

Bryant, C. R. (1973), 'The anticipation of urban expansion', *Geographica Polonica*, 28, 93–115.

—— (1974), 'An approach to the problem of urbanisation and structural change in agriculture: a case study from the Paris region, 1955–68', *Geografiska Annaler*, 56B, 1–27.

—— (1981), 'Agriculture in an urbanising environment: a case study from the Paris region, 1968–76', *Canadian Geographer*, 25, 127–45.

—, Russwurm, L. H. and McLellan, A. G. (1982), *The city's countryside: land and its management in the rural–urban fringe* (Longmans, London).

Buchanan, R. O. (1959), 'Some reflections on agricultural geography', *Geography*, 44, 1–13.

Bucksar, R. G. (1968), 'Significant changes in the American egg industry', *Journal of Geography*, 67, 36–41.

Bunce, M. (1973), 'Farm consolidation and enlargement in Ontario and its relevance to rural development', *Area*, 3, 13–16.

Bunting, T. and Guelke, L. (1979), 'Behavioural and perception geography: a critical appraisal', *Annals of the Association of American Geographers*, 69, 448–63.

Butler, J. B. (1960), *Profit and purpose in farming: a study of farms and small-holdings in part of the North Riding*, Department of Economics, University of Leeds, 68.

Buttel, F. and Larson, O. W. (1979), 'Farm-size, structure and energy intensity: an ecological analysis of US agriculture', *Rural Sociology*, 44, 471–88.

Byfuglien, J. and Nordgard, A. (1974), 'Types of regions?', *Norsk Geografisk Tidsskrift*, 28, 157–66.

Cabouret, M. (1976), 'Apercu sur la politique Helvétique en faveur de l'agriculture de montagne', *R. géog. Est.*, 15, 3–40.

Camm, B. M. (1962), 'Risk in vegetable production on a Fen farm', *The Farm Economist*, 10, 89–98.

Carlyle, W. (1983), 'Farm lay-outs in Manitoba', *Canadian Geographer*, 27, 17–34.

CCAHC (1978), *Agricultural co-operation, a policy review* (CCAHC, London). Incorporated into Food from Britain, March 1983.

—— (1979a), *Benefits of agricultural co-operation* (CCAHC, London). Incorporated into Food from Britain, March 1983.

—— (1979b), *Second-tier co-operatives* (CCAHC, London). Incorporated into Food from Britain, March 1983.

—— (1979a), *Benefits of agricultural co-operation* (CCAHC, London).

—— (1979b), *Second-tier co-operatives* (CCAHC, London).

Chapman, G. P. (1974), 'Perception and regulation: a case study of farmers in Bihar', *Transactions of the Institute of British Geographers*, 62, 71–94.

Chisholm, M. (1957), 'Regional variations in road transport costs: milk collection from farmers in England and Wales', *Farm Economist*, 3, 30–8.

—— (1964), 'Problems in the classification and use of farming-type regions', *Transactions of the Institute of British Geographers,* 35, 91–103.

—— (1979), *Rural settlement and land use* (Hutchinson, London).

Church, B. M., Boyd, D. A., Evans, J. A. and Sadler, J. I. (1968), 'A type-of-farming map based on agricultural census data', *Outlook on Agriculture,* 5, 191–6.

Clark, G. (1979), 'Farm amalgamations in Scotland', *Scottish Geographical Magazine,* 95, 93–107.

—— (1982), *The agricultural census – United Kingdom and United States,* Catmog 35 (Geo Books, Norwich).

Clark, G. and Gordon, D. (1980), 'Sampling for farm studies in geography', *Geography,* 65, 101–6.

——, Knowles, D. J. and Phillips, H. L. (1983), 'The accuracy of the agricultural census', *Geography,* 68, 115–20.

Clarke, G. B. and Simpson, I. G. (1959), 'A theoretical approach to profit maximization problems in farm management', *Journal of Agricultural Economics,* 13, 250–1.

Clawson, M. (1962), 'Urban sprawl and urban speculation', *Land Economy,* 38, 99–111.

Cloke, P. (1977), 'An index of rurality for England and Wales', *Regional Studies,* 11, 31–46.

—— (1980), 'New emphases for applied rural geography', *Progress in Human Geography,* 4, 181–217.

Clout, H. D. (1968), 'Planned and unplanned changes in French farm structures', *Geography,* 53, 311–15.

—— (1972), *Geography of post-war France: a social and economic approach* (Pergamon Press, Oxford).

—— (1975), 'Structural changes in French farming: the case of the Puy-de-Dome', *Tijdschrift voor Economische en Sociale Geografie,* 66, 234–45.

Coleman, A. (1976), 'Is planning really necessary?', *Geographical Journal,* 142, 411–37.

—— (1978a), 'Last bid for land-use sanity', *Geographical Magazine,* 50, 820–24.

—— (1978b), 'Planning and land use', *Chartered Surveyor,* 111, 158–63.

—— (1978c), 'Agricultural land losses: the evidence from maps', in Rogers, A. W. (ed.), *Urban growth, farmland losses and planning,* Institute of British Geographers, Wye College.

Cook, A. (1979), 'Resource assessment in East Africa', *Geography,* 64, 96–103.

Coppock, J. T. (1955), 'The relationship of farm and parish boundaries – a study in the use of agricultural statistics', *Geographical Studies,* 2, 12–26.

—— (1960), 'The parish as a geographical-statistical unit', *Tijdschrift voor Economische en Sociale Geographie,* 51, 317–26.

—— (1964), 'Post-war studies in the geography of British agriculture', *Geographical Review,* 54, 409–26.

—— (1965), 'The cartographic representation of British agricultural statistics', *Geography,* 50, 101–14.

—— (1968), 'The geography of agriculture', *Journal of Agricultural Economics,* 19, 153–75.

—— (1971), *An agricultural geography of Great Britain* (Bell, London).

—— (1976), *Agricultural atlas of England and Wales* (Faber and Faber, London).

—— (1976), *An agricultural atlas of Scotland* (John Donald, Edinburgh).

Cox, K. and Gollege, R. (1981), *Behavioural problems in geography revisited* (Methuen, New York).

Cromley, R. (1982), 'The von Thünen model and environmental uncertainty', *Annals of the Association of American Geographers*, 73, 404–10.

Cuddy, M. (1980), 'European agricultural policy: the regional dimension', *Built Environment*, 7, 200–10.

Dalton, R. T. (1971), 'Peas for freezing: a recent development in Lincolnshire agriculture', *East Midlands Geographer*, 5, 133–41.

Day, R. and Tinney, D. (1969), 'A dynamic von Thünen model', *Geographical Analysis*, 1, 137–51.

De Garis De Lisle, D. (1982), 'Effects of distance on cropping patterns internal to the farm', *Annals of the Association of American Geographers*, 72, 88–98.

Delamarre, A. (1976), 'Les bâtiments modernes d'élevage en France', *R. géog. Pyr. S-Ouest*, 47, 139–58.

Denman, D. R. (1965), 'Land ownership and the attraction of capital into agriculture: a British overview', *Land Economics*, 41, 209–16.

De Temple, D. J. (1971), *A space preference approach to the diffusion of innovations: the spread of harvestore systems through Northeast Iowa*, Geographic Monograph Series, Indiana University, Bloomington.

Dodds, P. R. (1965), 'Group marketing', *Journal of Agricultural Economics*, 16, 366–89.

Doherty, J. (1969), *Developments in behavioural geography*, Graduate Discussion Paper 35, Department of Geography, London School of Economics.

Edwards, A. M. (1969), 'Land requirements for UK agriculture by the year 2000: a preliminary statement', *Town and Country Planning*, 37, 108–15.

—— and Wibberley, G. P. (1971), *An agricultural land budget for Britain, 1965–2000*, Wye College, Kent.

Edwards, C. J. (1978), 'The effects of changing farm size upon levels of farm fragmentation: a Somerset case study', *Journal of Agricultural Economics*, 29, 143–54.

—— (1980), 'Complexity and change in farm production systems: a Somerset case study', *Transactions of the Institute of British Geographers*, 5, 45–52.

Erickson, F. A. (1973), 'Location of a system of storage distribution terminals for agricultural ammonia in the corn belt', Unpublished Ph.D. thesis, University of Illinois, Urbana.

Ewald, U. (1976), 'The von Thünen principle and agricultural zonation in colonial Mexico', *Journal of Historical Geography*, 3, 123–34.

Fielding, G. J. (1965), 'The role of government in New Zealand wheat growing', *Annals of the Association of American Geographers*, 55, 87–97.

Finch, V. C. *et al.* (1957), *Elements of Geography: Physical and Cultural* (McGraw-Hill, New York).

Fisher, J. S. (1970), 'Federal crop allotment programs and responses by individual farm operators', *Southeastern geographer*, 10, 47–58.

Fletcher, A. A. (1983), 'Agricultural information flows in North Wales', Unpublished Ph.D. thesis, University of Wales, Aberystwyth.

Floyd, B. (1976), *Problems in the modernisation of small-scale agriculture in underdeveloped tropical countries: a case study from the Caribbean*, XXII International Geographical Conference, USSR.

Fotheringham, A. and Reeds, L. (1979), 'An application of discriminant analysis to agricultural land-use prediction', *Economic Geography*, 55, 114–22.

Found, W. C. (1971), *A theoretical approach to rural land-use patterns* (Edward Arnold, London).

Foxall, G. R. and McConnell-Wood, M. W. (1976), *Member-society relations in agricultural co-operation*, Department of Agricultural Marketing, University of Newcastle upon Tyne, Report 22.

Freund, R. J. (1956), 'The introduction of risk into a programming model', *Econometrica*, 24, 253–63.

Fuller, A. M. and Mage, J. A. (eds.), (1976), *Part-time farming: problem or resource in rural development* (Geo Books, Norwich).

Garst, R. D. (1973), 'Spatial diffusion and information diffusion: a Kenyan example', *Proceedings of the Association of American Geographers*, 5, 75–80.

—— (1974), 'Innovation diffusion among the Gusii of Kenya', *Economic Geography*, 50, 300–12.

Gasson, R. M. (1966), 'The influence of urbanisation on farm ownership and practice', *Studies in Rural Land Use 7*, Wye College, Kent.

—— (1968), 'Occupations chosen by sons of farmers', *Journal of Agricultural Economics*, 19, 317–26.

—— (1969), 'Occupational immobility of small farmers', *Journal of Agricultural Economics*, 20, 279–88.

—— (1973), 'Goals and values of farmers', *Journal of Agricultural Economics*, 24, 521–42.

—— (1977), 'Farmers' approach to co-operative marketing', *Journal of Agricultural Economics*, 28, 27–37.

—— (1983), *'Gainful occupations of farm families'*, Wye College, Kent.

Gertler, L. O. and Crowley, R. (1977), *Changing Canadian cities: the next twenty-five years* (McClelland and Stewart, Toronto).

Gilg, A. W. (1973), 'A study in agricultural disease diffusion', *Transactions of the Institute of British Geographers*, 59, 77–98.

Gillooly, J. F. (1978), 'On the association of soil types and maize yields', *South African Journal of Science*, 74, 138–9.

—— and Dyer, T. (1979), 'On spatial and temporal variations of maize yields over South Africa', *South African Geographical Journal*, 61, 111–18.

Gold, J. R. (1980), *An Introduction to behavioural geography* (Oxford University Press, Oxford).

Goldsmith, H. F. and Cropp, J. H. (1964), 'Metropolitan dominance and agriculture', *Rural Sociology*, 29, 385–95.

Golledge, R. G. (1960), 'Sydney's metropolitan fringe: a study in rural–urban relations', *Australian Geographer*, 7, 243–55.

Goss, K. F. (1979), 'Consequences of the diffusion of innovations,' *Rural Sociology*, 44, 754–72.

Gould, P. R. (1963), 'Man against his environment: a game-theoretic framework', *Annals of the Association of American Geographers*, 53, 291–7.

Granger, O. (1980), 'Climatic variations and the Californian raisin industry', *Geographical Review*, 70, 300–13.

Gregor, H. F. (1957), 'Urban pressures on Californian land', *Land Economy*, 33, 311–25.

—— (1963), 'Urbanisation of South Californian agriculture', *Tijdschrift voor Economische en Sociale Geographie*, 54, 273–8.

—— (1979), 'The large farm as a stereotype: a look at the Pacific Southwest', *Economic Geography*, 55, 71–87.

—— (1982), 'Large-scale farming as a cultural dilemma in US rural development — the role of capital', *Geoforum*, 13, 1–10.

Griffin, E. (1973), 'Testing von Thünen's theory in Uruguay', *Geographical Review*, 63, 500–16.

Griffin, M. (1982), 'European challenge for English hops', *Geographical Magazine*, 54, 564–71.

Griffen, P. F. and Chatham, R. (1958), 'Urban impact on agriculture in Santa Clara County, California', *Annals of the Association of American Geographers*, 48, 195–208.

Grigg, D. B. (1974), *The agricultural systems of the world: an evolutionary approach* (Cambridge University Press, Cambridge).

—— (1981), 'Agricultural geography', *Progress in Human Geography*, 5, 268–76.

—— (1982a), *The dynamics of agricultural change* (Hutchinson, London).

—— (1982b), 'Agricultural geography', *Progress in Human Geography*, 6, 242–6.

—— (1983), 'Agricultural geography', *Progress in Human Geography*, 7, 255–60.

—— (1984), *An introduction to agricultural geography* (Hutchinson, London).

Griliches, Z. (1957), 'Hybrid corn: an exploration in the economics of technological change', *Econometrica*, 25, 501–22.

Hagerstrand, T. (1952), *The propagation of innovation waves*, Lund Studies in Geography (Lund, Gleerup).

—— (1953), *Innovations for loppet ur Korologisk Synpunkt* (Lund, Gleerup).

—— (1967), *Innovation diffusion as a spatial process* (University of Chicago Press, Chicago).

Haines, M. R. (1982), *An introduction to farming systems* (Longmans, London).

Hall, P. G. (1966), *Johann Heinrich von Thünen: Isolated State* (Pergamon Press, Oxford).

——, Gracey, H., Drewett, R. and Thomas, R. (1973), *The containment of urban England*, 2 vols. (George Allen and Unwin, London).

Hanham, R. Q. (1973). 'Diffusion of innovation from a supply perspective: an application to the artificial insemination of cattle in Southern Sweden', Unpublished Ph.D. thesis, Ohio State University, Columbus.

Hanneman, G. J., Carroll, T. W. Rogers, E. M., Stanfield, J. D. and Lin, N. (1969), 'Computer simulation of innovation diffusion in a peasant village', *American Behavioural Scientist*, 12, 36–45.

Harris, C. D. (1956), 'The pressure of residential-industrial land', in Thomas, W. L. (ed.), *Man's role in changing the face of the earth* (University of Chicago Press, Chicago).

Harrison, J. A. and Saare, P. (1971), 'Personal construct theory in the measurement of environmental images: problems and methods', *Environment and Behaviour*, 3, 351–74.

—— —— (1975), 'Personal construct theory in the measurement of environmental images: applications', *Environment and Behaviour*, 7, 3–58.

Hart, J. F. (1976), 'Urban encroachment on rural areas', *Geographical Review*, 66, 1–17.

Hart, P. W. E. (1978), 'Geographical aspects of contract farming, with special reference to the supply of crops to processing plants', *Tijdschrift voor Economische en Sociale Geografie*, 69, 205–15.

—— (1980), 'Problems and potentialities of the behavioural approach to agricultural location', *Geografiska Annaler*, 62B, 99–108.

Harvey, D. W. (1963), 'Locational change in the Kentish hop industry and the analysis of land-use patterns', *Transactions of the Institute of British Geographers*, 33, 123–44.

—— (1966), 'Theoretical concepts and the analysis of agricultural land use patterns in geography', *Annals of the Association of American Geographers*, 36, 362–74.

Harvey, D. W. (1968), 'Pattern, process, and the scale problem in geographical research', *Transactions of the Institute of British Geographers*, 45, 71–8.

—— (1969), 'Review of A. Pred, Behaviour and Location Part 1', *Geographical Review*, 59, 312–14.

Hatch, R. E., Harman, W. L. and Eidman, V. R. (1974), 'Incorporating multiple goals into the decision-making process: a simulation approach to firm growth analysis', *Southern Journal of Agricultural Economics*, 6, 103–10.

Havens, A. E. and Flinn, W. L. (1975), 'Green revolution technology and community development: the limits of action programmes', *Economic Development and Cultural Change*, 23, 469–81.

Hayter, R. (1975), 'Farmers' crop decisions and the frost hazard in east-central Alberta', *Tijdschrift voor Economische en Sociale Geografie*, 66, 93–102.

Hazel, P. B. R. (1970), 'Game theory—an extension of its application to farm planning under uncertainty', *Journal of Agricultural Economics*, 21, 239–52.

Heady, E. O. and Egbert, A. C. (1964), 'Regional programming of efficient agricultural production patterns', *Econometrica*, 32, 374–86.

Heiseler, S. (1977), 'The history and development of agricultural and horticultural co-operatives in East Anglia', *Oxford Agrarian Studies*, 6, 71–91.

Henderson, H. J. R. and Ilbery, B. W. (1974), 'Factors affecting the structure of agriculture in the Amman and Upper Tawe Valleys', *Swansea Geographer*, 12, 61–6.

Hewlett, R. (1967), 'Status, achievements and problems of agricultural co-operatives in Europe', in Warley, T. K. (ed.), *Agricultural producers and their markets* (Blackwell, Oxford).

Heyer, J. (1972), 'An analysis of peasant farm production under conditions of uncertainty', *Journal of Agricultural Economics*, 23, 135–45.

Higbee, E. (1961), 'Megalopolitan agriculture', in Gottman, J. (ed.), *Megalopolis* (The Twentieth Century Fund, New York).

Hill, B. E. (1974), 'Resources in agriculture: capital', in Edwards, A. and Rogers, A. (eds.), *Agricultural resources* (Faber and Faber, London).

—— and Ingersent, K. A. (1977), *Economic analysis of agriculture* (Heinemann, London).

Hill, R. and Smith, D. L. (1977), 'Farm fragmentation on western Eyre Peninsula, South Australia', *Australian Geographical Studies*, 15, 158–73.

Hilton, N. (1968), 'An approach to agricultural land classification in Great

Britain', *Land-use and resources: studies in applied geography*, Institute of British Geographers, Special Publication No. 1, 127–42.

Hirsch, G. P. and Maunder, A. H. (1978), *Farm amalgamation in Western Europe* (Saxon House, Farnborough).

Hoinville, G. and Jowell, J. (1978), *Survey research practice* (Heinemann, London).

Holt, C. C. (1970), 'A system of information centres for research and decision-making', *American Economic Review*, 60, 2–7.

Horvath, R. J. (1969), 'Von Thünen's isolated state and the area around Addis Ababa, Ethiopia', *Annals of the Association of American Geographers*, 59, 308–23.

Howes, R. (1967), 'A test of a linear programming model for agriculture', *Papers of the Regional Science Association*, 19, 123–40.

Hudson, R. (1980), 'Personal construct theory, the repertory grid method and human geography', *Progress in Human Geography*, 4, 346–59.

Hurst, M. E. (1974), *A geography of economic behaviour* (Prentice-Hall, London).

Hurwicz, L. (1950), *Optimality criteria for decision making under risk*, Cowles Commission Discussion Paper, Statistics, 350.

Ilbery, B. W. (1977), 'Point score analysis: a methodological framework for analysing the decision-making process in agriculture', *Tijdschrift voor Economische en Sociale Geografie*, 68, 66–71.

— — (1978), 'Agricultural decision-making: a behavioural perspective', *Progress in Human Geography*, 2, 448–66.

— — (1979), 'Decision-making in agriculture: a case study of north-east Oxfordshire', *Regional Studies*, 13, 199–210.

— — (1981a), 'Dorset agriculture: a classification of regional types', *Transactions of the Institute of British Geographers*, 6, 214–27.

— — (1982), 'The decline of hop farming in Hereford and Worcestershire', *Area*, 14, 203–12.

— — (1983a), 'Harvey's principles reapplied: a case study of the declining West Midlands hop industry', *Geoforum*, 14, 111–23.

— — (1983b), 'A behavioural analysis of hop farming in Hereford and Worcestershire', *Geoforum*, 14, 447–59.

— — (1983c), 'Goals and values of hop farmers', *Transactions of the Institute of British Geographers*, 8, 329–41.

— — (1983d), 'The renaissance of viticulture in England and Wales', *Geography*, 68, 341–5.

— — (1984a), 'Britain's uncertain future in the international hop market', *Outlook on Agriculture*, 12, 119–24.

— — (1984b), 'The marketing of hops in Great Britain: a study of changing structures and farmers' attitudes', *European Journal of Marketing*, 18, 45–55.

— — (1984c), 'Farm fragmentation in the Vale of Evesham', *Area*, 16, 159–65.

— — (1984d), 'Agricultural specialisation and farmer decision behaviour in the West Midlands', *Tijdschrift voor Economische en Sociale Geografie*, 75, 329–34.

— — (1985a), 'Factors affecting the structure of viticulture in England and Wales', *Area*, 17.

-- (1985b), 'Horticultural decline in the Vale of Evesham, 1950–80', *Journal of Rural Studies*, 1, 109–20.

-- and Hornby, R. (1983), 'Repertory grids and agricultural decision-making: a mid-Warwickshire case study', *Geografiska Annaler*, 65B, 77–84.

Ingersent, K. A. (1979), 'The variability of British potato yields: a statistical analysis', *Oxford Agrarian Studies*, 8, 33–52.

Jackson, B. G., Barnard, C. S. and Sturrock, F. G. (1963), 'The pattern of farming in eastern England', *Occasional Papers No. 8*, School of Agriculture, Cambridge University.

Jesse, E. V. and Johnson, A. C. (1970), 'An analysis of vegetable contracts', *American Journal of Agricultural Economics*, 52, 545.

Johansen, H. E. (1971), 'Diffusion of strip cropping in southwestern Wisconsin', *Annals of the Association of American Geographers*, 61, 671–83.

Johnsson, B. (1974), 'Uncertainty in the environment of the farm firm: a simulation approach', *European Review of Agricultural Economics*, 1, 391–413.

Johnston, R. J. (1979), *Geography and Geographers: Anglo-American human geography since 1945* (Edward Arnold, London).

Jones, G. E. (1963), 'The diffusion of agricultural innovations', *Journal of Agricultural Economics*, 15, 49–59.

-- (1967), 'The adoption and diffusion of agricultural practices', *World Agricultural Economics and Rural Sociology Abstracts*, 9, 1–34.

-- (1975), *'Innovation and farmer decision-making'*, D203 Agriculture, (Open University, Milton Keynes). Copyright © 1975 The Open University Press.

Jones, R. C. (1976), 'Testing macro-Thünen models by linear programming', *Professional Geographer*, 28, 353–61.

Jung, J. (1971), *'L'Aménagement de l'Espace Rural: une Illusion Economique'*, Calmann Levy, Perspective de l'économique: économie contemporaine, Paris.

Kaiser, E. J. (1968), 'Predicting the behaviour of predevelopment land-owners on the urban fringe', *Journal of American Institute of Planners*, 34, 328–33.

Kampp, A. (1979), 'Recent amalgamation of agricultural holdings', *Geografisk Tidsskrift*, 78, 57–60.

Kates, R. W. (1962), *Hazrd and choice perception in flood plain management*, Research Paper 78, Department of Geography, University of Chicago.

Kellerman, A. (1977), 'The pertinence of the macro-Thünen analysis', *Economic Geography*, 53, 255–64.

-- (1978), 'Determinants of rent from agricultural land around metropolitan areas', *Geographical Analysis*, 10, 1–12.

Kelly, G. A. (1955), *The psychology of personal constructs*, Vol. I and II (Norton, New York).

King, R. B. (1982), 'Rapid rural appraisal with Landsat imagery: a Tanzanian experience', *Zeitschrift fur Geomorphologie, Supplement Band*, 44, 5–20.

King, R. L. (1973), *Land reform: the Italian experience* (Butterworths, London).

-- (1977), *Land reform: a world survey* (Bell, London).

-- and Burton, S. (1982), 'Land fragmentation: notes on a fundamental rural spatial problem', *Progress in Human Geography*, 6, 476–94.

———— (1983), 'Structural change in agriculture: the geography of land consolidation', *Progress in Human Geography*, 7, 471–501.

Kivlin, J. E. and Fliegel, F. C. (1968), 'Orientation to agriculture: a factor analysis of farmers' perceptions of new practices', *Rural Sociology*, 33, 127–40.

Knowles, R. and Wareing, J. (1976), *Economic and social geography* (William Heinemann Ltd., London).

Krueger, R. R. (1959), 'Changing land use patterns in the Niagara fruit belt', *Transactions of the Royal Canadian Institute*, 32, 39–140.

—— (1978), 'Urbanisation of the Niagara fruit belt', *Canadian Geographer*, 22, 3179–93.

Künnecke, B. H. (1974), 'Sozialbrache—a phenomenon in the rural landscape of Germany', *The Professional Geographer*, 26, 412–15.

Laaksonen, K. (1979), 'The effect of climatic factors on the hectare yields of barley, oats, and spring wheat in Finland, 1972–7', *Fennia*, 157, 199–221.

Layton, R. L. (1978), 'The operational structure of the hobby farm', *Area*, 10, 242–6.

—— (1979), 'Hobby farming', *Geography*, 65, 220–3.

—— (1981a), 'Attitudes of hobby and commercial farmers in the rural-urban fringe of London, Ontario', *Cambria*, 8, 33–44.

—— (1981b), 'Horsiculture and land use', *Town and Country Planning*, 51, 47–8.

Leaman, J. and Conkling, E. (1975), 'Transport change and agricultural specialisation', *Annals of the Association of American Geographers*, 65, 425–32.

LeVay, C. (1975), *Co-operative theory and farmers' attitudes: a preliminary study*, Department of Agricultural Economics, University College, Aberystwyth.

—— (1976), *Farmers' attitudes to co-operation—the views of non-members*, Department of Agricultural Economics, University College, Aberystwyth.

—— (1983), 'Agricultural co-operative theory: a review', *Journal of Agricultural Economics*, 34, 1–44.

—— and Lewis, M. R. (1977), *Farmer participation in co-operatives—a study of the Brecon and Radnor area*', Department of Agricultural Economics, University College, Aberystwyth.

Linstrom, H. R. (1978), *Farmer to consumer marketing*, Washington: USDA, Economic Research Service.

Lloyd, P. E. and Dicken, P. (1977), *Location in space: a theoretical approach to economic geography* (Harper and Row, New York). Copyright © 1972 by Peter E. Lloyd and Peter Dicken.

Low, A. R. (1974), 'Decision-taking under uncertainty: a linear programming model of peasant farmer behaviour', *Journal of Agricultural Economics*, 25, 311–21.

Lynch, K. (1960), *The image of the city* (The MIT Press, Cambridge, Mass.).

McCarty, H. H. and Lindberg, J. B. (1966), *A preface to economic geography* (Prentice Hall, New Jersey).

MacEwen, M. and Sinclair, G. (1982), *New life for the hills* (Council for National Parks, London).

McInerney, J. P. (1969), 'Linear programming and game theory models—some extensions', *Journal of Agricultural Economics*, 20, 269–78.

McKay, R. D. (1976), 'The land use characteristics and implications of hobby farming: a case study in the town of Caledon, Regional Municipality of Peel', BES thesis, University of Waterloo, Ontario.

MAFF (1968), *Agricultural land classification map of England and Wales*, Agricultural Land Service. © British Crown copyright 1985.

— — (1976), *Standard labour requirements*, Guildford.

Malcolm, J. (1983), 'Food and farming', in Burns, J., McInerney, J. and Swinbank, A. (eds.), *The food industry* (Heinemann, London).

Marsh, C. (1982), *The survey method* (George Allen and Unwin, London).

Martin, A. F. and Steel, R. W. (1954), *The Oxford region: a scientific and historical survey* (British Association for Advancement of Science, Oxford).

Martin, L. R. G. (1975), *A comparative urban fringe study methodology*, Occasional Paper 6, Lands Directorate, Environment Canada, Ottawa.

Mattingly, P. F. (1972), 'Intensity of agricultural land-use near cities: a case study', *Professional Geographer*, 24, 7–10.

Mayfield, R. C. and Yapa, L. S. (1974), 'Information fields in rural Mysore', *Economic Geography*, 50, 313–23.

Mayhew, A. (1970), 'Structural reform and the future of West German agriculture', *Geographical Review*, 60, 54–68.

— — (1971), 'Agrarian reform in West Germany', *Transactions of the Institute of British Geographers*, 52, 61–76.

Menanteau-Horta, D. (1967), 'Diffusion and adoption of agricultural techniques among Chilean farmers: a sociological study on the processes of communication and acceptance of innovations as factors related to social change and agricultural development in Chile', Unpublished Ph.D. thesis, University of Minnesota, Minneapolis.

Merrill, R. (ed.), (1976), *Radical agriculture* (Harper and Row, London).

Michaels, P. (1982), 'Atmospheric pressure patterns, climatic change and winter wheat yields in North America', *Geoforum*, 13, 263–73.

Misra, R. P. (1969), 'Monte Carlo simulation of spatial diffusion: rationale and application to the Indian condition', MISRA, R. P. (ed.), *Regional Planning* (university of Mysore Press, Mysore).

Mitchell, G. F. C. (1969), *Application of a likert-type scale to the measurement of the degree of farmers' subscription to certain goals or values*, Department of Economics, University of Bristol.

Moran, W. (1979), 'Spatial patterns of agriculture on the urban periphery: the Auckland case', *Tijdschrift voor Economische en Sociale Geografie*, 70, 164–76.

Morgan, W. B. (1978), *Agriculture in the Third World: a spatial analysis* (Bell and Hyman, London).

— — and Munton, R. J. C. (1971), *Agricultural geography* (Methuen, London).

Moser, C. and Kalton, G. (1971), *Survey methods in social investigation* (Heinemann, London).

Muller, P. (1973), 'Trend surfaces of American agriculture: a macro-Thünen analysis', *Economic Geography*, 49, 228–42.

Munton, R. J. C. (1974), 'Farming on the urban fringe', in *Johnson*, J. H. (ed.), *Suburban growth—geographical processes at the edge of the western city* (Wiley, London).

— — (1976), 'An analysis of price trends in the agricultural land market of England and Wales', *Tijdschrift voor Economische en Sociale Geografie*, 67, 202–12.

–– (1977), 'Financial institutions: their ownership of agricultural land in Great Britain', *Area*, 9, 29–37.

–– (1983), *London's green belt* (George Allen and Unwin, London).

Murray, G. C. (1981), 'Cooperation, capital and control: a study of member and management behaviour in agricultural cooperatives in the East Anglian region of the United Kingdom', Unpublished Ph.D. thesis, School of Development Studies, University of East Anglia.

Muth, R. F. (1961), 'Economic change and rural–urban land use conversions', *Econometrica*, 29, 1–23.

Napolitan, L. and Brown, C. (1963), 'A type-of-farming classification of agricultural holdings in England and Wales according to enterprise patterns', *Journal of Agricultural Economics*, 15, 595–616.

Naylor, E. L. (1982), 'Retirement policy in French agriculture', *Journal of Agricultural Economics*, 33, 25–36.

Newby, H. (1979), *Green and pleasant land? Social change in rural England* (Hutchinson, London).

–– and Utting, P. (1981), 'Agribusiness in the United Kingdom—social and political implications', Paper presented to the British Sociological Association annual conference, University College, Aberystwyth.

Noble, G. (1980), 'Farm management problems of the energy crisis', *ADAS Quarterly Review*, 36, 1–13.

Norton, W. (1979), 'Relevance of von Thünen theory to historical and evolutionary analysis of agricultural land use', *Journal of Agricultural Economics*, 30, 39–47.

Norton-Taylor, R. (1982), *Whose land is it anyway?* (Turnstone Press, Wellingborough).

OECD, (1979), *Agriculture in the planning and management of peri-urban areas*, 2 vols., Paris.

Pacione, M. (1984), *Rural geography* (Harper and Row, London).

Parry, M. L. (1975), 'Secular climatic change and marginal agriculture', *Transactions of the Institute of British Geographers*, 64, 1–14.

–– (1976), 'Mapping of abandoned farmland in upland Britain', *Geographical Journal*, 142, 101–10.

Peet, J. R. (1969), 'The spatial expression of commercial agriculture in the nineteenth century: a von Thünen interpretation', *Economic Geography*, 45, 283–301.

Perry, P. J. (1969), 'The structural revolution in French agriculture: the role of "Sociétés d'Amenagement foncier et d'Establissement rural"', *Revue de Géographie de Montréal*, 23, 137–51.

Persson, L. O. (1983), 'Part-time farming—a corner-stone or obstacle in rural development?', *Sociologia Ruralis*, 23, 50–62.

Pickard, D. H. (1970), 'Factors affecting success and failure in farmers' cooperative associations', *Journal of Agricultural Economics*, 21, 105–19.

Pierce, J. T. (1981), 'Conversion of rural land to urban: a Canadian profile', *Professional Geographer*, 33, 163–73.

Platt, R. (1977), 'The loss of farmland: evolution of public response', *Geographical Review*, 67, 93–101.

—— (1981), 'Farmland conversion: national lessons from Iowa', *Professional Geographer*, 33, 113-22.

Pred, A. R. (1967a), *Behaviour and location: foundations for a geographic and dynamic location theory, Part 1*, Lund studies in Geography, B, 27 (Lund, Gleerup).

—— (1967b), *Innovation diffusion as a spatial process* (University of Chicago Press, Chicago).

—— (1969), *Behaviour and location: foundations for a geographic and dynamic location theory, Part 2*, Lund Studies in Geography, B, 28 (Lund, Gleerup).

Pryor, R. J. (1968), 'Defining the rural–urban fringe', *Social Forces*, 47, 202-15.

Raitz, K. B. (1971), 'The government institutionalisation of tobacco acreage in Wisconsin', *The Professional Geographer*, 23, 123-6.

Rasales, M. A. and Vargas, R. A. (1979), *The pea industry in East Anglia: relationships between pea growers, co-operatives, processors and technological innovations*, Master of Development Studies, The Hague.

Rayner, A. J. (1977), 'The regional pricing policy of the Milk Marketing Board and the public interest', *Journal of Agricultural Economics*, 28, 11-25.

Reitsma, H. J. (1971), 'Crop and livestock production in the vicinity of the US–Canada border', *Professional Geographer*, 23, 216-23.

Rhind, D. and Hudson, R. (1980), *Land Use* (Methuen, London).

Ricardo, D. (1817), *Principles of political economy and taxation* (Dent, London).

Richardson, B. (1974), 'Distance regularities in Guyanese rice cultivation', *Journal of Developing Areas*, 8, 235-55.

Ritson, C. (1977), *Agricultural economics* (Granada, London).

Rogers, A. W. (ed.) (1978), *Urban growth, farmland losses and planning*, Rural Geography Study Group, Institute of British Geographers, Wye College, Kent.

Rogers, E. M. (1962), *Diffusion of innovations* (MacMillan, New York).

—— and Shoemaker, F. F. (1971), *Communication of Innovations: a cross cultural approach* (Free press, New York).

Rose, A. J. (1955), 'The border between Queensland and New South Wales', *Australian Geographer*, 6, 3-18.

Russwurm, L. H. (1970), *Development of an urban corridor system: Toronto to Stratford area, 1941-66* (Queen's Printer, Toronto).

Saarinen, T. F. (1966), *Perception of drought hazard on the Great Plains*. Research Paper 106, Department of Geography, University of Chicago.

—— (1969), *Perception of the environment*, Commission on College Geography Resource Paper 5, Washington DC, Association of American Geographers.

Sargent, M. J. (1978). 'Success in horticultural marketing co-operation', Paper presented to British Association for Advancement of Science, University of Bath.

—— and Roxburgh, C. D. L. (1976), *Management and the growth and development of horticultural marketing co-operatives*, School of Biological Sciences, University of Bath.

Schmid, A. A. (1968), *Converting land from rural to urban uses* (Johns Hopkins Press, Baltimore).

Simmons, I. G. (1979). *Biogeography, natural and cultural* (Edward Arnold, London).

—— (1980), 'Ecological—functional approaches to agriculture in geographical contexts', *Geography*, 65, 305–16.

Simon, H. A. (1957), *Models of man: social and rational* (Wiley, New York).

Simpson, E. S. (1959), 'Milk production in England and Wales: a study in collective marketing', *Geographical Review*, 49, 95–111.

Sinclair, R. J. (1967), 'Von Thünen and urban sprawl', *Annals of the Association of American Geographers*, 57, 72–87.

Sit, V. F. S. (1979), 'Agriculture in the urban shadow: a review of the post-war experience of Hong Kong', *Pacific Viewpoint*, 20, 199–209.

Smith, E. G. (1975), 'Fragmented farms in the USA, *Annals of the Association of American Geographers*, 65, 58–70.

—— (1980), 'America's richest farms and ranches', *Annals of the Association of American Geographers*, 70, 528–41.

Smith, W. (1974), *Innovation and diffusion—a supply oriented example: hybrid grain corn in Quebec*, Studies in the Diffusion of Innovation (Ohio State University, Columbus).

Snyder, J. H. (1966), 'Toward land use stability by contract', *Journal of National Resources*, 6, 406–23.

Stamp, D. (1940), 'Fertility, productivity and classification of land in Britain', *Geographical Journal*, 96, 389–412.

Strauss, E. and Churcher, E. H. (1967), 'The regional analysis of the milk market', *Journal of Agricultural Economics*, 18, 221–40.

Symons, L. J. (1967), *Agricultural geography* (Bell, London).

Tadros, M. E. and Casler, G. L. (1969), 'A game theoretical model for farm planning under uncertainty', *American Journal of Agricultural Economics*, 51, 1164–7.

Tarrant, J. R. (1974), *Agricultural geography* (David and Charles, Newton Abbot.

—— (1975), 'Maize: a new United Kingdom agricultural crop', *Area*, 7, 175–9.

Taylor, C. C. (1949), 'Farm people's attitudes and opinions', in Schuller, E. A. and Taylor, C. C. (eds.), *Rural life in the United States* (A. Knopf, New York).

Theil, H. (1967), *Economics and information theory* (North Holland, Amsterdam).

Thomas, D. (1970), *London's Green Belt* (Faber and Faber, London).

Thompson, I. B. (1961), 'Le remembrement rurale en France: a case study from Lorraine', *Geography*, 46, 240–2.

Thornton, D. S. (1962), 'The study of decision-making and its relevance to the study of farm management', *Farm Economist*, 10, 40–56.

Todd, D. (1979), 'Regional and structural factors in farm-size variations: a Manitoba elucidation', *Environment and Planning A*, 11, 237–58.

—— and Brierley, J. S. (1977), 'Ethnicity and the rural economy: illustrations from Southern Manitoba, 1961–71', *Canadian Geographer*, 21, 237–49.

Townsend, J. G. (1976). 'Farm failure: the application of personal constructs in the tropical rainforest', *Area*, 8, 219–22.

—— (1977), 'Perceived worlds of the colonists of tropical rainforest, Columbia', *Transactions of the Institute of British Geographers*, 2, 430–58.

Van der Vliet, E. (1972), 'The nature of farming on South West Gower: a study of some factors affecting farmers' choice of enterprise', Unpublished M.Sc. (Econ.) thesis, University of Wales, Swansea.

Van Otten, G. (1980), 'Changing spatial characteristics of Willamette valley farms', *Professional Geographer*, 32, 63–71.

Van Valkenburg, S. and Held, C. C. (1952), *Europe* (Wiley, London).

Varjo, U. (1979), 'Productivity and fluctuating limits of crop cultivation in Finland', *Geographia Polonica*, 40, 225–33.

Vasquez-Platero, R. E. (1976), 'Decision models for livestock production in Uruguay', *Dissertation Abstracts International*, 37, 1693–4.

Von Neumann, J. and Morgenstern, O. (1944), *Theories of games and economic behaviour* (Princeton University Press, Princeton).

Von Thünen, J. H. (1826), *Der isoliente Staat in Beziebung auf Landwirtschaft und Nationalökonomie* (Rostock).

Wallace, J. (1985), Towards a geography of agribusiness (forthcoming).

Ward, J. H. Jnr. (1963), 'Hierarchical grouping to optimise an objective function', *Journal of the American Statistical Association*, 58, 236–46.

Watts, H. D. (1971), 'The location of the beet-sugar industry in England and Wales, 1912–1936', *Transactions of the Institute of British Geographers*, 53, 95–116.

–– (1974), 'Locational adjustment in the British beet-sugar industry', *Geography*, 59, 10–23.

Wehrwein, G. S. (1942), 'The rural-urban fringe', *Economic Geography*, 8, 217-28.

Whetstone, L. (1970), *The marketing of milk*, Institute of Economic Affairs, London, Monograph 21.

–– (1975), *The UK dairy industry since 1970*, Institute of Economic Affairs, London, Monograph 21 supplement.

Whitby, M. C. (1968), 'Lessons from Swedish farm structure policy', *Journal of Agricultural Economics*, 19, 279–99.

White, R. L. and Watts, H. D. (1977), 'The spatial evolution of an industry: the example of broiler production', *Transactions of the Institute of British Geographers*, 2, 175–91.

Whittlesey, D. (1935), 'The impress of effective central authority upon the landscape', *Annals of the Association of American Geographers*, 25, 85–97.

–– (1936), 'Major agricultural regions of the earth', *Annals of the Association of American Geographers*, 26, 199–240.

Wibberley, G. P. (1968), 'Pressures on Britain's rural land', in *Land use or abuse*, Report of the 22nd Oxford Farming Conference.

Wilbanks, T. J. (1972), 'Accessibility and technological change in Northern India', *Annals of the Association of American Geographers*, 62, 427–36.

Wilkening, E. A. (1954), 'Techniques of assessing farm family values', *Rural Sociology*, 19, 39–49.

Williams, M. (1976), 'Planned and unplanned changes in the marginal lands of South Australia', *Australian Geographer*, 13, 271–81.

Williams, W. M. (1963), 'The social study of family farming', *Geographical Journal*, 129, 63–75.

Winsberg, M. (1980), 'Concentration and specialisation in US agriculture, 1939–78', *Economic Geography*, 56, 183–9.

Wishart, D. (1969), 'An algorithm for hierarchical classifications', *Biometrics,*
    . 22, 165–70.
Wolpert, J. (1964), 'The decision-making process in a spatial context', *Annals
    of the Association of American Geographers*, 54, 537–58.
Wood, L. J. (1981), 'Energy and agriculture: some geographical implications',
    Tijdschrift voor Economische en Sociale Geografie, 72, 224–34.
Wrathall, J. E. (1978), 'The oil-seed rape revolution in England and Wales',
    Geography, 63, 42–5.
Yapa, L. S. and Mayfield, R. C. (1978), 'Non adoption of innovations: evidence
    from discriminant analysis', *Economic Geography*, 54, 145–56.

INDEX